D0986289

Caged In America

A Woman's Journey Through The Veil
A Memoir

By Zubaida "Jasmine" Sharif

To order additional copies of this book, contact:
Xlibris Corporation
1-888-795-4274
www.Xlibris.com
Orders@Xlibris.com
88946

Dedication

I give all my light and glory to Allah who has made the writing of this book possible. I send love to my mother for the strength she passed on to me. I thank all those dedicated people at the women's shelters and safe houses who helped me find a new life, especially those at the Rise. I send my deepest appreciation to my friends in Bloomington who have become my new family. I especially wish to thank my neighbor Gail who has been a true sister. She has been a healing medicine for both my body and soul. I give all my love to Susan, my ghostwriter, and very patient friend. Last, but not least, I send my most profound devotion to my only true cousin, Hanna, and my three darling children, Danya, Mohamed and Soloman.

Author's Note

This is the true story of my life in America. Names have been changed to protect the identities of those involved.

Chapter 1

Dreaming of Prince Charming

The morning of Tumasha's wedding, our house strained with excitement and anxiety. Strident love songs boomed from the radio in her bedroom. Dishes rattled in the kitchen below and our parents' staccato conversation echoed up the stairs. I blinked tired eyes, having slept little in the small room I shared with my younger sister, Huria. She had no such problem, curled beneath a tan blanket on her ratty bed, white skin looking less Arabic than the rest of us, too young to realize the importance of the day.

I was old enough to know. This was the day every Yemeni girl dreamed of, the marriage to her Prince Charming, the day she transformed from daughter into wife. In our world there were few things for a girl to look forward to, making those moments and days precious.

I slid from bed until my feet touched the wooden floor. The single fixture marking the sloped ceiling had been turned off overnight, but our room brightened with morning sun from the window overlooking the street. I gathered the purple dress spread neatly across my dresser and held it between myself and the foggy mirror, trying to get a sense of my reflection. At eight years, my body was like a boy's. I lacked thirteen-year-old Tumasha's breasts and hips, but that was fine with me. When it came to boys, I preferred playing soccer to romance, though that did not dim my envy for her impending marriage.

"I don't care!" Tumasha yelled above her music. "If they do not marry me to him, I'll run away. I swear!" My older brother, Mouzi, said something and Tumasha screamed back at him. A door slammed.

Returning the dress to its place, I cracked open our door and peered out in time to see Mouzi stride to his room across the unlighted hallway. No doubt he had been badgering Tumasha as he bullied everyone in the household.

Thinking myself safe, I opened the door wider and crept past Mouzi's room toward the stairs, but I was neither quiet nor fast enough. Mouzi's door flung open and he suddenly stood in front of me, blocking my way with his wide body, an evil look on his usually handsome face.

1

"No, Mouzi," I whispered.

Without a word, he grabbed my arm and punched me deeply in the stomach. Gasping for air, I crumpled to the floor.

"Gahba!" Mouzi cursed, as he had heard Father do countless times.

"Stop, Mouzi," I whimpered.

"Little bitch."

It was no use fighting, so I laid there, waiting for his shadow to move. Normally, after one punch, Mouzi would leave me in peace. That morning he was more agitated than usual. He paced down the hallway and returned to kick me.

"Why do you do this?" I pleaded. "Why must you beat me?"

"Shut up," he hissed.

Father had pitted us siblings against each other since we were born. Mouzi and Munsee were encouraged to dominate, while we girls were put down. Mouzi was actually second-born, but father told everyone that he and Tumasha were twins so that he would have a firstborn son, not a daughter. Maybe that was why Mouzi was more angry than usual. Tumasha was marrying first and getting too much attention.

I crawled to Tumasha's door.

"Where do you think you're going, bitch?" Mouzi's foot swung toward me, but missed. From my knees, I turned the doorknob and escaped into my sister's domain.

"Get out of here," Tumasha said over the slow drumming of another love song. Her room was a mirror image of my own, except she had a large bed all to herself. She sat on rumpled sheets and thick woolen blankets, back propped against the wooden headboard. While Huria was light in complexion, Tumasha was darker than any of us.

"Mouzi hit me."

"I don't care." She glared through dark eyes void of compassion. In our house there was no room for pity. Only the strong survived, and to be strong you had to bury your emotions.

My lip trembled. Though Tumasha ignored me most of the time, I held on to the hope that one day we would be intimate the way sisters should be. I had thought that since she was getting married, she might soften her heart for me as she had for her new husband, Asser.

"I said, get out," she said. "I have other things to do than worry about that bastard."

"I just--"

"Now! Get out of my fucking room!"

"Okay!" I opened her door and saw Mouzi had gone.

Walking on tiptoes, I went downstairs to the kitchen, which now occupied two adjoining rooms. In one, a metal pot of Yemeni tea simmered on the stove, spilling scents of clove and mint. The sink was filled with dirty pans and dishes waiting for me. In the other room, a long wooden table mottled with black knotholes held a plate containing half a dozen Yemeni cookies and two empty cups. Tall closets lined the walls except for the spot where Mom's sewing machine stood.

Like all women in her home village Mom had learned how to sew in her youth, but by all accounts she had been something special. Even after marrying Father, she retained a passion for sewing and it showed in the fine detail of her work. Now she sewed for many Yemeni wives and was popular because her work was quick and perfect. She earned lots of money making dresses, which was a godsend to us girls. Father gave my brothers money and gifts, but if we girls needed shoes and clothing, it was up to Mom to provide those things.

Hissam cried from the bedroom at the front of the house. Mom would be too busy nursing the baby to care about me, but I was used to that. I cooked, cleaned and babysat younger siblings most days and had expected to be in charge of the house while Mom and Tumasha prepared for the wedding.

I helped myself to tea, pouring it through a sieve to filter loose tea leaves, cloves, cardamom and mint leaves. Evaporated canned milk had already been added to the mix. For the best tea, one should let it simmer until it is brown and thick. This tea was not dark enough, but I lacked patience to wait. Sipping gingerly from the steaming mug, I walked to the adjoining room and helped myself to leftover Yemeni cookies. The crunchy sesame seed treats made a good breakfast with tea.

Alone in the kitchen, I sat on a chair facing Mom's sewing machine. I had looked forward to this day. Weddings were always a fun time. Even in summer heat, women would remove their scarves and dance late into the night. They would laugh and sing and be free for a time. I should be happy. Instead, I felt a deep emptiness.

"My sister is getting married," I whispered. "I cannot believe it." I missed her and she was not yet gone. I rubbed my stomach where Mouzi had punched me, but refused to acknowledge the pain.

☪

"Shabat!" Mom called. My name is Jasmine, but Mom had a nickname for each of us. Mine was Shabat, or Lefty, because I was left handed. It is really an insult to be called Shabat because the left hand is unclean, but I was just a girl and did not understand the implications then. Maybe if she had called me by my real name, my life would have turned out better. Maybe that is why nicknames are forbidden in the Qur'an. *Neither defame one another nor call one another by nicknames. Bad it is to be called wicked after having professed the faith and whoso repent not of this are doers of wrong.*

I stopped washing dishes and dried my hands.

"Jasmine!"

"Yes, Mama." I hurried from the kitchen and through the living room. Dark blue tapestries on the wall made the room dim. Mom seemed to find shadow comforting. I found it depressing.

Mom and Tumasha were in Mom's bedroom with the two youngest kids. Hissam looked like a little angel in his white sleeper. Toddler Jerraf clung to Mom's leg to steady herself.

"Tumasha and I are going to get her dress," Mom said. Her wide face and cheeks were a reminder of her Beni Musleh roots. Today, she covered her hair with a black scarf as usual, but instead of a plain house dress, she wore a dress with silver trim and a red bead necklace. "You watch the babies."

"Yes, Mama."

"And get the kitchen cleaned up. The women are coming this afternoon."

I nodded.

It was difficult to clean while caring for babies. When I asked for help, Huria ignored me. Mouzi left the house. He had been spending less and less time at home. I often smelled cigarettes on his breath and clothing and suspected he was hanging out with the wrong kind of boys, but said nothing. No one would listen to me anyway.

By mid-afternoon a dozen women had gathered in the kitchen. One brought henna to paint Tumasha's body. Others brought flat breads, tabouleh and hummus. Gossip and good wishes echoed through the house.

The women played drums and sang village songs. When Tumasha complained that her dress pinched or her hair wasn't quite right, Mom rushed to and fro, trying to get things just perfect. In the excitement, I forgot my sadness. I could not wait for the wonderful celebration.

☪

Weddings I had attended before were held in large halls, but Tumasha's was being hosted at Uncle Gaban's house, just five blocks from ours. Since Tumasha was taking so long to get ready, Huria and I were allowed to run ahead. Mom usually spat on a napkin and told us we needed to be home before it dried. This day she was too busy to bother.

We slipped into our worn dress shoes at the door and ran to the sidewalk. I held her hand and we rushed past two story houses built one next to the other along our street. We cut down a side alley and were soon at my uncle's door.

When we entered, heat hit my face. The living room was crowded with women in handcrafted dresses made of silks and accented with embroidery and glitter. Aunt Mouzia was meticulous with her house, not believing in clutter. There were no pictures or knickknacks, only three long couches and a huge shelving unit on one wall housing a TV and stereo. I wondered what she thought of all these Arabic women sitting shoulder to shoulder on her floor. Soon they would be dropping crumbs and grinding dirt into her carpet with their dancing. Already, the room so sweltered with body heat that her glossy white walls were sweating. Only women were allowed in my uncle's house; the men would gather at another location.

Free from prying eyes, women let down their scarves, revealing faces covered with so much makeup they looked like ghosts. I recognized many of them anyway because they had either come to our house to buy dresses from Mom or deposit something in the battered metal security box she kept under her bed. They would bring jewelry or cash or important papers for safe keeping, *so my husband will not find them.* Women united in a common deception.

A little later I noticed Aunt Absa, Mom's half-sister. She was a bad memory in our family, divorcing her husband and running off with another man, leaving six children behind. Like everyone, I blamed her. She was the woman and automatically in the wrong.

Uncle Gaban had not punished her, which made him weak in everyone's eyes. If Father had been in his place, Aunt Absa would not be alive.

Yemeni weddings take place behind closed doors, usually at the bride's house. The sheikh, local head of the mosque, oversees proceedings. Fathers sit across from each other and other men attend as witnesses according to Islamic law. Promises of payment in money and gold are made and the husband and bride, often strangers to each other, are married before being presented to the crowd. That is when the celebration really begins.

It seemed we waited forever for the bride and groom to appear. When they did finally arrive, Asser's entrance drove the women into a frantic rush to cover themselves. Tumasha was beautiful in a full white wedding gown that accentuated her breasts. Asser cradled her elbow, looking shorter than usual in his white tuxedo. His jet black hair and mustache had been neatly trimmed, but, to me, he still seemed greasy. As much as I tried, I could not understand why Tumasha was attracted to Asser. Something about him made my skin crawl.

Women cheered and clapped; many *zaghreeded,* trilling their tongues so loudly it gave me goose bumps. Mom was loudest of all.

Asser seated Tumasha and she sank into the folds of her dress, her entire body nearly swallowed in fabric. I had always seen Tumasha as the big sister; in that moment she looked so tiny and fragile I could not help but to fear for her. She seemed happy, but she was still a child like me, and now was expected to be a wife to this greasy man. Asser sat before the audience, fed Tumasha cake, and excused himself to attend the men's party at Beit Hanina Hall.

Women removed their scarves once again. Yemeni music filled the room; Faisal Alawi's fast paced melodies had everyone dancing. Breads and pies and Arabic coffee were served. Mom ordered pizza and opened bottles of soda pop. I played with other children in the basement where it was cool and soon forgot Tumasha. I forgot I would have added responsibility with my older sister gone. It was a night for celebrating and merriment.

At midnight Father came into the house like a dark storm, bad leg clomping on the floor overhead. "Quiet down," he bellowed. "Shut off the music!"

The music stopped.

"It is time to go home. None of you should be out this late."

Huria and I climbed from the basement. Father stood with hands on hips. He was much older than Mom, with gray hair and fine dark eyebrows. His eyes were bloodshot and his thin lips formed a scowl. Uncle Gaban stood behind him, eyelids heavy from drinking.

"Go home!" Father said.

Women scurried, tightening scarves and gathering dishes. A few spiteful eyes glanced Father's direction, but no one said a word.

I took Huria's hand. "Time to go," I said.

"Hurry," Father barked. "The party is over."

Asser pushed through the flow of fleeing women and whisked Tumasha outside, leaving my parents, Huria, me and my aunt and uncle alone.

"Look at this mess," Aunt Mouzia said. "Now I am left to clean it all."

Father looked at Uncle Gaban and nodded. He had been worried neighbors would call the police about the noise, that they would discover Tumasha had been married. She was only thirteen and this was America, not Yemen.

☾

Unlike most of the girls in our Dearborn community, Tumasha chose the man she would marry. She had met Asser through someone at school and, for weeks, had been obsessing over him and making plans. She even convinced Asser to step up to his father and demand to marry her. Asser's father finally gave in and met with Father at our house, where they agreed on a bride price of $20,000. When anyone puts money into Father's hand he is usually happy. But this time he was anxious.

"So, how the hell are we going to pull this off?" I overheard Asser's father ask.

"We will keep it secret." Father's voice was steady, but I sensed some doubt.

"I'm not going to jail over this," Assar's father said. In America there were laws against marrying a girl so young. Asser was over eighteen and they could all be in serious trouble. But that did not stop them.

"We will have a small wedding at her uncle Gaban's house. Nobody will bust us."

"Are you sure?"

"The key is not to invite too many people," Father said. "My wife is crazy, she'll invite the whole world if I let her. If we keep it small, no one outside will know."

☪

The wedding had been small by Yemeni standards, but the woman enjoyed celebrating anyway. As the last of them exited, Mom stood quietly next to me, her beautiful light complexion accentuated by a dark scarf. I noticed tears in her eyes.

She will not cry at my wedding. I wouldn't marry too young. I wouldn't marry a greasy man. She would be proud and happy on my wedding day.

"Let's go," Father said, hobbling through the door. Mom followed several paces behind, holding her scarf tight against the night breeze.

Chapter 2

Rays of Light

Everyone in our Yemeni community knew that Tumasha and Asser were married, but no one outside suspected. Asser spoke freely of his wife. As long as Tumasha was hidden away at home like the other wives, no one would see how young she was. No one would check. No one would care. That was how the traditions continued.

When Tumasha and Asser moved into Father's house I was overjoyed; my sister was still with us and I saw them as the romantic couple. But Father did not see it that way. He complained whenever he saw Tumasha and Asser together. If he found them wrestling in the living room and having fun, he would call Tumasha a whore. Tumasha complained to Mom, but dared not talk back to Father. Asser, however, would not tolerate this treatment. Many times I heard him talking to a cousin on the phone about jobs. After living with us for only two months, Asser announced they were moving to California.

"You cannot leave," Mom said. Tumasha was her favorite even though she never said the words.

"We're not staying here," Tumasha said. "Baba can bitch at someone else."

☪

After Tumasha moved, the house settled into a new routine. I was now the oldest girl. As a younger child, I would often break the tension by making jokes and expressing situations with humor. With Tumasha gone, my humor was not viewed in the same way. Mouzi took out his frustrations with his fists. Father's cursing became more frequent. Nothing I said seemed to stop it.

"Do not let them get to you," Mom advised. "If you feel anger, show them a smile. If you feel fear, stand your ground. Never let them know what you are thinking."

I tried to follow her advice, but it was difficult to disregard Father's cutting tongue. When I ran crying to Mom, she would suggest her alternate strategy, "Eat. It will make you feel better."

In summer, I spent as much time outside as I could. When Mom was in a good mood and didn't mind hearing eight kids screaming, I invited my friends in the neighborhood to play soccer, even the boys. They were more challenging and I enjoyed playing boys against girls. Mom was fine with them being there as long as she could keep an eye on us.

Other days, I went across the street to the home of the Beni Abee family. They had two small girls. Although I didn't officially babysit, Mr. Abee would often pay me a few dollars to watch them. He adored me, but thought I was too high-spirited; I needed to be shyer, because I was going to be a woman. He always had a smile and jolly laugh that brightened my day. It was nice to see a cheerful father. It made up a little for my own father's dark, dusty face, and the way his forehead wrinkled when he called me a "go-go" girl.

One day I was outside with the girls when a man arrived in a shiny car. He had a nice tan, was slender, and his black hair was glossed and neatly brushed like Elvis. His eyes were large and dark, and he had a beautiful smile.

I turned to Ursa, the older sister. "Who is that man?"

"That's my brother, dummy!" Ursa had a mean mouth on her. She laughed and ran toward the man. Little Habubah also ran to the street. "Gais! Gais!"

I followed, keeping my distance. Once I got to know people I was talkative, but I was shy around strangers, especially men.

"Gais," Habubah begged. "Do you have candy?"

Gais reached into his pocket. "You," he said to me. "What is your name?"

"My name is none of your business," I said. It was not appropriate for him to talk to me, but I could not help but be intrigued. He was a handsome man like New York models I had seen in magazines.

He laughed. "None of my business? Then I guess you don't want candy." He pulled a fistful of colorful hard candy from his pocket.

I liked him immediately. In future visits, when he arrived with his movie star sunglasses and fiery red Grand Am with the bird painted on the hood, I teased him without mercy. "You stay away from my car," he would warn me. I would sit on the hood and make fun of his American clothing. Then I would imitate him and his father, using phrases they used and their particular hand gestures.

He giggled at my antics. "You're witty, do you know that?"

I loved his laugh because it made me laugh too. I thought he was funny and kind, but had no romantic interest.

☪

When summer ended, I returned to Salina School, just two blocks from our house. No one asked where Tumasha had gone and I was careful not to mention her marriage.

After school, I was sometimes allowed to visit two of my friends, Farta and Zeena. Farta was my cousin, a blood relative through Mom's family. We looked almost alike. She had my long black hair and smooth skin, but a smaller nose.

Zeena was from Lebanon, but was considered lower class because she lived in our Yemeni neighborhood. She had beautiful brown hair and was tan for a Lebanese. I used to tease her about her nose being shaped like a hawk's beak.

Together, we were the Three Musketeers, always on the verge of getting into trouble. Farta's one-eyed father spoiled her, but her mom was strict. Nevertheless, Farta was a dare devil. She used to do things behind her mom's back, like take off her scarf at school. Sometimes she would even take off the tights under her dress. It was wrong when she did these things, but she was my favorite cousin. I would never tell on her.

Two weeks before Christmas, Farta decided that we should celebrate by giving each other gifts. I was nervous about the idea. We were Muslim, not Christian. My family never gave gifts for any occasion, not even birthday presents, except for one time when my half-brother, Naseem, came to visit. He was half Vietnamese, the son of Father's first wife whom he had divorced long ago. Naseem was cheerful and fun, a ray of sun in our dreary house. He took us to *Toys R Us*, and bought everything we pointed to. We ended up with three baskets of toys that day.

"It will be fun," Farta said, stretching across the flowered blanket on her bed. The wind blew fine wisps of snow against the windows, making scratching noises.

"I don't know. What if we get caught?"

Even though Mom wished people "Merry Christmas", she would be devastated if she found out. She was devout in her belief and took each of us children aside to teach the Holy Qur'an individually at home. I loved these times with her. It was the one

11

chance we had to be mother and daughter, protected in Allah's mercy. "Qul Hu-wallahu Ahad," Mom would *tagweed* the Al-Iklas, the Purity of faith. *Say: He is Allah the One*. There was such song and poetry in these words!. "Allahus-Samad; Lam yalid, wa lam yuulad." *Allah, the Eternal Absolute; He begotteth not, nor is He begotten*. "Walam yukul-la-huuu kufiwan ahad." *And there is none like unto Him*. I loved following her lead, sounding out the Arabic words. Soon I could *tagweed* the Qur'an better than my siblings. Mom was proud of my accomplishment and I was happy, for I wanted to be like her more than anything. She was strong and beautiful and outgoing. She taught us the true teachings of Islam, not Father's selfish interpretation that allowed him to use profanity and earn money selling his daughters as brides.

Farta shrugged. "We won't get caught. They won't even notice."

"But I--"

Farta jumped from her bed. "Come on. Baba will take us to the store."

I reluctantly followed her downstairs to the living room. Green curtains were pulled back from the windows to let in the winter sun. Black and white photos of relatives hung on one wall, the women totally covered except their eyes. On the opposite wall, Farta's twin brother sat on the couch beside her father watching TV. He was the only person I knew who was mentally challenged and I was afraid to get to close to him. Sometimes he said hello to me, but most of the time I avoided him.

"Can we go to the store," Farta asked her father.

"Sure," he said, glancing with his good eye.

After dressing in warm coats, we scraped the wide Oldsmobile's windshield and climbed onto the cold vinyl front seat. Trembling, I blew on my hands to warm them. Farta's brother climbed onto the back seat, but didn't say a word.

The car started with a roar. We often rode to the store with Farta's father. He had trouble telling red lights from green lights, so Farta would let him know when to stop. Sometimes he would drive through the red lights and I was scared to ride with him. That day I was doubly scared, afraid we would wreck and afraid Farta would get caught buying Christmas presents.

"Green," Farta called out as we made our way down Dix Avenue, passing grocery and clothing shops and doctor's offices. "Green. Green. Red."

The car idled with an intermittent squealing noise. I concentrated on warming my hands.

"Can I have five dollars?" Farta asked while we waited for the light.

"What for?"

"I need some things for school."

When we reached the store, Farta's father slid his wallet from his pocket and gave her five one dollar bills. I was jealous. Father never gave me anything, and any money I made at the Abee's he took away.

We strolled, looking at jewelry, perfume and makeup as well as pencils and school supplies. "I don't think this is a good idea," I said. "What if your father sees us?"

"He's busy." Farta's father was at the front of the store talking to the owner. Farta took her time choosing a ring and bracelet along with a couple of pens and a ruler.

"He's going to notice the jewelry," I said.

Farta shrugged. "He won't say anything."

I followed her to the front. When we reached the cashier, my heart was racing.

Farta's father did not say a word. He didn't even pay attention to what she was buying. I should have been relieved, but my heart didn't slow until we returned to her house.

"I have to go home," I said.

"We will meet on my porch on Monday," Farta said. "We will give gifts then."

I nodded, but now I had another worry. I had nothing to give her.

A few days later, I ran three blocks of snow-covered alley from our house to hers. In my pocket was some candy, the only thing I could find to give to my friends. I could not help but look over my shoulder, certain that Mom or Father would discover what I was doing and come after me. Mouzi would be more than happy to teach me a lesson.

I stopped to catch my breath on Farta's porch. Zeena arrived a few seconds later.

"Where is Farta?" she asked. "She is not playing a trick on us, is she?"

I knocked. "She should be here."

"If Father catches me, he'll beat me." Zeena had an alcoholic father too.

I thought of my father coming home drunk with his belly inflated like a hot air balloon. His face would be ugly gray and covered in sweat. Mom would scream he was in America to provide for us, he wasn't a good Muslim, while I sat silently on the sofa with my brothers and sisters, hoping she would finally kill him in his weakened state and put an end to our suffering. "Saba, help me," Father would cry. "I'm going to die! I'm going to die!" She would yell back, "I hope you do!" Then she would send us children to bed and I would lie awake, sleepless from fear that Mom might be dead in the morning.

The door opened and Farta came onto the porch.

I hugged Zeena. "See," I said. "Farta is here."

"We must hurry," Farta said.

We exchanged presents quickly. I gave them both a piece of candy. Even though I feared we would be caught, I was thrilled about getting their small gifts in return.

Chapter 3

An Ill Wind

I always knew Mom was brighter than Father. Local women looked up to her and confided in her. She read and understood the Qur'an. Maybe that was why Father treated her so cruelly. He feared others would see she was the better person.

For years Mom had wanted to take citizenship classes and he had promised many times that she could, but never let her sign up for the classes offered at Salina School. When I was thirteen, Mom decided to go without his blessing. I do not know what gave her such courage. It might have been a result of my half-brother, Mathloom, coming to live with us. She wanted to get back at Father for taking him in.

Mathloom was the son of Father's second wife, a woman he divorced before coming to America. Mathloom had traveled with us to the U.S., but had been living with other relatives for ten years. Most of the time he was nice, but there was a strangeness about him. Sometimes he did not know where he was or he would sit and listen to some invisible person. I'm certain Mom was not happy having him in our household.

Citizenship classes started at five in the evening, a time when Father usually stopped at a Dix Avenue coffee shop after his job at Ford Motor Company. On days Mom walked to Salina School, I babysat my younger siblings, worried that Father would come home early and I would be the one to absorb his wrath. But I was lucky and she came home before he did on that day and every other day of her classes.

Unlike many women, who were still studying after five years, Mom learned her lessons in one semester and passed her test. The others could not believe she finished before them, but I knew she could do it. She was smart and could have gone to college under other circumstances.

Mom was proud the day she came home with her citizenship papers. When Father returned later that evening, she tossed them onto the table before him.

"There. I have done it."

"Done what?" Father stared at the papers.

"I passed my citizenship exam."

I expected him to go for her throat. Instead, he sat calmly, fingering the edge of the papers with his rough hands. "Prepare the *irgeelah*," was all he said.

If Mom was relieved, I could not tell. She was an expert at keeping her feelings hidden. She went to the garage and returned with a tin of charcoal. Smoking was prohibited by Islam, but our garage was like a coal mine, full of bags of charcoal to be burned in the *irgeelah*.

"Get some water, Shabat."

I filled the teapot and followed her to the living room, where Mouzi, Mathloom and Munsee sat watching TV. Blue light from the screen reflected off a tapestry behind the couch, making the room seem underwater. Little Munsee cuddled in a blanket and looked half asleep.

"Get to bed," Mom said.

"This show isn't over," Mouzi complained.

"Your baba wants to smoke," she said. Mouzi groaned as he left. Munsee darted from the room like a scared deer.

Mom placed the silver water pipe on the coffee table. I poured water into the main chamber while she lit charcoal and filled the pottery cup with fresh tobacco. Soon, water gurgled, creating a soothing sound.

Father brought up some *khat* from his basement stash. Also prohibited by Islam, *khat* is a euphoria inducing herb grown in Yemen. It was illegal in the United States and Father kept it hidden like Tumasha's marriage.

Father sat on floor pillows and sucked smoke from one of the *irgeelah's* tubes. Breathing out like a contented dragon, he watched smoke drift and vanish into darkness. Smooth, peppery odor filled the room and I found myself relaxing. Mom seemed relaxed too, placing a wad of *khat* into her cheek. The only time Mom and Father seemed happy was when they smoked and chewed together.

"Go up to bed," Mom said.

As I climbed the stairs, I hoped this was a good sign, but still remained uneasy.

☾

It was on a sunny afternoon the next week that Mom paid for her success. I was washing dishes while my youngest sister, Jerraf, and Munsee ran around playing and laughing. Hissam slept in his baby seat atop the kitchen table. Mom sat at the table drinking a cup of Yemeni tea.

The phone rang and she answered it.

"Mohsen! How are you?" Mom's cousin had just come to America from Yemen. "I am so pleased you called." Her face lit with a radiance I rarely saw. I took that happiness inside me, inhaling it like smoke, and wondered if life would be happier in Yemen with her family nearby.

The kitchen door banged open and I jumped. Father's bad foot thumped and the stink of alcohol bled into the room. Mom's conversation stopped.

"Who is that?" he barked.

"My cousin, Mohsen." All the light had drained from Mom's face, as if the sun had gone behind a cloud. "He is here from Yemen."

Father ground his teeth and stumbled toward her. I dried my hands on a towel. Mom often said "*Albab thee tighee mineh areeh, sidah wastareeh*". The door that the wind comes from, seal it and relax. If only we could close that door to Father.

"Your cousin?" Father's brow furrowed. An instant later, he ripped the phone from the wall. Cords snapped and bells jangled. I ran to Mom's side, but not before Father crashed the phone into her skull. Once. Twice. *Ring! Ring!*

"Talking to your cousin, huh?" he screamed.

"Stop!" I yelled. I tried to grab the phone. I tried to be Mom's guardian angel, but this monster from Hell was too strong. Huria ran from upstairs, screaming. Jerraf and Munsee returned to the room. Soon they were all crying.

The phone crashed again. *Ring!* Blood sprayed onto my hands. Blood splattered the Monster's face.

"Look what you've done!" I yelled, using all my strength to help Mom push him away. He stumbled back.

"Mama! Mama!" Munsee cried.

Mom gathered Munsee and Jerraf into her arms. "Everything is okay."

The Monster limped to the door, breathing heavily.

"Get out!" I screamed. When he stumbled through the door frame, I hoped he would trip and fall, but he held himself upright. I slammed the door, wishing it would crush his fingers.

"You're bleeding," Huria cried. Blood speckled our clothing and pooled on the floor. Mom pulled herself up against the table. I shook so hard my teeth chattered.

"We need help," I whispered. "Huria, get a towel."

For a few minutes it seemed I walked through a cloud. I called the ambulance on our other phone and calmly told them where we lived. I reassured the little ones that Mom was going to be okay. I worked with Huria to mop up blood.

"Everything is okay," I repeated over and over. "Mom is okay."

When the sound of the ambulance siren reached my ears, I realized that everything was *not* okay. Mom was bleeding badly. What would we do without her? What would happen if we were left alone with only the Monster to care for us? Panicked, I ran across the street.

"Help us!" I cried, banging on the door. I couldn't catch my breath.

Busa's mom opened the door. A blue flowered scarf covered her head.

"Mom needs help."

She came outside and took my hand. "It's okay. Everything is all right. I'll help you."

"My mom," I sobbed, as we walked across the street. "She's bleeding."

Busa's mom walked faster. "Did your father hurt her again?"

The ambulance siren grew suddenly louder as the vehicle turned onto our street. I showed two paramedics to the kitchen. They put their stretcher on the floor. A woman in a white uniform went straight to Mom while a man opened a blue case stocked with medical supplies. He handed the woman a stethoscope and opened the case to reveal numerous bandages.

"Did somebody do this to you?" the woman asked.

"No," Mom said.

"You're sure?" The woman listened to Mom's heart. It is broken, I thought.

"Yes," Mom said. "I'm sure."

I took Mom's hand. Jerraf and Munsee clung to her like grapes while the woman checked her eyes and wrapped gauze around her head. Huria stood to one side, gnawing her fingernails.

"It looks like someone hit you with the phone," the woman said calmly.

"No," Mom said. "I fell."

Tell her the truth!, I screamed inside.

"You can tell us," the man said. "We'll protect you."

Mom didn't answer. *Tell her how the Monster beat you*, I thought.

"My father," I said.

Mom grabbed my wrist. "Quiet!" she said in Arabic.

"Your father?" the woman asked.

I wanted to spill everything. This wasn't the first time Father had beat Mom. It wouldn't be the last. He would kill her someday. Instead, I kept quiet, as Mom had commanded.

"We need to take you to the hospital," the woman said. "Your head should be checked."

I had no way to get to the hospital, so I spent the rest of the day and evening terrified that Mom was dying. We stayed in the living room watching TV and waiting to hear from Mom or even Father. Afternoon turned to night. I cooked dinner, but was too upset to eat anything.

Afterward, Hissam fell asleep on my lap. *Maybe in a few years Father will be dead, and you will grow up to be a good kid*, I thought. I hoped he wouldn't be like Mouzi and Munsee who were becoming the worst part of Father. They hated like him and disrespected women like him. I feared for their wives and children.

Mom finally returned with a neighbor. They had stitched her head, but she refused to stay in the hospital for observation. She had a smile on her face, but it was a shattered smile, as if to say, *I'm back here again for some more rounds*. I hated that she would not put her foot down and leave Father. That night I prayed to Allah, could he please kill Father?

A year later, I was still praying. Mom was pregnant again and Father continued his abuse.

Father

I have tried so many times to describe
The vicious living thing
To say that this is who you are

You are the dark
You are empty

You are estranged from your soul
You are far.
Far away from feelings or sympathy

You... you! You are agony!
You are the executioner
You are disturbance
Dangerous
You are ammunitions!
You are hell, burning us to unlimited degrees.
Leave this lifetime, leave us be!

You are?
You cannot be my father.
You can't be biological, for you have no blood.
You can't be saved, even if you were to be cut!

Why? Why am I so angry even after the escape?
I've lost my senses
You've taken away my shape
The shape of life or love
And my mother; you have hurt her,
You've damaged the soul of her.
She was the beauty in us.
But in your eyes we were all a blur.

Say something! Damn you!
I hate that you will not speak
Just admit, confess so this curse on us will break

So help me God
My mission
I strive to live in me, to become flawless one day
Just to come back to you father.
And feel I am real
I am someone
One day, I pray
I will say everything
To heal my soul from your fire
Father.

Chapter 4

Proposals

As a young teen, most of the time it was a relief to be at school. But school was not free from troubles. In gym, girls were supposed to strip and shower in front of everyone. Most of the American girls were not bothered by this. They would run around the locker room in towels or naked. We Muslim girls were taught not expose our bodies even around other women. Some of us would change clothes quickly and pretend to shower. Others would giggle from nervousness as they showered. None of us were happy. Many girls complained until some parents got together and asked the local sheikh to write a letter. As a consequence, doors were installed on the shower stalls. After that, I looked forward to gym class and spending time with my friends, Dayabah and Shigah, from Yemen.

Dayabah was a jolly girl, who looked up to me. "Jasmine, you are so beautiful," she said one day, holding her hands across her flat chest. "I wish I had perfect breasts like you." I laughed as if it were one of her jokes. In truth, such compliments embarrassed me. We did not speak of these things in my house. Shigah and Dayabah's families had accepted the freedoms offered in America, while mine had not.

Shigah reminded me of Lucy Lawless, who played the character Xena on TV. She was athletic and brave. Shigah could run faster than the whole class and should have been in the Olympics. She did not let any wrong go by and protected anyone she cared about. She was even brave enough to fight for me when a girl in our class teased me.

"What's the matter? You afraid to show your ugly hair?"

I turned away, wanting to avoid conflict.

"Can't you speak? You probably don't even know English."

"Shut up!" Shigah said.

"Are you going to let your friends talk for you?"

"Don't you *ever* make fun of my good friend," Shigah said, her eyes burning. She pushed the other girl backward.

"She's just a--"

"Just a what?" Shigah said. She pushed harder and the girl fell to the cement sidewalk. "Just because you think you are better than everyone, doesn't mean you are!"

The girl climbed to her feet. Shigah shoved her down again.

"Tramp!" Shigah grumbled. "Come on. Let's get out of here."

On the way home, Dayabah asked if I could come to her house to visit. I *so* wished I could spend more time with them, but now that I was a teenager I was not allowed to go anywhere. The only time I could see them was when they came to my house so that Mom could keep an eye on us.

C·

When I was fourteen my menstrual period started. Of course, I had to tell my mother. To me it seemed a curse, but Mom was overjoyed that I was now a *woman*. Even Father was happy. He rarely spoke to me, but when he heard the news he took me shopping. He insisted I buy a bra and let me pick out any kind I wanted. He was even in a good mood several days later and I wondered if he had been chewing too much *khat* in his basement lair.

Barely a month later, I discovered why. Mom took me aside in the kitchen after school.

"I have good news," she said, bubbling like a tea pot.

I couldn't imagine what it was that would make her so happy.

"Gais Abee wants to marry you."

"Gais, our neighbor?" Goosebumps raised across my arms. "Mom, no. I don't want to. I don't want to get married."

She smiled gently and guided me to a chair then poured me a cup of Yemeni tea.

"Gais is a man," I said. "I can't marry him."

"Listen," she said. "You are going to get married, settle down and he will be good to you. We've known him all our lives. His family is generous and sweet and kind. You have to get married, you're a woman now."

My hands shook. Tea spilled onto the table. "What about school?"

"It is better than living with your father for the rest of your life," she said. "You will have a husband. You will have someone who will treat you better."

"No," I said. "I don't want to get married!" I liked going to school. I liked having friends. I didn't want to be stuck in the house every day cooking and cleaning and waiting for my husband to come home drunk.

Mom nodded. "I know you are afraid. We were all afraid. But it is time."

It is not time, I thought. We were in America, not Yemen. Girls finished school here before they got married. Many American girls even got jobs before marrying.

Mom stood and patted my back. "I will give you some time to think about it," she said. "You will see. It will be good for you."

Trembling, I ran upstairs to my room. The afternoon sun was hot through the window, but not as hot as my worry. I sat on my bed and stared at the blue sky. Allah, please help me, I prayed. Don't make me do this. I am not a woman! I am not ready for a husband.

The next day, my uncle's wife, Mouzia, sat at the kitchen table with Mom when I came home from school. A black scarf covered her head and a smile brightened her usually sour face.

"Salam, Jasmine," she said. "Come," she said. "Sit with us and have some tea."

I barely knew this woman and she had never been nice to me. I thought it strange that she would visit. Hesitantly, I sat beside Mom.

"I hear that you are a woman now," Mouzia said. "It is a happy time for you."

I glanced at Mom. This was all her doing. She had invited Aunt Mouzia to join her side.

"You'll have a big wedding. There will be singing and dancing."

"I am not getting married," I said.

"You know marriage is good." Aunt Mouzia said. "Everyone will be happy."

I shook my head.

"You will wear a beautiful dress and your new husband will treat you like a princess. You will get gold and gifts and have a house of your own."

"I don't want those things." When I was younger the dream of becoming a princess had appealed to me, but those dreams had given way to the reality of what was expected of a wife. I wasn't ready to have a man touching me.

Impatience started to show beneath Aunt Mouzia's smile. "I don't know why not. Gais is a very nice man. He has a good job in New York. He will make a wonderful husband."

The conversation ended there, but the next morning Mom was waiting when I walked downstairs.

"I have been patient with you, Jasmine," she said. "But we must not make Gais wait. If you do not accept his proposal, he will not ask again. You may have to marry someone you have never met."

I didn't understand how arranged marriages worked at the time, but the thought of being married to a man I had never met was even more terrifying than being married to someone I knew. "A stranger?"

"Yes," Mom said. "Agree to marry Gais. He comes from a good family. Only Allah knows who your father will pick next time. It may be some old man with gray hair."

An old man! At least Gais was young and attractive. I didn't want to be married to someone Father's age.

"Okay," I whispered.

Father arranged our marriage that same day with the sheikh who had married Tumasha. He bargained with Gais and his father for a bride price and I understood why he had been so happy. Money. If he had gotten $20,000 for Tumasha, he would get at least that much for me.

It was dowry money, I found out later, that should have gone to me. The Qur'an says to "give women their dowry freely; but if of themselves they give it up to you, then enjoy it as convenient and profitable." Father's perverted understanding of the Qur'an and Yemeni traditions was colored by greed. He would keep my money, just as he had kept my sister's.

When Father returned, he informed me that Gais and I were to be engaged for a year. It would take that long for Gais to earn my bride price. I could not have been more relieved.

Following tradition, Gais and I met in our living room with our families present. He was dressed in a fine New York suit, his face aglow. I was dressed like a thirty-year-old, with too much face makeup, a fancy party dress and gaudy jewelry. My long hair hung free, cascading to my waist. Mom was so happy. Father looked like a tiger that had just stuffed itself.

We were not allowed to be alone, which was good. Though I had teased Gais many times as a girl, the thought of him becoming my husband embarrassed me. I could barely look at him.

In the weeks that followed, Gais bought me gifts, including a gold watch. He had to return to his job in New York, but called me from the store.

"Salam, Jasmine," he said. "How are you?"

"Fine." I didn't know what else to say. I couldn't tell him about my friends at school. I couldn't tell him about Father's outbursts. I had just finished washing the dishes. That didn't seem an interesting thing to talk about either.

"I miss you," he said. "You are the most beautiful woman in the world."

I felt my cheeks warm. How could I explain that I didn't feel like a woman? I came up with the idea of writing letters instead of talking on the phone. That way I could take time to write my thoughts.

"What is your address?" I said.

"Why do you ask?"

"I want to write you a letter."

He was more than happy to write to me and I found out why. Gais' letters were long and romantic. His handwriting flowed as if an artist had painted rows of beautiful flowers across the page. I was entranced. More easily than I expected, I began to fall in love with this man. He was ten years older, but the difference vanished as our chemistry grew. I found myself talking to him two or three hours at a time. Maybe he was my prince charming after all.

Chapter 5

Too Hard to be Broken

Weeks dragged into months. My relationship with Gais flourished, but things at home were falling apart. Mom was taking on more and more sewing. People from California were sending her boxes of fabric for wedding dresses. She'd sew all day and late into the night, leaving me to care for the kids. I saw the tired look on her face and the slump in her posture. I knew she was working too much, but no one else seemed to care. She deserved so much better.

Mathloom grew more and more belligerent toward Father until one night they got into a knife fight. Father kicked him out of the house. Mouzi went out of control. At seventeen, he saw himself as a man, able to do as he pleased. He stopped praying. He stayed out late and often didn't come home at all. He dated American girls and smoked and drank openly. He even dropped out of school. When Mom questioned him, he said he would never succeed at anything because of Father.

In a desperate attempt to save Mouzi from himself, Mom made an offer. She told him she had twenty-five thousand dollars saved from her sewing. She promised to give it to him if he would shape up and go back to school. "You must do something with your life. I will give you the biggest wedding, find you the best girl. Just finish your schooling."

Of course, marriage was everything in our world so my brother agreed. Father convinced Mom to let Mouzi put his name on the bank account so that he could take out money when he needed it. Three months later, while Tumasha was visiting from California, Mom received a bank statement in the mail. She opened the envelope, but couldn't decipher the information.

"Tell me how much is in it," she said, handing me the paper.

I was shocked. "There is only five dollars," I said, feeling sick to my stomach. Had Mouzi taken *all* of it?

"Five dollars!" She yanked the paper from my hand "You don't know how to read a damn thing! All these years in school and you don't know how to read."

"Here, Tumasha." She handed the statement to my sister. "You read it."

Tumasha's eyes went wide. "Jasmine is right. There's only five dollars in the account."

"No! It cannot be!" Mom took the paper and stared at it. "Allah, help me." Her face turned to stone. She didn't cry or scream, but walked calmly to her room, took the Qur'an from the bedside table, and began to pray.

I went to my room. From the window, I could see Gais' father's house. I wished he were there. I wished I could turn into a butterfly and fly away from this family. Mom had been saving money for years. I wondered how much more she could endure.

Darkness descended. Stars winked into view. The slamming of the back door told me Father was home. Hairs tingled on my neck. Mom would not allow Mouzi to take so much money without bringing it to Father's attention. I expected a big fight this time.

I crept to the top of the stairs.

"I have been robbed by your son!" Mom screamed.

The Monster laughed.

"I don't mean twenty dollars from the kitchen," she said. "He has taken twenty-five thousand from my bank account."

"You should have known better than to put his name on it," Father said.

There was a long pause. My heart beat rapidly.

"It was you!" Mom said.

"Of course. I am the man. The money is mine."

"I earned that money," Mom shouted. "It was mine. What did you do with my money?"

"It doesn't matter." The Monster laughed again. No doubt he had spent it entertaining the men in town, buying them food and drink as if he were the ruler of the neighborhood.

The back door slammed again.

"La tighaa gasee fa-tinkasir wala-ridib fatinasir," Mom said aloud. *Do not be too hard, lest you be broken; do not be too soft, lest you be bent.*

For months Mom was depressed. She rarely talked. She no longer made jokes. She didn't sing her poetry. She barely ate. Even when Tumasha and Asser moved back from California, she was not comforted. I was supposed to be happy because of my upcoming wedding, but how could I be? I felt as if Mom had died, leaving an empty shell in our house.

☪

One morning I was downstairs watching Hissam and Jerraf, when Mom cried out. I ran to her room and found her on the floor.

"What's wrong?" Her face was so wrinkled I almost didn't recognize her.

"Pain," she gasped.

"What's hurting?"

"Everywhere," she said. "It hurts everywhere."

I didn't know what to do. I helped her sit up and tried massaging her shoulders.

"No!" she cried. "Stop! It hurts."

Tumasha took her to an Arabic doctor. He was next to useless, prescribing Tylenol. When the Tylenol did little to help, I begged her to see an American doctor. She refused.

For the next six months, she tolerated that pain. By the end, her round face had thinned to a gaunt mask and I could see the bones of her wrists through her skin. Tumasha finally convinced her to see another doctor and she was finally diagnosed with lupus.

Doctors put her on Prednisone, which helped until she overdosed and ended up in the hospital. Tumasha and I took turns at her bedside while she hallucinated about the end of the world. She described flames of lava and people screaming. She told me one night I should move away from her side because she saw heaven on me. All I could do was cry and hold her.

"Allah, compassionate and merciful," I prayed. "Why have you done this to her? Hasn't she suffered enough? Why hasn't Father been punished for his evil deeds instead?"

I was so confused, I lost hope. The world became a dark place, darker than our black veils and *baltos*. I could see no future for myself, not even my marriage to Gais.

After many days, Mom began to recover. She stopped talking about heaven and hell fires and seemed more herself. One day, she even made a joke. I knew then that she would live.

She had survived, but I wasn't sure I had. My engagement lay heavily on my mind. My stomach twisted with guilt. How could I abandon Mom when she was in such a state? I was the middle daughter. I was the one who should stay home and care for her. Gais was a wonderful man, but how could I leave Mom?

When she returned to the house, I found the courage to approach her.

"Mom," I said. "I've been thinking about this. Someone should help you with the housework. I do not have to get married."

A smile crossed her taut face. "I have been looking forward to this wedding for years. You cannot disappoint me now." She touched my cheek. "Everyone is destined to their own life, Jasmine, and yours is to be married."

I hoped she was right. I was deeply in love with Gais by then.

Mama

I *feel* your pain and the faith that you gain
We both *believe* yet are tied on the same chain
You walk this road, while I am in the passing lane.

We try to break it, but we face each others' backs
I focus on the pain, my only attack!
Yet mother, your fear is that you lack.

You stand like a statue of liberty and charm
You see my strength as yours, but you have done harm.
Not to me... all is forgiven
It is your pain you have buried and hidden.

Is this why I confuse faith with patience?
You said beatings for control test our tolerance.
Yes, when accepting it!
Instead, I crumble bit by bit.

This poem is not to hate you, it is an encore!
We have been destined to this for sure
Accept me as I have come from your womb
The reality of me is your way out of *doom*
Don't tell me you have no room
Who else but God is close to your heart? *Whom?*

When there is no more me to blame
Our faith as one will remain the same
I will not disgrace, there is no shame
I carry Allah and Allah carries me
Along the roots of my inner journey

It's your love that nurtures my soul
You and I eat from the same bowl
We will reunite in a happy first feast
A painless reunion with peace at least.

Chapter 6

Closed Part of Her Mind

With Mom recovered from her bout with lupus, life returned to normal. Her anger toward Father seemed to vanish and she focused again on taking care of the house and children. It seemed she could lock the bad things away in some part of her mind and move on. I admired her for that. A weaker woman would have given up.

Not long after she returned from the hospital, we received news of an engagement party next door. Mom brought up the subject with Father, but he refused to let her go. After washing dishes and doing my homework, I found Mom in the kitchen. She wore her good black shoes and blue embroidered dress trimmed with gold sequins. Makeup was caked on her face, making her seem thinner than she already was.

"I can't believe it," she said. "Laylah is finally getting married." Colorful dresses she had sewn were spread on the table like flowers in a garden. Arabic coffee boiled on the stove, creating a strong spicy aroma. I thought of my steadily approaching marriage to Gais.

"Laylah has invited us," Mom said. "She will be insulted if we don't go." It wouldn't be such an insult, but Mom was dying to get out of the house and be among other women.

She removed the coffee from the stove and poured a cup. "Jasmine, could you please take this coffee to your father? And could you ask him about the engagement party for me? He told me earlier I could not go, but I am already dressed. Maybe he will change his mind."

I wanted to say no, but Father would beat her if she asked again. I was her only chance. This was the least I could do for her, but still I was terrified.

The coffee cup trembled in my hand as I descended to the Monster's lair. I heard music and TV voices coming through the closed door. Maybe he was asleep. Maybe he had passed out. Maybe he was dead. I knocked softly.

"What!" the Monster yelled.

"I have coffee," I said, slowly opening the door. Father's room was lined with red and blue wall tapestries. An end table was cluttered with a tray of pills, dirty cups and plates and a table lamp. Beside it, Father leaned in his recliner. His eyes were bloodshot. Gray hair pressed to one side of his head. I extended the cup to him.

The Monster grunted. My heart raced until I could barely get my mouth to speak. "Baba, you know Mama wants to go next door for a party."

He sipped coffee.

"It's not far. I'm home to babysit."

He sat up in the chair.

I stepped back. "She won't be gone long, I promise."

The Monster leaned forward and stared into my eyes. I braced, expecting him to strike out. Instead, he cleared his throat.

"Tell her she can go," he said. A shiver ran down my neck and spine. Something was wrong, but I couldn't identify it. He didn't seem angry, but I felt danger. He was like a tiger watching me from the trees, waiting to pounce.

"I'll tell her." I ran up the basement steps.

"He said you can go." The moment the words left my mouth, I regretted saying them. *Don't go, Mom*, I thought. I have a bad feeling. But maybe I was just imagining danger because I had walked in fear my entire life. Maybe Father was being generous.

Mom quickly wrapped her scarf around her head and left through the back door.

"Be home early," I said when it was too late for her to hear. *She will be in trouble for this*, I thought.

I fed and bathed Hissam and Jerraf and put them to bed around nine-o-clock, but I was too worried to sleep. I paced in the hall.

Ten PM. I went to the kitchen and listened at the door. Party music thumped from the neighbor's house. "Go to bed," Mouzi said when he came in. He smelled of cigarettes and marijuana and his eyes were glazed.

Ten-thirty. I wandered into Mom's room and sat on the corner of her bed. The only light came from a streetlight across the road. The room was colored in blacks and grays. My stomach wound into knots. "What are you doing up?" Mouzi came into the bedroom with a glass of tea in one hand and several Yemeni cookies in the other.

"I'm not going to sleep until Mom comes home," I said.

"Go to sleep!" he said, scowling.

I tried to sleep on Mom's bed, but only grew more and more nervous. I smelled cigarette smoke and thought Mouzi must be smoking in the living room. But when I looked, Mouzi was asleep on the couch. The TV painted the room with bluish light. To my horror, Father was smoking in the kitchen.

Eleven PM. I didn't have to pee, but it was a good excuse to leave Mom's room. It was while I tip-toed past Mouzi that I saw the rifle in the kitchen, propped near one of the old steam radiators.

A gun! my thoughts raced. The Monster was going to kill Mom. How could I save her? If I ran to the party to warn her, she would just return home that much sooner. I couldn't talk to the Monster. He would laugh and push me aside.

"Jasmine, what are you doing out of bed?" The Monster stood before me with searing red eyes and fiery smoke breath.

"I..."

"Go to sleep, Sweetheart."

No, I thought. I couldn't let him kill Mom. Instead of going upstairs, I went back into the living room, sat beside Mouzi, and nudged him with my elbow. "Mouzi?"

"What the fuck!"

"Baba has a gun."

"What?"

"Baba has a gun. He's going to kill Mama when she comes home."

"A gun? Where?"

"By the heater," I said. "He's going to shoot her."

"You go to bed," he said "I'll take care of this."

Mouzi slid from the couch and staggered from the room. I stayed behind, shaking so hard I couldn't control myself.

"What are you doing?" the Monster said. "Go to sleep."

"What the fuck is this, Dad? What is this?"

"Go to bed!" I heard footsteps upstairs. The argument had awakened the kids.

"This is a rifle," Mouzi said. "What are you planning on doing with it, Baba?"

"None of your damn business."

"Do you plan to kill my mother? Is that what this is for?"

"Give me that!" A chair toppled.

Unable to bear this any longer, I ran to the kitchen. Huria and Munsee clattered downstairs. Mouzi and the Monster struggled for the gun.

"Stop it!" I grabbed at the rifle stock, trying to keep the muzzle from pointing at anyone. "You're going to shoot someone!"

There were more footsteps on the stairs. "No, Baba!" Hissam cried.

"Give me the gun," Mouzi screamed.

"Please, don't do this," I sobbed. It seemed like we wrestled for hours. The children's cries echoed in my ears.

Suddenly, the Monster staggered back and the gun was in Mouzi's hands. "You are not going to kill my mother," he said.

"It's okay." Father leaned against the wall, panting like a dog. His face was as red as his eyes. "I was going to scare her, that's all."

Mouzi opened the gun and pulled two rounds from the chamber. The brass casings sparkled. "It looks like you were planning on more than scaring her."

Father held out his hand. "Just give me my rifle. I'll put it away."

"No," Mouzi said. "I'll lock it up in the basement. Give me the key."

Father hesitated, but finally handed Mouzi the key. I couldn't believe what I was seeing. Mouzi had stood up to Father. All these years I had thought him a spineless copy of the Monster. Now, I wasn't so sure. Maybe Mouzi had some backbone after all.

Father returned to the basement. I got the kids settled in Mom's room and waited. Every creak and groan of the house sounded like Father walking up the basement steps. I would hold my breath and listen, waiting to hear bullets sliding into the gun, but he didn't return.

When Mom got back, we broke into a chorus of tears.

"What is the matter?" She sat on the bed and embraced the young ones. "Please tell me."

We explained about the gun and Father's fight with Mouzi, about the bullets and Mouzi taking the key. Mom was unusually quiet.

"He was going to kill you," I said.

"May God punish this man," she said. "It's time for everyone to go to sleep."

While we tried to settle down in her bed, Mom went to the living room and readied some tobacco in the *irgeelah*. She sat in the shadows, sucking in smoke and sitting quietly. When the younger ones were asleep, I tip-toed into the living room.

"You should be sleeping," she said.

"Mom, I don't want you to stay here anymore. You have to leave. You have to do something."

She blew out a smoke-filled sigh.

"He's trying to kill you," I said. "Look how far it has gone. He had a--"

"He's not going to kill me," she said. "He wouldn't dare kill me."

"But he had a gun," I said. "What kind of proof do you need? If I hadn't seen the gun, you might be dead now."

She kissed me on the forehead. "Allah guides us toward what is right. If we become good women, He will protect us." She held me close. "I believe in God. I believe in Allah. He will never betray us."

The *irgeelah* bubbled. Already, she had put the incident in that closed part of her mind. The next morning she would act as if nothing happened, while I would suffer for months with the memory of Father and Mouzi wrestling over the gun. The scars ran deep, so deep that I doubted even Allah could heal them.

Chapter 7

Floating in a Sea of Stars

In the months leading up to my wedding, Mom began acting like herself again. She was still so thin that none of her clothes fit and her eyes had lost some of their sparkle, but Mom was still inside. She put all her energy into my special event. I had never seen her more excited. Even when Gais' came to inform Father he could not pay for the wedding, Mom was not bothered.

"We will pay for it," she said.

Father was less accommodating. "The man's family pays for the wedding."

"Gais has been working to save for the dowry," Mr. Abee said. "He will be lucky to have that paid by the wedding date."

"We made a deal before the sheikh," Father reminded him.

"I know, but I cannot grow money on my trees. Either it goes to the dowry or to the wedding."

"So you are breaking our contract?"

"If I must."

"No!" Mom said. "Jasmine is going to be married if I have to sew one thousand dresses to pay for it."

Father looked disgusted, but after Mom's stay in the hospital he had been less quick to lash out. "Okay," he said. "We will handle the wedding, but I expect the dowry paid in full, do you understand?

"Of course."

We didn't have a car, so an American friend of Mom's drove us all over town to find a hall and buy supplies. The first hall we went to was near Warren Street, a big facility. The Lebanese owner was a squat man with black hair combed strait back and a mustache. He showed us into a large room decorated with panels of wall paper and brass sconces.

"It's beautiful," I said. "This will be perfect."

Mom was not as enthusiastic. "How many people will it hold?"

"Six hundred."

"What kind of meals?"

"We can do traditional Arabic or American food. We can

even do a combination." He looked at Mom's friend, assuming we would have many Americans at the wedding.

"That's good," I said.

"How much for five hundred people and traditional food?"

"Six thousand for a sit down meal."

"Six thousand! That is robbery."

"We can do it for maybe fifty-five hundred."

Mom shook her head. "This is my daughter's wedding. I want it perfect, the best of everything. It will be a day she remembers for the rest of her life."

"We can do a buffet for forty-five hundred."

"Do I look like the queen of Sheba?" Mom held out her hand to show him how boney it was. "I have been a sick woman and only Allah knows when he will take me. This may be the last wedding I attend. I want my daughter to have the best, but at a price I can afford."

She turned to me. "You see how beautiful she is. She will make a wonderful bride. This is a wonderful place for her wedding, but not at that price."

"Four thousand," the man said. "That's the lowest I go."

I saw the hint of a smile on Mom's face. "You are a generous man," she said. "We will take it."

At the bakery, I found the cake of my dreams. It had a rectangular base with white frosting with red roses. At the each end white staircases led to two central round cakes of the same design with a bride and groom perched on top. The cake's middle held a water spring with red and white water.

The wedding dress took more than one day. I tried on more designs than I can remember. I wanted something form-fitting, tight at the waist.

"You might as well go naked," Mom said. "That is not appropriate for a Muslim woman."

I finally found a long sleeved dress with a full skirt covered in heart embroidery and decorated with rhinestones. In the mirror I resembled a princess ready for my prince. Inside, my nerves were jangling. I might be ready for the wedding, but not the wedding night. I'd heard the talk. "It will be like a knife going into you." "He will throw you down and take you by force if you do not go along." "It is something all women suffer through." "There will be blood." The prospect was terrifying.

☾⋆

The evening before my wedding, half a dozen women came to the house. Tumasha brought her video camera to record the event. Mom made tea, fresh bread and hummus and roast lamb. Hailah brought henna and drums.

She spent hours meticulously drawing roses and other intricate patterns on my hands and arms with burgundy dye outlined in black. Then she painted my feet and legs up to the knees. The other women chatted, sang traditional Yemeni songs, and helped themselves to the food Mom had prepared. When Hailah finished, I looked like an exotic creature from a faraway land.

"You are beautiful," Mom said. Some of the women *zaghreeded*. Others applauded. Even Tumasha said I was gorgeous. When the women left, Mom took me by the hand to her room.

"Sit," she said. She took a box from her closet. "I bought you a wedding present."

I opened the box. Inside, were a yellow gold necklace with a rose patterned design and matching bracelet and earrings. "This is beautiful, Mom!" Tears fell from my eyes. Mom seldom showed the affection I craved. When she did, those times were precious.

"It will be your special day, Jasmine. Now, go upstairs and take your bath. You have a big day tomorrow."

I spent the next hour bathing and shaving. All my body hair must be removed so that I would be pure for my husband. Afterward, in the darkness of my room, I looked across the street at Gais' father's house. The room lights upstairs were dark. I wondered if Gais was sleeping or lying awake in the dark. Would we both be up all night?

☾⋆

My wedding day, I was a jumble of emotion, tired from lack of sleep, but also tremendously excited. I would be beautiful in my painted body and flowing white dress, yet I could not feel completely happy. Despite what everyone said, I did not feel like a woman. I was still that girl who played soccer with the boys. I was still the teen gossiping with her friends in gym class. I did not feel ready for a man, even a prince.

In the morning Hailah and her daughter, Adila, came to style my hair. It was so long and thick they had to lay me down on the floor to comb it out and curl it. It took three hours. Then they helped me into my dress and placed the veil on my head while Mom ran back and forth like a crazy woman, making sure everything was set.

"They're here!" Huria yelled.

"He's coming," Mom said. She straightened my veil. "Go stand by the door."

There was a knock and one of the women opened the door. Gais stood outside in a white tuxedo, hair combed back and face freshly shaved. He looked more handsome than ever.

"Hi, Jasmine," he said.

I managed a quick smile, but my stomach was so nervous I feared I would throw up if I said anything. Hands darted all around, opening the door and guiding me outside into the sunny afternoon. I heard Father's gruff voice complaining while Gais and I walked to the white limo. Everything was in slow motion. A man in a black suit opened the door. Gais' sisters darted around us, sprinkling glitter and hearts. Mr. Abee stood across the street. I saw no sign of Gais' mother.

"You look beautiful," Gais said. Women *zaghreeded*. Cars lined up behind the limo for blocks. An egg flew past us and broke in the street.

"What are you doing?" Father grumbled.

"It's for luck," Mom said.

Luck, I thought. Allah, protect me, I was going to need all the luck I could get.

Gais helped me into the limo, gathered the train of my dress and veil, and tucked them inside. Cars honked and reved their engines. Soon, we were in motion, heading for the hall.

Gais took my hand and smiled. "Isn't it fantastic! This must be the biggest wedding in Dearborn history. I think your mother invited everyone in town." He pointed out the back window. The line of cars extended as far as I could see.

After touring several Dearborn streets, we arrived at the hall. Gais helped me from the limo and I heard live Yemeni drumming and loud *zaghreeding* coming from inside the hall. Men and women had gathering outside. It was a gorgeous, sunny day and he walked me in slow motion past the crowd. Glitter clung to his hair and he held my hand gently.

Men wore their best suits; women wore colorful silk dresses, many with veils. Yemeni men, mesmerized by my "beauty," called to Allah and the prophets to protect me from the evil eye. Women commented on my loveliness as well. These were not the bitter, gossipy comments I usually heard. They truly seemed enthralled. I felt like an angel come down from the sky. I was in this natural high with Love, Love, Love. I felt only love for Gais and his love for me.

Inside, we paraded between tables covered in white linen and decorated with flowers. Only the women followed us, for this was the women's party hall. Gais would stay for an introduction and then leave to join the men. On the stage at the front of the room, we sat in high backed chairs, our thrones of the journey of commitment. Some women took pictures. Tumasha kept busy with her video camera.

"Kiss each other," she said. Kissing was not acceptable in this situation, but Tumasha had become more open since living in California. After some coaxing, we finally kissed. I did not look to the crowd to see their reaction, but only hoped this did not curse my wedding. *Bakhat elsharayif a'maa.* The luck of the original is blinded by the curse.

Once we were presented to the crowd as man and wife, the women hurried Gais out. Veils came off and everyone could be themselves. Servers carried silver trays to the buffet table and aromas of curried lamb, and spiced rice lifted through the room. I wasn't very hungry, but forced myself to eat a little.

After the meal, the drum beat intensified and everyone danced. I searched the floor for Mom. She had always been a good dancer, but I could tell she held herself back because of her pain. She was fragile beneath her silks.

I felt a rush of tears about to erupt, but bottled them up. The bride is not allowed to cry on her wedding day. She must be an example of pride and dignity. She must prove she has the strength to take on whatever happens in the marriage.

Gais returned midway through the evening to help me cut the cake. I did not see him again until midnight when it was time for the women to *zaghreed* us out of the hall. My prince in white took my hand. I wanted to go with him and at the same time run away as fast as I could. My stomach seemed to fill with buzzing bees. My hands shook by the time we reached the limo.

"I love you," Gais whispered. "Everything will be all right."

Gais was very sensitive about the situation and had arranged for our night to be at the Hyatt Regency, away from prying eyes and ears. Most girls had their wedding night at their parents' house or their new in-law's house. But it was not all roses. Even though we would not have to worry about parents on my wedding night, we were expected to produce a bloody sheet as proof of *sharaf*, my pride of being a virgin. It was a ridiculous tradition. There was no excuse for it, and no religion, especially Islam, condoned the practice.

Gais unlocked the door to our suite. It was a richly decorated room with floral paintings on the walls and a large bed. An expansive window overlooked Dearborn's golden lights and I could almost imagine we were floating in a sea of stars.

"This is it," he said. His voice sounded nervous and I realized I was not the only one expected to perform. Gais did not want to hurt me. He was not that kind of man. He went into the bathroom for a few minutes and when he returned, came toward me slowly.

"You are as beautiful as the stars," he said, touching my face gently and kissing me, "I have been waiting for this day to be with you." His manly tone reverberated in my heart, setting free a harmonious song. I was lost in his kisses.

"I want you more than anything," he said.

"Me too," I whispered. My body grew hot with passion, but I wished he would not stop kissing me. Maybe we will not do this tonight, I hoped.

"Do you want to change into something comfortable?"

"Yes." I was ready to get out of the wedding dress and this would give me time to catch my breath. I rushed into the bathroom and took my time removing the dress. I bathed myself and let my long hair fall free. Keeping on my panties, I slid into a *dira*, a nearly see through garment decorated with swirling designs to cover most of my nakedness. The fabric was light and I should have been cool, but my body steamed nonetheless.

When I looked at my nearly naked body in the mirror, I broke down crying. I kept seeing Mom's face and what the lupus had done to her. I heard Father's voice calling me a whore. Even outside his house and with my new husband, I was not free of the Monster. I felt unworthy. I felt dirty. Damn, why did it have to be this way? I sobbed quietly, hoping Gais did not hear, not wanting to insult him. I could not help myself. I was the first from my group of friends to marry. I could not see myself facing them after this happened.

It felt like an hour before I left the bathroom. My long hair brushed against my knees as I walked to Gais.

"My love," he said. He had removed his wedding clothes and wore only a *foutah,* a white wraparound skirt worn by Arab men. His chest and arms were muscular and I felt suddenly safe with him. The Monster's angry voice faded until I was alone with my love.

"Here," he said. "Sit next to me." He removed the *foutah* and tossed it aside.

I sat nervously. Gais caressed me and my heart pounded wildly, too fast too soon. I had never been touched before. I became tense.

"Don't be afraid," he said. "I will never hurt you." He was patient, taking time to make me comfortable. I was glad not have the typical Yemeni man on the first night, ready to rip off my clothes and tear me up. But eventually, even Gais' patience ran out.

"Let's get this over with," he said. He reached his hand between my legs and found I still wore my underwear.

"You can't wear these," he said. It would have been funny if I had not been so nervous. I had heard the story of one girl wearing eight pair of underwear on her wedding night.

I took off the panties myself and soon we were in position for intercourse, the full flush of excitement and fear coursing through me. I bled when he entered me, blood from my loins and tears from my eyes.

"It's okay," he said, wiping my cheeks, dark with *kuhil* eyeliner. He cried with me, and I realized the sensitivity inside this man who was my husband.

☪

The next two days we enjoyed each other's company and discussed our future. We went shopping and dined at the most expensive restaurants. At night we walked under starry skies. I felt free to talk and laugh as I never had in Father's house. I was happy. I was joyous. I was in love with love. I was a new person. My face felt aglow with contentment.

On our third day at the hotel, as I lay in Gais' arms, he pulled me close.

"I have decided to buy tickets to Hawaii," he said. "We're going to have a real honeymoon. We'll take romantic moonlight walks on the beach and go dancing."

I was shocked. I remembered thinking how romantic Tumasha's wedding had seemed. But she had nothing compared to this. Mom was right. Getting married was the best thing I'd done. Life after this would be wonderful.

Chapter 8

Darkness Covered Us

It wasn't long after Gais mentioned Hawaii that the phone rang.

"Hello." The light drained from his eyes.

"What is it?" I asked.

"My father," he said. "He said I have to come home."

I soon discovered that Mr. Abee controlled Gais and his finances. Gais respected his father's wishes because he had no choice. So much for our new life free from the chains of the past. After two days of heaven, I found myself living across the street from Father.

When we arrived at the Abee house, my mother-in-law stood with arms crossed over her chest. Her dark wrinkled face reminded me of a chimpanzee. I kissed her cheek with no welcome in return. This was a bad sign. In Yemen, mothers-in-law are behind most divorces. They can make a marriage miserable for a newly married couple with their nagging and complaining. I refused to see this situation as hopeless, though. At fifteen and madly in love, I was ready to do whatever it took to make my marriage work.

My dreams were further dashed when I learned we were to live with the Abees. When Tumasha and Asser married they had a bedroom on the second floor of my parent's house. We did not even get that luxury. We were to occupy a bedroom right off the kitchen. We would have little privacy with Gais' mother lurking on the other side of our door.

I tried to stay positive, but it was difficult. The house was a mess. A layer of dust covered everything; the floors had not been swept in months, mold grew rampant in the bathroom and roaches skittered through the kitchen. Gais' mother had obviously not trained his sisters to do housework. I decided to take the task on myself. If Gais' mother was bothered by something I had done, I could get on her good side by helping with the house.

The next morning, after a night of lovemaking, Mr. Abee rousted Gais early.

"Jasmine," his mother yelled. "Get out of bed. Will you not fix your husband breakfast?" By the time I got to the kitchen, Gais was gone. His mother sat at the table with a cup of hot tea. She glared at me as if I'd killed her son, not married him.

After a quick breakfast, I set about scrubbing the kitchen and bathroom floors. I spent the rest of the week washing walls and windows, scrubbing mildew and grime, dusting and polishing. Not once did I get a compliment.

"You would get more done if you didn't sleep all day," Gias' mother said. I was used to waking up at ten in Father's house.

"What else do you need me to do?"

She had no answer to that. The house looked much better than it had when I arrived. So she just scowled and drank her tea. All those years I had babysat her kids, she never acted this way. I didn't understand. I hadn't done anything to her. Wasn't she happy to have her son married? Instead she treated me like a slave.

A week after the wedding I went outside to hang laundry and saw Mom across the street. She waved and walked to the road. I set down the basket and met her at the sidewalk.

"Are you already doing chores?" she asked.

"Yeah, Mom," I said. "How are you feeling?"

"But the henna has not even faded from your arms."

"Mom, it's fine." In Yemeni, a wife does not show sadness or make complaints lest she be seen as the *bad* wife and *bad* daughter-in-law. It was a cultural pride thing. You honor your family when you take the bullshit.

Days wore into weeks. My mother-in-law remained cruel and cold, a dark cloud over us both. I discovered from Ursa, her oldest daughter with the sharp tongue, that she was upset about Gais and me staying in our room for long periods, sometimes a whole day. She would eavesdrop at our door. Of course, she did not like what she heard. We were newly married and passionate. There was a lot of laughter and talking and making love.

"You look tired, Jasmine," she said one day as I brought tea and cookies to some of her woman friends. "I don't know why. You sleep in every day until almost noon." The other women frowned. "Of course, she does stay up all night," Gais' mother added.

I refused to react. I did my chores without complaint, no matter what she said. I think she was surprised and maybe frustrated that she could not get me to break. She did not realize the childhood I had suffered. She did not know I had been fighting a terrible monster for years. Besides, now that I had Gais, I could face anything. When he arrived home each night, my worries melted.

She tried a different tactic. "I am so miserable. My oldest son has married and nothing is the same. I have been sick ever since."

I only smiled in a friendly way. At the end of the day, after cleaning and cooking, I asked if she needed me for anything else. She stared with her sour face and said nothing. I had won that round. Yemeni women say you rank high in your family if you can endure more than a man. My mother-in-law tested my strength and endurance and unloaded her own pain on me each day. My love for Gais gave me the strength to hold on.

But I didn't want to keep fighting forever. When Gais and I were alone I suggested we get an apartment. We were husband and wife. We needed a house of our own. Gais agreed, but his father controlled him. The time was not right.

In the fall, Gais suggested I return to school. That freed me from his mother during most of the day. When I returned to the house, I would keep busy until Gais and his father came home. Then I could breathe a sigh of relief. Mr. Abee was always nice to me and Gais' mother never said anything harsh when the men were home.

In fact, Mr. Abee was the same kind man I had known as a girl. His opinion didn't change when I married his son. I decided to replace my real father with him. He would be the "dad" I never had. It was a good feeling to trust again.

Then, one afternoon I overheard a conversation.

"I am telling you," Mr. Abee said, "your wife is using birth control behind your back. This can be the only reason she is not pregnant yet. It has been one year. I want you to put her in her place and demand an answer."

"She has no reason," Gais said. His voice sounded timid.

"I tell you, she's a liar. She cannot be trusted."

It was if a sledge hammer had struck my mind. You backstabbing son of a loser, I thought. Here Mr. Abee was all this time smiling to my face while accusing me behind my back. I felt trapped. I could only trust Gais and he was gone most of the day. How was I to survive in this house where I was unwanted?

I ran to my room and threw myself onto the bed, tears streaming from my eyes. I could see my destiny with the one I loved being destroyed by our families. How typical for the Yemeni people to wallow in sorrow. Where happiness existed, they tried to tear it down.

Moments later, I heard Gais coming. The door opened and closed quietly. I felt the sudden tension in the room, but I dared not look at him. Instead I listened to his heavy breathing.

"Are you okay, Gais?" I finally asked.

"No!" he snapped. I blinked back tears.

"I'm sorry, Jasmine," he said more calmly. "It's something Father said."

I wiped my eyes and faced him. I saw pain in his expression.

"Are you taking pills?" he asked.

"Huh, what do you mean pills?"

"Birth control, or anything like that. I want a baby from you."

I shook my head. "First of all, *why* would I take anything to prevent having a baby? Second, how would I get them? I am only allowed to go to school." I pointed around the room. "Search the drawers and my purse and everything I posses and see if you find anything."

He took my hand gently. "I'm sorry. Forget I ever asked."

We made love. Passion was our "escapeland", our way to shut out the harsh reality that surrounded us. It was our way to solve problems after we cried and to celebrate happiness after we laughed. As long as blood pumped through our veins, we would remain together. We were full like the moon and hot like the sun, full of fascination and lust, so hungry after years of deprivation from love. We did not talk; we made love. It was a fantasy, but also the most intense experience I have had. Even today I cling to those passionate memories.

☪

I thought the birth control issue was settled, but a few weeks later Gais charged in and started ripping open cabinets and closets.

"Gais, what are you looking for? Can I help?"

"Nothing," he yelled. "Just leave this room!"

"What is it, Gais? Are you looking for pills?"

"Fuck this!" he said, tossing clothes about the room. He stormed out, leaving me to clean up the mess. I cried as I folded clothes and put them away. It was my fault entirely. If only I could get pregnant, everything would be all right. Gais' father would be happy and Gais would not feel so much pressure.

When Gais returned later, he apologized.

"I'm not taking pills," I assured him. "I'm even afraid to take Tylenol."

"I know," he said. "It's my father. He won't let this be."

Gais went to sleep, but I could only lie there. Darkness surrounded me, a deep dark hole. We had been married a year and no matter how I tried I could not make anyone happy.

After midnight I crept to the darkened kitchen. The floor was cold against my feet, cold like this house of hate. I walked to the bathroom and looked at myself in the mirror. Eyes once beautiful brown were now swollen with grief. The smooth face that had awed men and women at my wedding had been etched by pain. This was the end. I would never see another happy day.

I looked for a straight blade, but found only Gais' double-track razor. Desperate to stop my pain, I emptied a bottle of Motrin pills into my palm and swallowed them. Would that be enough? Maybe not.

I returned to the razor. Sitting on the floor, I ripped at my arms with the small blades, digging as deep as I could, feeling the burn of physical cuts blend into memories of verbal abuse and neglect. Blood welled and sheeted. It would be over soon. No more pain. No more suffering. Gais would be free. Blood dripped a steady rhythm onto the bathroom linoleum. I listened and let my thoughts drift like balloons overcoming gravity.

Suddenly I remembered Mom. It was if she stood before me, face streaked with tears.

"Oh. Mama." I imagined her at my funeral, standing over my body. I didn't want do that to her. But it was too late. Blood pooled on the floor, bright red. I felt the warmth draining from my body. My vision spun, my ears rang.

As if from a great distance, I heard a knocking.

Mama, is that you? I didn't want her to see me like this.

The knocking got louder.

I was amazed at the lack of pain. *It must be the Motrin.*

"Jasmine!"

Mama?

"Jasmine, please open the door, it's me, Gais."

My love, I thought.

"Open the door!"

"I just want to die," I said. *Better than to live this dark life.*

The door crashed open. Arms pulled around me. His skin was warm.

"Jasmine! Jasmine!"

His family would not let Gais take me to the hospital. They didn't want to make a scene for the neighbors. Instead, Gais wrapped my arms with gauze and bandages. He wiped blood from my body and helped me change clothes.

"Allah, help me," he said as he carried me to our room. "Don't ever do this again, Jasmine. Every slice to your skin cuts my heart."

"I'm sorry," I said as he laid me on the soft bed. I would never do this again, I promised myself, no matter how bad things got. Consciousness drained away.

Chapter 9

The Monster's Return

After my suicide attempt, Gais never mentioned getting pregnant, but the stress of living with his parents became more and more intense. I began to have nightmares. I tried to keep them from Gais because he had enough problems of his own. But one dream I could not deny. I woke at three in the morning gasping for air and calling out.

"What's wrong, Jasmine?" Gais wrapped his arm around me.

"Nothing." My heart still pounded in my chest.

Gais was troubled. "Please, tell me. What did you dream about?"

"I can't say."

"Why not? I am your husband."

"Mom says if you tell your nightmare before three days has passed it will come true."

"That's just superstition," Gais said.

"I suppose. But what if it *is* true?"

Gais stroked my hair. "No dream can be so bad that I cannot keep it from happening."

Once my heart calmed, I finally gave in. "In the dream I was this little girl running in the sunshine between long rows of sunflowers."

"That sounds like a nice dream," Gais said.

I began to cry. "I was running because we were divorced." There. I had said it. "Divorced."

"No," Gais said. "As long as I am alive that will never happen." He kissed me and I felt brand new. He snuggled me from behind. I felt safe. He was medicine to my heart.

Gais

He was my reason for bliss.
When I looked at the stars at night he was the reason for their being.
He was the awakening of spring and the roar of water falls;

And the shine of the sun.
Earth was transformed, becoming paradise and peace
And every second was that way with him.
Nothing else mattered because life was so good.

Others in the Yemeni community started to talk. They seemed fascinated by the passion we shared. Men didn't have to beat wives and women didn't have to bow down to husbands. We were redefining the meaning of a happy marriage, at least within our neighborhood.

Father could not stand the idea. One night in a drunken rage he came to the house and started cursing outside our window loud enough for the entire block to hear.

"Get up you bitch! I see you. You are on the bed. Is that all you do is let him fuck you like some donkey?" His voice echoed to the sky and beyond. Even Allah must have heard his profanity.

I felt humiliated. I wished for Allah to strike the Monster hard from his throne. The Qur'an says, *Satan's handiwork is to stir up enmity and hatred among you by means of liquor and gambling and to hinder you from remembrance of God and from prayer.* Was this not just cause to punish Father?

"You're drunk," Mr. Abee yelled from the front door. "Mr. Amag, you have no fear of Allah, or respect for these kids. Go home."

Despite Father's outburst, the marriage remained intact through the long summer. In September, high school resumed. At sixteen, I was both wife and student, but the school was large enough that no one knew. I was just another face lost in a sea of faces.

One day after school Gais took me on a shopping spree. I was stunned. I didn't tell Gais that I had never been to the mall before.

"Buy whatever you want." He pointed to racks of women's clothing. I picked several outfits. When the woman at the register totaled the price, it came to over four hundred dollars.

"I'm sorry," I said to Gais. "That's too much. I will put some back."

"No," he said. "They are yours. I want my wife to have everything she wants."

I was shocked when he suggested I wear one of the outfits to school.

"Gais, how am I supposed to do that? I always wear my black *balto* and scarf."

"Wear your outfit under the *balto*, and when you get there, take it off."

Farta and other girls did such things. If I been caught doing it Father would have killed me for sure. "I don't know," I said.

"You will like it," he assured me. "Try it just once."

Once I worked up my courage, I enjoyed showing off my new clothes. God did not strike me dead and if Mouzi was at school that day, he never spoke a word to me. When Gais picked me up, I was again dressed in my *balto* and scarf. I thought I was home free.

I should have realized that in a closed Arabic community someone was bound to tell. I had not been home long when Father charged across the street.

"I want my daughter!" he yelled. The Monster had returned.

I peered out the window while Mr. Abee went to the door. "Go home, Mr. Amag."

"Your son thinks he can act American and ruin my daughter."

"Oh Allah," Mr. Abee muttered, "give me patience on this man." He went outside and I followed, standing in his shadow.

Father's face was bloated and red. "He is even teaching her how to drive. I tell you I will take my daughter from you all if this continues." He lunged past Mr. Abee and grabbed my hand. "In fact, you are coming home right now!" I smelled alcohol on his breath.

"Stop," I yelled. "I am a married woman."

His fingers dug into my arm like claws. He dragged me across the street.

"Get into the car."

"Where are we going?'

"To see the sheikh." He shoved me inside. "You're getting a divorce right now."

"You can't do that." Tears flowed from my eyes. I looked back at Mr. Abee, but he only watched helplessly.

Father started the car and sped from the curb.

"Stop this, Baba," I sobbed. "Please, stop."

He turned his ugly face toward me, lips pulled tight against his teeth. "Have you given your husband a blow job, huh?"

I was stunned. That was none of his business

"You are nothing to him," he screamed. The car veered and settled.

"Gais is my husband," I said, trying to sound calm. "You are the one who wanted me to marry him. You are the one who got the money!"

He slammed the brake so hard my head nearly hit the dashboard. Suddenly, he was too calm. Without another word, he turned the car around.

When we reached Mr. Abee's house, an argument broke out, first with Gais and then Mr. Abee. Father again threatened divorce, insisting that Gais was corrupting me with his evil ways. In the end, Mr. Abee agreed to go to the sheikh and settle the issue once and for all.

Of course the argument was not really about my reputation or purity. Like it always was with Father, it was about the damned money. Father wanted more. Gais agreed to pay.

☪

One day, Gais came home with unexpected news. "I'm getting a job in Hawaii."

"Hawaii?"

"On a boat." He bubbled with excitement. "The pay is real good, my love. We'll have money to leave this mess forever."

I couldn't believe it. This was our chance to escape. "We're moving to Hawaii?"

"No, only I will go at first."

"Oh." My heart thudded. Gais would be thousands of miles away and I would be alone with his mother. How would I survive her vile tongue without his comforting touch?

A week later, he bought his plane ticket. He knocked on the bathroom door. When I opened it, he grabbed my arms and slowly leaned me against the wall. Looking deep into my eyes, he said, "Give me four months. I promise to come back and take you to Hawaii forever."

There was a determination in his look. I felt his words, but my intuition objected. I wanted to scream, "Don't go, don't leave me alone here, you will never return." But I said nothing. I trusted Gais. He needed to get away from his controlling father. I fully understood that.

"Whatever happens with my parents, just take it," he said.

I nodded. Four months. I could survive that long. Even though I would miss him terribly, I would be strong.

While time passed, I listened to music. Every time I heard a beautiful song, I would absorb it slowly into my veins and remember my time with Gais. Sometimes, I could hear him singing these songs to me, and sing along with him. We soared in blue skies among fluffy happy-face clouds. I heard the tenor of his voice, how it made my heart race and my palms sweat. I saw his angelic face, innocent and powerful. I remembered the way his eyes spoke to me and his tender kisses.

I began writing poetry. I wrote of my love for Gais and my hatred for his family. I wrote of desolation and yearning. I promised myself that no one would keep us apart.

Gais called often from Hawaii, but Mr. Abee would cut our time short. Sometimes Gais' mother would not answer the phone in order to keep us from talking. When Gais sent me a tape recording of him singing a romantic song, I hung on his every word. Soon, I thought. Soon we would move to Hawaii, far from our parents.

☪

When Gais returned, he was so thin he looked malnourished.

"What happened to you?" I asked.

"I couldn't eat," he said. "I hated it there. I missed you so much."

We made love that night and Gais described seeing the stars at sea. "Venus appears just after sunset or before sunrise," he said. "You can tell it's a planet because it doesn't sparkle. It's the brightest thing in the sky. Like you."

I snuggled against him. Even working at a miserable job, he could see the romance in things. How lucky I was to have found such a man. He was also smart and would often tell me how stars and planets were formed as I fell asleep in his arms. That night, Venus was his subject.

"It's the second planet from the sun," he said, holding me close. "The Greeks thought it was a beautiful goddess." He yawned. "If they only knew the truth. Their goddess is a cauldron of sulfur and poison gas."

Gais decided he could not return to Hawaii, not without me. Unfortunately, he did not have the courage to stand up to his father and move out. He was the man and had greater advantage than I did, but even for Yemeni men tradition is often stronger than need.

Gais found a job working at an amusement park. He had to leave early every morning to catch the Bablo ship at the docks. I told him to wake me so that I could fix his breakfast, but he never did, giving his mother an excuse to complain. I was a neglectful wife because I refused to cook for my husband.

Her cruelty escalated as time went on. She began pinching my breasts and pubic area when I walked near. One day when I called Gais to have him pick up some tuna on his way home, she went into a rage.

"Why don't you leave my son alone? You are trying to drive him away from his family. I know what you are, up to."

"I just wanted some--"

"Well, I will make sure he divorces you!"

Without another word, I went to our bedroom and shut the door. There was no use trying to talk to this crazy woman. When Gais came home, her ranting continued.

"What have you been doing?" he asked me. "Mom is so angry. Why did you hit Habubah?"

Tears welled in my eyes. "I didn't hit Habubah. It's a lie to drive us apart. You have no idea what I have been dealing with your mother." I explained the problems I had had while he was in Hawaii and how she had gotten worse since he returned. "I haven't told you because I did not want to cause more stress for you. We have to get out of this house, Gais."

"Father will never permit it."

"We have to do something."

"I'll save money. In a year--"

"This marriage will not survive a year." I pulled him close. "I'll go to my father. Maybe he will help us." The last thing I wanted to do was confront the Monster, but I had no choice if Gais could not stand up to his father.

"I forbid it," he said.

"I'm going." Wiping tears from my eyes, I left the room. I was determined to get us out of that house and away from his crazy mother.

I found Father in his basement room. He smelled of alcohol, but was not yet his monstrous self. Surprisingly, he listened to my complaints and said he would take care of everything. I suspected he was up to something, probably figuring a way to demand even more money from the Abee family. Nothing would make him happier.

A few days later I discovered he had made another appointment with the sheikh. I prayed to Allah that this would be the end of our problems. Once Gais and I were free, we could have a happy life together.

☪

As chance would have it, there was a wedding scheduled the same day as Father's meeting. Father was in an exceptionally good mood and told Mom, my sisters and me to go have a good time. I was happy to go, but my stomach would not settle.

While we celebrated, Father met with the sheikh, Mr. Abee, mediators and men from our Yemini village. When we returned home from the wedding at 10:30 PM, he wasn't there.

"Baba," I called out. He was not in his room.

"He is probably drinking with the men," Mom said.

"He was supposed to meet the sheikh," I said. He would go there sober.

"He will be home soon."

When midnight struck, I knew something was wrong. It should not take this long to decide whether Gais and I should have our own apartment. I paced back and forth in the kitchen.

At 1:00 AM, Father came through the back door.

"Well, Sweetheart, we solved everything." He smiled. "Your troubles are over."

I nearly cried with joy. An apartment of our own! Gais and I would be alone and I would feel like a real wife rather than a slave to his mother.

"You are divorced."

Divorced? The word echoed in my head. My arms fell limp to my sides and I swear the kitchen lights went dark. It felt as if I had been shot.

The Monster smiled. "The sheikh and the men have agreed according to Islamic law. You are better off divorced."

The men have agreed. That was not Islamic law; that was men making excuses for how they feel a woman should be treated. They called it Islam, but even at sixteen I knew there was no religion that did not speak of equality and compassion to every living thing. I was not an expert on the Qur'an, but this was not what Allah would want.

"You should be happy," father said. "You are free from that husband and his horrible family."

I said nothing. Father had done this to destroy my happiness. I hated him so much. I hated the blood that ran through my veins. It was Father's blood, the Monster's blood. It was poison. *I am not like you*, I screamed inside. I was not like any of those so-called Islamic Yemeni Arabs. I walked upstairs to my old bedroom and sat on the bed. My head pounded.

Across the street, light shown from Mr. Abee's house, but I could not see Gais. I wanted to scream out his name. *Gais! Gais! Rescue me. Take me out of here. Let us escape this madness. Let us run away*. I was drowning in toxic waste. I was suffocating. The room grew smaller and smaller. The ceiling descended to crush my bones into powder, leaving nothing but pain.

"Allah!" I whispered. "Why?" I struggled to find any ray of hope, but there was nothing. Nothing could heal me, not even the best doctor in the world. I was caught in a tidal wave of darkness and despair.

I was divorced.

Chapter 10

Lessons from the Qur'an

If the pain of losing Gais was not enough, I found out from Mom that Sheikh Mosa sanctioned the divorce thinking *he* had a chance to take me in marriage. I also discovered that my ex-in-laws had found the poems I had written about them. Mr. Abee had taken the hateful ones to the meeting as proof that I wanted divorce. He asked for a $5000 penalty. Father ended up giving them my gold belt and money to pay the debt.

In the days after the divorce, I was insulted and pushed around by Father, Mouzi and now Munsee, who had begun to mimic the other men in his life.

"Gabha," they would say. "Tramp. No one will marry you. You embarrass our family, bitch!"

Father's "good morning" consisted of spit in my face and a reminder, "you are a slut." He criticized me in front of my siblings and mother. They laughed as though it was funny, but they were really crying for help from the hellfire. We were all trapped in this endless cycle of abuse.

Buckets of curses overflowed in my head. I never talked back. If Father had heard my thoughts he certainly would have beat me. *It is better not to speak*, I told myself. People who cannot talk are the lucky ones. Better to have no voice than a voice that cannot express thoughts or pain or even laughter. I prayed that Allah would seek his revenge on the Monster.

What is This Tragedy?

Away from my chest you tore my heart
You made true lovers forever part.
You scarred me for life, took my soul away
How do you expect me to live every day?
This love is in ashes, burnt to the ground
All because of voracious blood hounds!

Vying for money and eroding earth between us
AAH, the world is at end

Nothing is left
We are shattered, broken

I was reborn with you, then killed
Justice stained, cuts inside me filled!
Now I live, breathing but dead
The throbbing continues, screaming pain in my head!
Stop it!

My only escape was to my bedroom window at night. I would turn on my alarm radio in the darkness and listen to soul music or pillow talk. Across the street, Gais' house was dimly lit and I would imagine myself together with him again. As the music flowed, so did my tears. Slowly, it began to heal me.

During the day, I turned to the Qur'an. In my everyday life it seemed that men were born to suck the life out of women and run us out of this Earth that was made for both Adam and Eve. I had read the Qur'an in Arabic as a young girl, but now I was determined to *understand* it. I began to read and translate it into English. In doing this, I saw passages I had never heard from my parents. Women *do* have rights. Yes, we have rights.

The woman is the teacher of children and the man is provider. That does not mean she cannot work. If she has knowledge or a gift she may use it. The Prophet's daughter was a poet. His wife not only owned a silk company, *she* asked for *his* hand in marriage. If a man does not make love to his wife she can ask for a divorce. If a man slaps his wife, the price is beyond what he can pay. When a woman is divorced, she may ask a man to marry her. Love must be involved and she should not marry the next day.

The Qur'an offered other wisdoms too. When a woman has her period, the husband should help her around the house because the blood flows from every vein in her body. The Prophet says not to have kids every year and to take time to teach them the Qur'an. God says to cover modestly, not wear all black and cover everything. The scarf represents respect for women.

All of this was opposite to what I had been taught. Confused by my discoveries, I took my questions to a teacher at the mosque.

"This is all true what you read, Jasmine. The translation is correct."

My view of life changed. I purified myself with ablutions, washing my face, washing my hands to the elbows and feet to the ankles. I prayed every day as instructed by the Qur'an: *And observe prayer at early morning, at the close of the day, and at the approach of night; for the good deeds drive away the evil deeds.*

I had been raised in a house of battles, right versus wrong. It was the only way my parents knew. I saw now that being Muslim did not fit my parents' profile. My only guidance now was Allah. It was a relief to learn how loving and holy the Prophet was, how pure the teachings of the Qur'an. It healed my senses, my way of feeling, how I expressed things. I had the *right* to express myself. A mission grew inside my spirit.

I did not understand everything, but that did not stop me from trying to teach my family what I had learned. One night as we watched an Arabic news report showing "our" people dying, one of the boys said, "*All* Americans should die." Someone else answered, "Yes, infidels go to hell. Only Arabic people are worth saving."

"You should not speak that way," I said. "Didn't the Prophet Muhammad say you must do good to neighbors who are near and neighbors who are strangers? He did not say your Arabic neighbor, he said neighbor!"

The others looked at me dumbfounded.

"Allah says none of this hatred," I explained. "Quit lying to yourselves. People like you give Allah a bad name."

Mom stared at me as if I had been possessed by an American ghost.

"Why are you defending the disbelievers?"

I looked into her eyes and said, "If it is the right way, so be it."

My comments were followed by some of the biggest beatings I have ever received. They did not stop me. I went to the Qur'an and read it aloud with a beautiful *tagweed* that came from my heart. I prayed harder and more times than I could count. The more I did, the more my family problems escalated. Yet I was becoming more solid inside. It felt good to speak, and the words sang from my mouth were *freedom* born from the softest and purist airs of my spirit.

While I fought for the Qur'an by day, my nights were given over to Gais. In bed each night, I felt we were still married. He would come to the window in my dreams and we would talk and laugh. I loved being close to him again. But dreams were not the same as reality. Mornings brought disappointment.

☪

I decided I wanted to go to Arabic school to learn translations of the Qur'an. It was something I needed for myself. I asked Mom one afternoon when she was in the living room smoking the *irgeelah.*

"Ask your father," she said her relaxed mood.

Asking anything from Father was like crossing a broken bridge with the chance of falling into burning flames below. Yet, you take risks. That is what life is about, right? I found him in his dungeon room. His eyes were bloodshot, but he didn't stink of alcohol at least.

"Mom said I should ask you if I can attend Arabic school."

"Arabic school," he mimicked. "You are *divorced.* Stay home, huh. You have enough knowledge to get you in trouble."

So much for crossing the bridge and facing the Monster. I could have started an argument, but thought of the Qur'an instead. Even if the world is corrupted, the Prophet says, walk and talk and think in peace. Somehow I would have to find that peace with my father. That would be my most difficult lesson.

My studies continued even without Arabic school. Particular passages in the Qur'an took on deeper meaning. When I had a problem, I recalled the Iqraa or Pen of the Qur'an which tells of the angel Gabriel appearing to Mohammad. Mohammad did not feel worthy of being chosen because he could not read or write. Gabriel commanded him to read. *Recite thou! In the name of thy Lord who created man from clots of blood. Recite thou! Thy Lord is most beneficent, who, taught by the Pen, taught man that which he knoweth not.* I was becoming a new person. I saw people as equal and beautiful and appreciated them for who they were. As my respect for others increased, self respect grew in equal measure. All this time, even as a child, the beauty was in me.

Tears welled up when I saw that my mind was on the right path. Allah gave me strength. He did not *talk* to me, but filled my heart with truth. I responded without fear or doubt. I believed. When I found myself being punched by Mouzi or degraded by Father, I sought strength in Mohammad's story. He listened to God's messenger and was called to greater things. This was all happening for a purpose. Someday, from all this abuse would come good. I was sure of it. We are all chosen for something in life.

I had not spoken to my ex-in-laws since the divorce. The prophet Muhammad tells us that if we remain upset with someone more than three days, Satan will create stories in our mind to hold a grudge even when there is a solution to the problem. I had to do something. It was time to reflect the light and glory found in the ways of Islam and break through the cultural darkness that imprisoned me. I would talk to my neighbors in friendship, not hatred.

The next day I saw my ex-mother-in-law hanging laundry in her yard. Father had gone to his usual hangout to drink coffee, so I crossed and walked toward their fence.

"Good afternoon, neighbor," I called out. The excitement of making it that far without anyone making a commotion thrilled me.

She looked up, astonished by my "too close" presence; we both knew the rules. I extended my hand and she came close enough for me to respectfully kiss the top of her head. To my amazement, she started to cry.

"Salam." I walked away feeling as if a weight had been lifted. I waved to her as I crossed back to my parents' house.

Inside, I found Mom sitting, reading the Qur'an.

"Mom, I need to talk to you".

"What?" she asked absentmindedly.

"I did something," I said. "Listen first to everything I have to say, please."

She looked up.

"You remember what our prophets taught us about forgiveness?"

"Uh hum," she responded.

"Well," I said, smiling. "I just crossed the street and greeted my ex-mother-in-law with peace."

"What!" Her gaze grew fearful. "Did your father or anyone see you?"

"No, Mom. We are only to fear Allah, not people. Remember? You read the Qur'an. I have done nothing wrong."

"Did she call to you?" She wanted Gais and me to get back together and hoped a peace offering from his mother would change the past. I loved Mom for understanding the passion I bore for

Gais, but she did not know how my ex-mother-in-law had treated me. It would truly be a miracle of God if that woman ever accepted me into her house again.

"No," I said. "I just decided it was the right thing to do."

"You must be careful, Shabat. A woman's life is filled with peril."

"Jasmine, Mom. Call me Jasmine." In the Holy Book, Allah tells of his ninety-nine names and one of them is *Al-rahman*, merciful. Allah states that daughters and wives and sisters are his *Al-rahman*, and admonishes men to be merciful and gentle to them. Allah is good.

Chapter 11

The Girl of His Dreams

A year after my divorce from Gais, I overheard Father and Mom talking in the basement.

"As long as he has the dowry money I don't care," Father said. It was the first inkling I had that a marriage was in the works. I felt sorry for Huria that Father didn't even care what man she married as long as the money was there.

It brought to mind the Qur'an sura, The Backbiter. *Woe to every backbiter, defamer, who amassed wealth and stored it against the future! He thinks surely that his wealth will be with him forever. Nay! For he shall be thrown into the Crushing Fire.* There was no saving Father. I could only pray that he did not drag us down with him.

A couple days later when I walked into the house after school, Mom was waiting for me. Before I could drop my books, she whispered, "Your cousin, Habul, is here from Yemen. I want you to go and welcome him. Make sure you shake his hand."

Something was up. Mom was not only encouraging me to see a man, she wanted me to *touch* him. She would never normally do such thing. It was improper. It would be bad for my reputation. I should never touch a stranger, even a cousin.

Out of respect for Mom I walked to the living room, but I worried the entire time. Father would beat us both if he caught us being familiar under his roof. I tightened my head scarf and approached my cousin, keeping my eyes downcast. From the chest down, he was a big man, with muscular torso and legs. I extended my hand.

"Salam," I said quietly. He took my hand in his powerful grip.

"Salam" he said. His voice was deep. I pulled away and quickly walked from the room.

"There," I said to Mom. "I have met him." I ran upstairs and sat on the edge of my bed to gaze out the window. It was my comfort zone. While Mom was busy talking to the cousin downstairs, I hoped I might see Gais across the street.

The next day, I overheard Uncle Gaban talking to Father.

"Amag," he said, "this is all he can afford. We are all pitching in for your daughter's dowry."

"It is not enough," Father said.

Poor Huria, I thought. Maybe Uncle Gaban wouldn't have enough money and there would be no wedding.

"Maybe we can find two thousand more," Gaban said, "but no more."

"I thought Habul already had a fiancé. He can marry her if you don't have the money."

"Habul does not want his fiancé. He wants Jasmine and only Jasmine."

My mind froze. Jasmine? I couldn't believe what I had heard.

"Do you know," Gaban said, "he kept me up all night telling me she is the girl of his dreams."

That was why Mom had acted so strange. I stared at my hand.

"All right," Father said. "I will accept your amount, but I want it up front."

I soon discovered that the marriage had been Mom's idea. Habul was Mom's cousin's son, who had come to America for a "visit." Of course his visit was actually for the purpose of finding an American wife in order to gain citizenship. Mom didn't mind that. A romantic at heart, she wanted this man to be the one. He was already family, after all.

It had been easy for Mom to convince Father. He just wanted the money. I wondered how much I was worth this time. What a mockery our lives were. I had barely been divorced. Why did I have to be the girl of Habul's dreams?

The girl of his dreams. Those words repeated again and again in my mind. People had told me I was beautiful all my life. I always seemed to attract the eyes of men and the jealousy of women. This *beauty* was no gift but a curse.

The rest of the day, I acted as if I had not heard anything. Who knew? Maybe I had heard wrong and the situation would go away. It did not.

Habul returned the next day. Mom was thrilled. "He is going to be real good," she said. "He will respect you three times more than someone who is not blood."

"He's a stranger," I said. At least I'd had a year to get to know Gais.

"He is one hundred percent from our root. He can never disappoint us."

"You can't be sure of that," I said. If I had not already been married and divorced, I might have been happier with their choice for me. But I was not over my love for Gais. He was on my mind all the time. We were a tragic tale like Romeo and Juliet. Women would see me on the street and ask what had happened. "Oooh, you guys were so perfect for each other. You were destined to be together. Maybe an evil eye was done out of jealousy." All I could say was, "Well, it is destiny that I find someone better someday." I knew in my heart that jealousy was not the reason for my divorce. It was greed, plain and simple. Father's greed for money. My mother-in-law's greed to keep her son. The sheikh's greed to possess me. Hearing what Gais was telling people cut an even deeper wound. "I will always love her in my heart and I swear no one will take her place." How could I handle that pressure on my heart and get married for a second time?

"You must put Gais behind you," Mom said. "Habul will be a good husband. He will give you wonderful children."

I might have gotten over Gais sooner if he did not live across the street. Until that day with Habul we still existed, unchanging like a picture in a frame. I still had hope that one day we would be together again.

"Gais is dead to you now," Mom said, reading my mood. "You must move on."

I nodded, but inside I wondered if maybe someone *had* cast an evil eye. A devout Muslim wasn't supposed to believe in superstition, but after living with Mom all those years I had picked up some of her habits. No matter how strong my spirit was with God, I felt that if I was living wrong no success would come out of it.

Later that day, as I watched out my window, I tried to clear my mind of bad thoughts. I prayed to Allah and looked for a sign. Would this marriage work or not?

Suddenly, a beautiful blue bird hit the screen and got caught in a tear along the edge. Was that a sign? What was the bird telling me? If it freed itself quickly, did that mean I should not get married? If it struggled, would I be trapped in unhappiness? I focused on the bird's frantic flapping. Downy feathers fluttered to the ground.

In the end, it did not matter. At seventeen, I had no voice. I couldn't tell Father I refused to marry Habul because a bird got snagged on my screen.

C˟

The next day, the sheikh came to approve Father's arrangement. I wanted to be loved by my husband and hoped this new marriage would succeed, but a fear of failure overwhelmed me. This was no way to start a new life.

At the time, Uncle Gaban was also arranging a marriage for his daughter, Owra, who was three years younger than me. Mom convinced Gaban to pay for a small wedding for the both of us in the same hall.

As with my previous wedding, we were decorated with henna the night before. Owra was not happy. She refused to wear a wedding gown because she had been forced into the marriage. Instead she wore a figure fitting sequined dress, vertically half blue and half white. I wore the same dress in black and white.

That night, I felt alive for the first time in months. Good marriage or bad, I was going to enjoy the women's celebration as if it were my last day on Earth. Owra, on the other hand, looked as if someone had died. While we sat on a long couch being "presented" with our husbands, I could not wait until they left. I longed to grab Owra's hand and dance and sing, show her it was all right to smile for the moment at least.

When the music began, Owra's husband left, but Habul stayed. It was obvious the women were growing impatient to uncover themselves and dance. I saw my aunt whispering to Mom, undoubtedly asking when my stubborn husband was going to leave. Some of the women looked ready to carry him out by force.

Suddenly, Habul grabbed my hand and pulled me across the stage. His shoe caught a wire and he nearly tripped over some big black speakers. Undaunted, he led me onto the dance floor. The mood in the place shifted at once. The women adored this surprise and started *zaghreeding* loudly, even young girls "ripe" enough to be the next bride.

Wow, I thought, he's a romantic. We danced to the fast beat of Fasil Alawi and the women clapped hard, turning the hall into an exotic frenzy. Habul twirled me like a merry-go-round. I couldn't believe what a fine dancer he was. I didn't lose my balance once despite the fast beat. As we danced face to face he whipped off his tuxedo jacket and tossed it to Mom. Grinning, she held it to her chest and danced too. Women filled the hall with screams and craziness. We had all gone wild.

Finally, I had to tell Habul it was time for him to go. He got his tuxedo coat and kissed me in front of the women. They roared, convinced by his actions that he was madly in love. And I had to admit, I was caught up in the moment too. Maybe now I could let go of Gais.

Chapter 12

A Daughter's Luck

Habul moved into Father's house and we stayed in Tumasha's old room. I continued with my schooling. Instead of attending the regular high school, I went to Miller School, a smaller program for students to make up their credit work. I liked it. Too many people at the high school intimidated me and I did not fit in. At Miller school I felt more like myself.

Every morning when I got up, Habul would greet me with, "A pleasant morning my beautiful dove."

He showed me books of poetry and stories he had handwritten in Arabic. He even read some to me, but it was hard to understand his dialect. He told me he had written poems and stories about me before he had even met me. I must admit I was taken by this romantic talk and his interest in poetry. I found his masculine body attractive. He had a broad, hard chest and soccer-player legs from his days playing the game in Saudi Arabia. Every day he would brush my hair and make me laugh with his facial expressions and antics. He had such humor. I couldn't help picturing myself in love with him.

School mornings, he would watch me walk to the end of the sidewalk to meet the bus.

"Do not let anyone bother you, and if anyone does, you let me know," he would yell.

I would giggle. "Okay, Habul. See you later."

Of course, in America boys and girls attended school together. Once as I was getting off the bus, one of the boys asked me about our homework.

"Who was that guy?" Habul snapped as soon as I came through the door. There was a fire in his eyes that I had not seen before. "What did he say to you? I don't want to have to go to school to keep watch over you."

"He was just asking about homework," I said. "I have him in my class.'"

"Well, do not talk to him in the future."

"Okay," I said. It was no big deal to me.

A month into our marriage, Habul came home from his job at a restaurant in Wyandot looking depressed. He sat me on the blanket on the living room floor. "Talk to me."

"Are you okay?" I said. I wondered if someone had died in his family. He didn't talk much about his life overseas, only that his father had eight wives and twenty-five children and his parents had divorced when he was young. His mother lived in Saudi Arabia.

"I am okay," he said with a strained smile. He went on to talk about his poetry. I thought I smelled alcohol on his breath. After living with Father, I certainly could recognize it. No. Maybe it was my imagination. Sometimes I smelled alcohol on Father even when he wasn't drinking. I leaned closer to get a better whiff.

Habul laughed. "Why are you sneaking up so close?"

"Habul, I want to ask you a question. Did you drink alcohol?"

He shook his head. "No."

"Are you sure?"

He glanced at the ceiling, avoiding my eyes.

"I am your wife," I said. "Tell me the truth."

"I can only write well," he said with a little sigh, "when I am intoxicated."

Allah, help me. Here I imagined I had married the perfect man, a romantic poet who would care for me. Instead, I had married an alcoholic. Bad luck followed me like a dog.

"Where did you learn to drink alcohol?" I felt acid building in my stomach. "Yemen does not allow drinking."

"In Arabia," he confessed. "Alcohol is everywhere, it is just hidden."

"The land of sacred Mecca? Are you kidding me?" Suddenly I saw Father sitting by me, not my husband.

"Don't cry," Habul said. He reached his arm around me "I only had a sip or two. I won't do it again. Ever. I promise."

I believed him. I wanted to believe he would never drink again. I wanted to believe in him so badly.

Over the next few weeks Habul became belligerent. He hugged me in the kitchen while Father watched. He stomped across the floor and talked in a booming voice late into the night. He got so noisy during our lovemaking that Mouzi pounded on the door and told us to be quiet.

When Habul came home drunk one night, Mom opened the door quietly, trying not to let Father hear anything. Tension had been building between the two men, and she was afraid Father would get his gun out if he saw Habul in such shape.

"Son, you did not call to say you were coming late," she said. "We worried about you."

He looked her straight in the face, and said, "Neither you nor anyone has the right to ask me anything. This is my life."

"Really?" Mom said. She had been so happy to bring Habul into our family and now he insulted her. "Well Habul, just go to sleep. I have nothing to say to you." He was so drunk, he had to crawl up the stairs.

"My daughter's luck," Mom mumbled. We were both disappointed.

I followed Habul to our room, but did not say a word. I huddled under a blanket on the floor and tried to sleep. When I got up for school the next day, he was still sleeping.

I spent the rest of the day worrying about what I was going to do. What he would say to me? With his moody ways, I did not know what to expect. I felt sick inside. Heat poured through my body and mind. I could not concentrate. Would my second marriage end like the first, over when it had barely begun?

When I arrived home, Habul opened the door for me. "Make some Arabic coffee," he said. His eyes were bloodshot and he looked rumpled, as if he hadn't slept in a week.

"Sure." I dropped my books onto the table and went to the stove. *Would you like that with rum?* I put water on to boil.

"Jasmine, come here and put socks on my feet," he commanded. "Hurry! You have been raised like a cow. Can't you move faster?"

Instead of Habul, Father sat before me. Habul's toned chest had sagged into a bloated belly and his arms had lost their strength. I was married to Father. My mind spun in circles. As I slid a sock over his callused sole, I thought of how Gais used to rub and kiss my feet, telling me how cute they were. Burning tears flowed from my heart. I swallowed them back. *Please help me Allah. What have I done to deserve this?*

☾

Each night Habul came home from work he insisted I fulfill my wifely duty and open to him. I could not refuse. I was his property. My opinion did not matter. But as time went on, his drunken behavior disrupted the household beyond our bedroom. Father became grumpier than usual. Mom hinted we should move into our own place.

One day Father called from the kitchen, "Habul! Habul!"

"Where is that worthless blood cousin of yours?" he asked Mom loudly.

He was in bed, of course. Habul put on his pants and strolled from our room.

"What is it?" he asked from the top of the stairs.

"Get your clothes on," Father said. "We're going to immigration and get your alien papers started."

"I don't want immigration papers," Habul said. He must have thought it was a trap. "I only want Jasmine. I can do those papers--"

"If you are not ready in thirty minutes, you are leaving my house!"

Habul chuckled. "All right," he said. "I will be ready, commander." He saluted from the top of the stairs. What a Charlie Chaplin he was. If only he wouldn't drink, I could love this man.

I never understood why Father was so concerned over Habul's papers. He still had time on his work visa, plenty of time to see how the marriage went before we supported his citizenship request. Maybe deep down, Father liked him despite their clashes. They were one and the same under the skin, the same view of life, the same temperament. *Allah, help me.*

Chapter 13

A Place of Our Own

Eventually, even Father would not put up with Habul. One night when he came home drunk, they got into a big fight about my dowry. Father gave us one month to get out.

Uncle Gaban decided to be *Mr. Generous*. He offered us his basement, which had a small kitchen with a linoleum floor and a yellow kitchen table with two chairs. The remainder of the floor was carpeted and one wall was covered in mirrors. He gave us four planks and two blankets to use as a bed. I figured that was to make sure we did not get too comfortable, which was good. Habul would get his shit together quicker and we could move out.

Mainly, I was uncomfortable living with Aunt Mouzia. We always called her *CNN* because she knew everyone's news. In all of Dearborn no one gossiped as much as Aunt Mouzia. Living in their house was like walking on broken glass. I suspected she listened to every conversation and kept track of our comings and goings.

But I did not know how nosey the woman really was until we had been living in the basement for a few days. There was a piece of plywood leaning against a stairway that led upstairs to a bedroom. The board gave us some privacy because it blocked people's view until they reached the bottom of the stairs. This was especially welcome since Habul had decided we should be naked most of the time. I didn't like being so exposed. It was not proper for a Muslim woman, even in her own home, but I had no choice.

The first time I heard someone coming down the steps, I went over and no one was there. The second time, instead of going to the stairs, I listened. Someone was sitting there watching us through cracks in the board. I heard them breathing.

I put on my *dira*. "Someone is watching us," I whispered to Habul. "They've been watching everything." Not only were we in the open, the mirrored wall opposite our bed was in view of the stairway. I expected Habul to get angry and go running after them.

"Let them see everything," he said. "I want the whole world to know I hold the most beautiful woman naked in my arms."

He was always erotic in his word choices, but not in bed. It was a shame. His intimacy was only on paper. I never complained about his lovemaking, but he must have suspected I was unhappy. He was always trying to get me to compare.

"So, did you love your precious Gais," he would ask. "Do you still love him?"

I lied to him with my lips. "No, of course not. You are my husband. I love *you*." Fortunately, he could not read my heart.

When I wore my shiny pink slip, he would ask, "Did you wear this for him? Did you?"

"I don't remember." That was true enough. It was not what I wore with Gais that stayed in my mind, but the feel of his fingertips on my body, the touch of his lips to mine.

Habul didn't stop there. His questioning would get so graphic and personal I couldn't help but be disgusted. He made me feel filthy sometimes.

"Let us talk about something else," I would suggest. "Your poetry?" Sometimes that would work and sometimes it would not, but the questions about Gais never stopped. I heard from Mom it was because Habul was listening to the men on Dix Avenue. Many Yemeni men talked about what a shame it was that Gais and I had been divorced, blaming Father.

Sometimes Habul would come home angry and test me. He would twist conversations around or tell me stories and ask me how I felt about them. He wanted to hear that I still loved Gais. He wanted to confirm his suspicions.

I was determined not to feed his jealousy. The harder he tried to make me admit my love for Gais, the more determined I was to show him that I loved only him. I began dressing sexy for him each evening when he came home. He thought I looked like an American prostitute. Nothing seemed to help his insecurity. He was like that wall of mirrors, bending every event or gesture to a different angle.

☪

Habul and I moved to a one bedroom apartment owned by a religious Yemeni family. I hoped things would be better once we got our own place, but Habul became even more possessive. With the exception of attending Huria's wedding, I was only allowed to leave the apartment to go to Miller School.

School became the highlight of my day. I had two American girlfriends there, Gena and Lisa, who asked me a lot about Islam. I answered their questions with pleasure. Eventually, they became so interested in Islam they converted. I felt good being their guide to the faith, but that did not improve my life at home.

The more Habul drank, the more unpredictable he became. His emotions were a roller coaster, blissful one moment, outraged the next. I wanted a way out, but was sealed in a little box with duct tape. I had nowhere to go and no one to turn to.

Alone in the apartment, I fanaticized about freedom. I would finish my education and become useful to society. My world would be happy and peaceful. Nobody would die in war; we'd have cures for every disease. Therapists would help families deal with alcohol and drug addictions. Everyone would have smiles on their faces and each and every person would become both a leader and a follower. That was the hope I clung to in days of darkness and isolation.

I considered going to A.C.C.E.S.S., a social center run by Lebanese that helped the Arabic community with food and other support. A playground separated our apartment from the building, but I was afraid to trust anybody there.

Near the end of the school year, Habul quit his job. The stress of having him always at home and not being able to pay bills made me physically sick. I would wake up feeling nauseated and be unable to eat most of the day.

I started to plan my escape. I would go to Hawaii and work on a ship like Gais had. I would change my identity. I might even see Gais working there. I imagined us living happily ever after for a while, but realized that could not be. No. I would be independent. I did not need a man in my life. I would be a revolutionary!

The nausea got worse and I felt cramping low in my belly. Afraid something serious might be wrong, I convinced Habul to let me see a doctor and ended up at an Arabic female gynecologist. It did not take her long to find what was wrong.

"Congratulations," she said. "You are pregnant".

Fuck! That was not part of the plan. "You are sure?"

"Oh, yes," she said.

I returned home, stunned. The first person I told was my cousin, Aura.

"You have to get rid of it," she said. "No baby should be raised by Habul."

"Hell, no!" I said.

"It is the only way. You will be trapped forever if you have his baby."

"Don't mention that again," I said. "It's murder."

"Life is murder," Aura said. She hung up.

☪

I decided to tell Habul I was pregnant right away. Maybe then he would stop procrastinating and get a job. On the other hand, he might react badly. A baby would be another mouth to feed and we couldn't even afford rent.

I waited until he was comfortable in his chair, reading the paper.

"Habul, I want to know, are you ready for children in any way?

"Of course, all boys. Yeah. Why do you ask?"

"What about this apartment that you cannot pay for? You don't even have a job. Are you sure you know what you want in life?"

"I am busy," he said. "You take my focus off the newspaper, trying to seduce me with your conversations. This beauty of yours is a curse." He chuckled.

"Habul, I'm pregnant."

He leapt from the chair so fast it startled me. "Hurray!" he yelled, grasping my shoulders. He jumped up and down like a crazy man. "Now I can continue my writing."

I was relieved. Later, as we lay in pitch dark, his voice broke the loud silence. "Jasmine, I am truly happy for us. Really I am. Just make sure it is a boy." He kissed my forehead.

"Sure," I said. "No problem." As if I had a way to make it a boy.

I was three months pregnant when graduation day arrived. The hall bulged with parents and families for all the students except me. Education had never been important in our house and neither was I, but I had dreamed that Allah would send me a miracle. While other students celebrated, I took the bus home.

I should have been happy with my achievement, but it was hard to keep my spirits up. Like the cloudy day, my heart remained gray as I walked to our dreadful apartment with nothing to look forward to but more of Habul's poetry and suspicious questioning.

I noticed a car slowing. I didn't pay attention until I saw Gais behind the wheel. *Gais. My one true love.* Suddenly, the day was sunny.

Gais stared directly at me as he passed. He made no indication that he recognized me, but when our eyes met, lightning flashed between us. My heart raced and I fought the urge to run to him. *Gais! Gais!* I wanted to jump in his car and flee with him.

He stopped at a stop sign and I saw him looking in the mirror. I stood in place, frozen to the ground. *Come back to me, Gais.* He never got out of his car or called me closer. He couldn't, of course. We were no longer husband and wife, but unrelated man and woman. Simply speaking to me on the street could start a firestorm.

My thoughts turned cartwheels as I walked upstairs to our apartment. I sat on the couch, not bothering to remove my graduation gown and hat. I was giddy. I had seen Gais! If only we could have one day alone, I would ask him what happened the night the men met with the sheikh. Why had they decided to divorce us? Why had they torn us apart?

Reality brought me back to the shoddy sofa and the tears bulging from my eyes. I hated my life. I hated Habul. I should not live in the same neighborhood as Gais. It opened up old wounds. I must forget him and concentrate on caring for my child, the one thing I had left in this life to love. The baby in my stomach was my survival and my strength.

☪

Mom was the happiest I had seen her in a long time. I was pregnant and Huria was married to a man from New York. Even Mouzi wasn't hateful. When Habul allowed me to visit, Mom made sure I ate *safargal,* a yellow Indian apple that is supposed to make the baby beautiful.

As months passed, I watched my stomach grow and felt this life moving inside me. I loved my baby more than anything. I prayed to Allah to give me a girl, voiding everyone else's prejudices. This baby needed me and I needed it. I would never let it down.

The larger my stomach grew, the more jealous Habul became.

"When you have this baby, it better not steal your love from me." He said this as if making a joke, but I knew better. In this disguised manner, he warned me day after day not to give too much attention to the baby. I knew he was serious.

"I do not want this baby to ruin *us*," he told me one evening.

"Look, Habul, this thing inside me is part of you and me. It was given to us by the Creator. How can you not love it?" No matter what I said, he would not be comforted. He could not get past his fear that I would love the baby more than him. In different ways, we were both vulnerable and lost.

"Sit next to me on the couch," he said. "I just want to lie against you."

We held each other for a while and I prayed for a sign. Habul needed therapy if he was going to accept the baby in our marriage. For me, I just wanted to be free of him.

My belly grew so large it seemed to take over my body. Habul became more and more unpredictable. One day he broke open the door to the bathroom while I was in the shower.

"What are you doing?" he said. His voice was rough and angry.

"Taking a shower," I said, shaking with fear. *What else would I be doing?* "Please close the door."

"Well, you are taking too long," he said. "What are you really doing?"

"Habul, I am begging you to close the door." I started crying like a terrified child. As water ran warm down my body, I tried to cover my nakedness with my long hair.

Habul laughed. "You are my soul, Jasmine. I did not mean frighten you. Just hurry up."

"Okay, I'm actually done now." I tried to make my voice bright and encouraging. He left, humming the sound of one of his poems.

A few days later, he burst into the bathroom again, insisting he look behind the curtain. I wasn't as startled this time.

"Why do you keep barging into the bathroom, Habul?"

"What if you have Gais in there with you?" he said with all seriousness.

I didn't know whether to laugh or cry. "Habul, there's not even a window in the bathroom. How would Gais get in? He is the past. You must stop thinking about him."

"Why should I stop? You love him."

"Don't you trust me?"

He didn't answer. We both knew he did not.

"What if I did love him? I'm in the present with you. I'm married to you. I want to make a life with you."

"Do you love me?"

"Of course. I'm carrying your baby." The tone sounded insincere even to me. Who was I kidding? I didn't love Habul, but admitting it would bring consequences. My divorce from Gais had been painful enough. I could not imagine how my family would treat me if I went home pregnant and asking for a second divorce.

I started taking showers when Habul was at work. Our nights became a series of repetitive arguments after watching TV or watching him write his poetry. I was not allowed to leave his sight, even to go to bed. Sometimes I would doze off and open my eyes to see his face inches from mine, his sour breath hot on my cheek.

Habul was sick, maybe seriously mentally ill. All I could do was avoid him as much as possible and try not to set off his paranoid behavior. I felt like fragile china about to drop to the floor and break at any moment. The only thing that kept me going was the baby. I had to hold myself together.

☾

"Good morning, my beautiful dove," Habul said one morning, as if everything was perfectly normal. "I can't help watching you sleep." The thought of him sitting there all night sent shivers ran down my spine. "I heard you talking," he said. "It is not clear what you are mumbling."

Oh God. I hoped I had not mentioned Gais. "Well, I don't even remember dreaming, Habul." I sat up in bed. "I have some advice for you. Pray to Allah. We all need him, sad or happy, poor or rich, sick or healthy."

Habul stared with a puzzled look.

"What is a Muslim without his prayers five times a day?" I said. "If we remember Allah, he will remember us and grant us security from this crazy world."

"I don't need to pray," he said, posing like Shakespeare. "I am Habul and I am a Poet. I pray through my poetry."

What did he know about prayer or what God expected of us? We had no food in the house and he chose not to find a common job or work in a factory because he believed he was better than that. He thought he deserved royal treatment because he could write? Yes, he did place words into beautiful patterns when the spirit moved him, but it wasn't putting food on the table. We have to eat before we can laugh or cry or dream. I could not believe

Habul was from Mom's Musleh family. He was such a sad excuse of a man, trapped in his narrow perspective.

"You should read the chapter in the Holy Qur'an about poets," I said angrily.

That was the first time Habul beat me.

Chapter 14

Crazy Man

My pregnancy continued, and Habul continued his abuse, slapping me hard across the face with both hands, ripping off my clothes and raping me. I cried for him to stop. I reminded him that I carried our child. Finally, in desperation I yelled, "Okay, do whatever the hell you want with me! Rape me! Just do it!" Many times I wished he would rip me in half. I would rather die and go to Allah than live through this torture, which seemed to have no solution or end.

Habul was always sorry afterward.

"I am so sorry, my love," he would cry. "I didn't mean it." He would get on his knees and literally kiss my feet for forgiveness. There were times I did forgive him from my heart, thinking nobody in my household ever said *I am sorry*, at least to a woman. I would forgive, but I could never forget my cheek bones numbing from the pain or my eyes swelling almost shut.

Habul got an assembly line job at a factory and I thought things would calm down. He would be gone during the day and tired at night. Too tired for beatings, I hoped.

His first day on the job, he returned at midnight. I opened the door to his knocking. He looked tired and dirty.

"Do you want to eat right now?" I said. "Shall I serve you?"

"No, just sit and talk with me."

I sat beside him on the couch.

He took a deep breath. "I am so sick of those American, ignorant dogs treating me like a foreigner. Do they not know who I am! I am Habul!" His voice had risen already to a shout.

"Habul," I said calmly, "this is only your first day. It will get better."

"Bastards," he hissed.

"If you want a better job in America you need an education. You have lots of opportunities here. First, you need to learn English."

"No!" he yelled. "I am already educated from my own country. I do not need the English language."

Fuck your ignorance, I thought. If he didn't like it here, he should go back to Yemen. *Asshole.* "Would you like your dinner now?" I said.

"Serve me."

"Of course." I went to the kitchen to prepare his food.

After Habul ate, he went to bed and was soon asleep. I had relief for the night, but that didn't last long.

☪

On his days off, Habul would hang around with his cousin. Antar was bad news. He often brought his wife over to our apartment and the men would go out and get drunk. At least I had company, but Habul was only getting worse.

"Habul," I suggested one day, "let's go to A.C.C.E.S.S. and see a therapist for this drinking problem. Please? They are Arabic and everything is confidential."

"No," he said, shaking his head.

"We need to do something," I said. "You're drinking all our money. We can't afford rent or food. What will happen when the baby comes?"

Habul broke down and cried. "Go to bed," he said brusquely. "I do not want to see you right now."

I did as he commanded, but lay awake for a long time. What was he thinking? Was he angry at me for suggesting help? Would he beat me? I didn't want to be hurt again. I was still sick everyday from the pregnancy and now I had developed itching sores on my scalp. I was still a young woman, but my body was crumbling under the stress of this existence.

Eventually I dozed off only to awake to the sound of heavy footsteps approaching. I opened my eyes to see Habul leaning toward me. He straddled my stomach, his weight pressing against the baby. *My baby!*

"I called you," he said. "Why did you ignore me?" His eyes looked fierce, but unfocused.

"I did not hear you," I said. "I fell asleep."

"Bitch!"

"Please, Habul, I'm pregnant. You're hurting me with your weight on my stomach."

"Take your clothes off!" He rolled from atop me.

I removed my *dira* and stood naked before him. My belly was so large I couldn't see how he could find me attractive, but I don't think attractiveness had anything to do with it.

He might get my body, but he would never take my soul. I returned to the bed and let him have his way. After that, he was satisfied enough to let me sleep.

☪

One afternoon, still suffering from morning sickness, I tried to relax on the bed. Habul reached for me, wanting to have sex.

"I have to cook before you go to work," I said, hoping he would let me go. "I do not feel good." My body tensed, expecting rough treatment.

"I will cook for you," he said with a grin. I was speechless. Had the Habul I married returned, or was he just here for a moment to give me false hope?

"Just tell me how to make chicken soup," he said, climbing out of bed.

"Sure," By the time he finished the soup, it would be time for him to leave for work.

I talked him through the process. He cut up pieces of chicken and put them into a pot on the stove while I watched from the living room. My mouth watered as a meaty aroma drifted through the apartment. He worked in the kitchen for a while longer then came to sit beside me.

"Come on honey," he said, fondling my breast. "While the chicken cooks, let us stir ourselves on the floor!" He grabbed my hand.

I pulled back, nauseated. "No, Habul. The chicken will burn. I smell it already."

He darted to the kitchen where smoke billowed from the pot. He grabbed a spatula and waved it, hitting the ceiling light and breaking the cover. Glass flew, some even hitting me where I sat on the couch.

"Shit," he said. He turned off the stove, tossed the meat into the sink and returned to me. "Let's go have sex."

"But the glass...."

He pulled me from the couch and threw me onto the bed. I gritted my teeth to keep from vomiting the whole thirty seconds it took him to relieve himself inside me.

Like a mad man, he climbed off and jumped up and down, naked and cheering. Who was this crazy man? Would he leave me in peace or lash out? I slipped my clothes on and ran to the bathroom. Only after he settled down did I let him in to shower.

Before leaving for work, he joined me at the kitchen table for a cup of lemonade. "You are a worthless wife," he said. "You ruined the food."

"Well," I said. "If you were a man--"

He tossed his lemonade into my face.

"Oh!" I shouted. Lemonade ran down the front of my dress. "What have you done?"

"I am so sorry," Habul said. He went down onto his knees. I let him kiss my feet. *This is the last time*, I thought. Kissing my feet would be the last memory he had of our marriage. Let it burn forever in his mind.

Habul left and my anger turned to despair. I had my hand on the phone, ready to call Father about Habul's behavior, but hesitated. I didn't want to admit to Father or even myself that I was in a failing marriage. Instead of calling, I sat in the kitchen feeling hopeless. *Gais*, I thought. *Where are you now that I need you?*

The next day was Saturday and Habul was off from work. We didn't say a word until after noon.

He asked me to sit by him on the couch. "Jasmine, do you love me? I will set you free from this marriage if you tell me the truth."

Allah knows I was tempted to unleash a whirlwind upon him. It was killing me inside, this holding back everything. I restrained my tongue. "It's not about love," I said. "This is a marriage. I do not like how you treat me or what you do to me, but we are married."

Habul looked unhappy. "My beautiful dove--"

"You took my holiday Eid money," I said, anger gaining the upper hand, "and you are paranoid. You did not trust in our marriage from the first day. You beat me and cage me in the apartment. You ask me if I love you? Love is not supposed to hurt, Habul."

He gazed at his lap. "Do you want me to divorce you?"

"Yes," I said. "Yes I do." There, it was finally out.

He looked up. Anger perched behind his eyes, ready to pounce. Apparently, that was not the answer he wanted to hear.

"Your family will never love you as I do," he said staring straight into my eyes.

"That would not be difficult," I said. "I never received love from my family."

"All right," he said, standing suddenly. "I am going to the mosque, and when I get back I will take you to your father's house."

I was relieved he was gone, but the thought of going to Father and asking for the divorce made my stomach churn. His rage would erupt, especially now that I was pregnant. Staying with Habul almost seemed better than facing Father's rage. Almost.

Less than an hour later, I heard banging at our front door. When I opened it, Father shoved his way past me into the apartment.

"Where is Habul?" His eyes blazed and he worked his teeth as if chewing tough meat.

"He went out," I said. Too little time had passed for Habul to speak with Father. Either this was a terrible coincidence or news had gotten to Father before Habul.

"I want my money. He owes me money for the dowry. If you were a good daughter you would remind him to pay me."

"I didn't know."

"Bitch," he said. "When is he coming back?"

I shrugged. "He went to the mosque."

"The mosque? What for?"

"A divorce," I said. "I've talked with Habul and he is willing to divorce me."

Father clomped closer and I tensed, waiting for his slap. Instead, he spat in my face. "You are a disgrace to me. Whore. Bitch. I will wait here until Habul returns." He plopped onto the couch, mouth working angrily.

The tension grew thick between us. I almost offered to make tea, but thought better of it. It was wise not to talk to the Monster any more than I had to.

It seemed like hours before we heard footsteps outside. Father sprang from his perch and headed for the door.

Before Habul could welcome him to our home, the Monster unleashed. "Where is the rest of my money, you worthless man? You and the rest of Beni-Musleh are shit!"

"Do not talk about my roots," Habul said. "Because you are part of it too, Father."

"So my daughter is pregnant, and now you want to divorce her? You don't want her no more, huh?"

"Who said that?" Habul puffed his chest out. "I will *not* give up my wife to you or anybody else."

I cringed, knowing what would happen next. Someone was going to get hurt.

Father delivered the first punch, hitting Habul in the right cheek. It did not faze Habul.

"Come on, Father," he taunted. "I will give you the other cheek, but not my wife."

A veil of silence fell around me. In my eyes it looked as if Father was fighting a mirror image of himself as the two men exchanged punches and insults. I felt like screaming at the top of my lungs, but all I could do was swallow my worry. *Please, Allah, save these men from their stupidity.*

Finally, Father broke off. He was breathing heavily. "I am taking my daughter," he panted. "You will never touch her again."

Still lost in a haze, I was pulled from the house by Father's strong hand. I had no emotions, going wherever the winds blew me. Nothing seemed real.

That night I was back in my old room, staring at the ceiling and praying with all my heart for an end to my torment. As I prayed, tension leaked from me. My heartbeat slowed and my sobbing stopped. A new energy entered me, full of light and promise. In that moment, Allah wrapped me like a baby in her mother's arms. No words could describe that sudden feeling of faith and belief. I had experienced so much sadness for my baby about to be born into this environment, but now I felt a sense of promise. Leaving Habul had been the right path.

"I will always be there for you," I whispered, touching my stomach. "You will not feel orphaned as I so often have."

Pity Habul

Just look at the tables turning
One last time Shakespeare, repeat the con words out your mouth
What is it that you say about me?
You have been my shame
Our child now your pointless game!

Do you even know where it's from?
You play so smart, but for the world are dumb!
You are the reason for this life in me
Because you took me so carelessly
You have no happiness and hide your true grieving
By indulging in intoxicated drinking!
I am in your life as a kindness
You are in mine as pity and crisis!

Chapter 15

Joy in my Soul

The next morning Father reminded me that I might be free of Habul, but I was not *free*.

"Your baby will be a bastard," he said as if making conversation. The sores on my scalp itched terribly, but I forced myself to ignore them.

"Is that what you want?" he said. "A bastard?"

I did not answer. I had chosen the Monster's verbal abuse over Habul's fists. This was the cost of that transaction.

"So," he said. "How will you make money to pay me to live here?"

According to Islam, it was a duty for men to provide for a divorced relative, but not in this dark hole of a house. I was on my own.

"I can apply for welfare," I said. "I can get cash and food stamps."

He smiled.

☪

The idea that I could get money from the government made Father happy, but at the end of the month he badgered Mom and me.

"This is all you get? Where is the rest?"

"She will get more when the baby is born," Mom said.

Father looked suspicious. "I know you have hidden money away in some bank. She should be paying me to stay here."

"Why? So you can drink it down with your friends?"

I expected Father to slap her, but he did not. Something had changed between them since her stay in the hospital. Maybe he saw how fragile her life was, or maybe the rest of my siblings were keeping him occupied. Tumasha was having emotional problems and her kids were at the house much of the time. Mouzi was engaged to a cousin and the both of them were selling cocaine to raise money for the dowry. Huria's marriage was in trouble. She called every day to complain to Mom. Soon, I expected Father would have two divorced women in his house.

Father left, grumbling, and I settled back with my tea. Shortly after, there was a pounding at the front door.

"Who can that be?" Mom said.

I walked to the front door and looked out the window. It was Habul. He had been making threatening phone calls for a couple weeks. He'd broken into Father's house a couple times. I feared him to the point I had nightmares.

He pounded again. "Let me in, my love."

"Who is it?" Mom asked.

"Habul."

"What is he doing here?" Mom joined me and opened the door.

"Don't let him in," I said.

Too late. He charged inside.

"Jasmine, my love."

I ignored him and walked into the living room.

"Come home," he said, following at my heals. "I love you! Your family will only use you."

"Like you use me? Only it's worse because you're my husband." I refused to look at him.

"If you don't leave," Mom threatened, "we will call the police." She looked scared.

Habul grabbed my hand and twisted me toward him. I slipped my fingers from his. His eyes widened when he saw how big I was.

"You see the mess you have left me?" I said. "How can I expect you to provide for a child when you cannot take care of yourself?"

"I just want--"

"You don't know what you want, Habul. I refuse to let you hurt my baby."

Tears overflowed from his eyes. "Please, Jasmine. I am lost without you."

"Go home, Habul."

Sadness turned to anger in the blink of an eye. "You are still my wife," he snarled. "You will do as I say."

"This marriage is over," I said.

With Mom there, he didn't have the courage to hit me. Instead, he stormed out, slamming the door behind him. I heard later he was telling everyone in town that Father had stolen his wife.

☪

I went into labor January 25, 1994. Mouzi was the only one at home with a car, so he volunteered to take me and Mom to the hospital. I expected him to degrade me and complain during the ride, but he was in a good mood.

"Hang on, Jasmine," he said as he sped through the streets. "You're doing fine."

Labor pains tore through my stomach, but they felt no worse than Habul's punches.

"Almost there," Mouzi said.

Everything happened so fast. I was taken to a room where a nurse examined me, but it was not long before I was in the delivery room. With Mom and the Qur'an at my side, it took only two hours for my baby to be born.

"It's a girl," I heard someone say.

Thank you, God. My heart overflowed with joy.

"I will call her Dignity," I said, holding the tiny bundle in my arms. She was the most precious thing to me. All the world's treasures could not replace the joy in my soul that day. Nothing could have been more wonderful than my new daughter.

Dignity

Dignity my love for you is too great, tears become stormy
Dignity you are a gift to me of the highest glory.
Dignity you are the song to my soul; you are my symphony
Dignity you have healed all of my wounds and agony
Dignity you are the fruit of my childhood
Dignity you the guidance and light to my motherhood
Dignity your name comes from the Qur'an
Dignity you are the skies from night to dawn
Dignity you made my heart sweet as a ripened fig
Dignity you are my fulfillment that is much too big
Dignity you are my joy and filled my heart to the core
Dignity you are my peace when the world around is still sore.
Dignity for once my soul is wildly enchanted
Dignity my wish for a girl has been gloriously granted.

Dignity was eight days old when Father asked, "When do you get money for the baby?"

I'd just fed her and put her down for a morning nap. "I have to go to the WIC office," I said. The weather had been cold and roads icy. I was still trying to recover from the birth and didn't want to venture outside.

"Do it today," he said. "It is bad enough I have Huria back in the house. I will not have a bastard living here for free."

Habul and I were not yet divorced and the fear of going back to him made me more obedient to Father's wishes. That afternoon I journeyed through snowy streets to an office that was gray and cold and filled with women sitting on plastic chairs, many holding small children on their laps. The room smelled of urine-soaked diapers and spoiled milk.

I registered at the desk, and when I turned was surprised to see Gais there with a friend. He still looked the same with his dark hair combed back like a movie star. I felt my cheeks warm. Before he could see my embarrassment, I looked away. Gais did not approach me, which was for the best. He had remarried and people would talk.

I managed to pass by him on the way to a seat. "Salam," I said.

Gais nodded. "How are you doing, Jasmine?"

"I just had a baby." There were so many things rushing through my mind, I wanted to blurt them all at the same time. Did he still believe I had used birth control during our marriage? I wanted to assure him that I had not. If we had created a child together, would he have fought the divorce? I wanted to tell him that I wished Dignity was his daughter instead of Habul's. I wanted to say I was sorry. I wanted to say I loved him.

"Congratulations," he said.

As I returned home, I wished my life had been different. But wishing did not make it so. The minute I walked through the door, the phone rang.

"Hello," I said.

"If I can't have you, nobody will," Habul said. "I promise." His voice was like ice in my ear canal. I hung up, but my hands shook uncontrollably. I had this madman following me. I had just had a baby, but was still expected to do housework. Worst of all, I was living across the street from Gais and his new wife. *Help me, Allah!* I wanted to escape my mind.

I tried reading the Qur'an, but even that did not work. Then I saw Mouzi's cigarettes where he had left them. I needed something to calm my nerves and decided to try one. He would never notice. He was too busy smoking weed and selling cocaine to miss cigarettes. I took a few into the bathroom.

Mouzi didn't notice, but Mom did. She had a nose like a blood hound.

"Jasmine! What are you doing?"

"Nothing," I said, putting the cigarette out in the sink. Steps creaked near the closed door.

"Open the door," she said.

I waved my hand to clear away the obvious smoke. She opened the door.

"I can't believe this." Her nose and mouth wrinkled. "You just had a baby. It is a disgrace. What kind of Muslim are you?"

"I'm sorry, Mom."

"Sorry!" Mom could cuss like Father, but most of the time she tried not to use such language. That day she cursed at me until I thought the skin had been stripped from my body.

I went to my room, embarrassed at disappointing her and failing my duty to the Qur'an. Only a year earlier I had been lecturing my family to follow the teachings of the Holy Book.

☪

My family was always full of contradictions. That same afternoon, Mom called me to come downstairs. She had the *irgeelah* ready to smoke with natural tobacco mailed from Yemen.

"Sit," she said softly. "Smoke with me."

I did not question her. We smoked and the *irgeelah* gurgled.

"Everything is going to be okay," she said with a rare bright smile. "You have a beautiful baby and a husband who loves you."

"It's not love, Mom."

"It is Habul's way of love," she said. "He is a temperamental poet. You have to be cautious with a man like that."

"He's crazy."

"You have to mold a man," she said.

"Mom, that doesn't work. Look at Father. After all these years, he's treats you worse than ever. You are perfect in everything you do and you are beautiful and too young for him. He's thirty five years older than you."

Mom got a faraway look and I wondered if she had had dreams as a girl. Certainly she must not have wanted to marry Father. Had she ever been in love?

"Habul is not like your father," she said. "Habul is wild for you."

"He is not *yet* like father," I said. "But he's worse in his own way, trust me."

"This is your second marriage, Jasmine."

"I didn't ask for it, Mom."

"Go back to him," she said. "It is better than living here with your father and brothers. Be a good wife. Do not burn yourself out thinking too much." *Too late*, I thought. I had been burnt out since I was eight years old.

"With all respect, Mom, I will never go back to Habul."

Mom shook her head sadly and sucked on a tube. *You can't teach an old dog new tricks.* No matter how many good points I raised, she just wouldn't let go of the old ways. She had given up the fight and would spend the rest of her life in misery. I could not see myself doing the same. Rather than starting a pointless argument, I released myself to the *irgeelah's* gurgle and settled in with Mom. Despite our different views, I valued my time in her company more than anything.

☪

Dignity brought love to Father's house. My brothers and sisters hovered over her constantly and for the first time we seemed like a real *family*. I thanked Allah over and over for bringing some peace into my life.

A couple months after Dignity's birth, Father helped me get a protective order against Habul. He told everyone he was making sure his daughter was protected from harm. Actually, I think he was sick of Habul breaking his doors.

I wanted to be divorced. Habul continued to plead with people to help him take me back. The Qur'an says we have the right to ask for divorce and it shall be granted on the day we ask for it. That is not the case, however, especially when a woman requests divorce. In Yemen, when a woman is not granted her divorce for a year or more, it is called *moalakah*, which means hung by the end of the rope. That was my case. I waited two years.

In the end, a group of men caught Habul outside the mosque and wore him down until he signed the Islamic divorce. Afterward, he made sure every man there heard what he had to say.

"This is unfair. My wife has been taken from me. But even if I do not have Jasmine in my life, I will see her through our baby."

Habul the poet was a liar. He never looked for his daughter or called to see her, and he certainly never paid child support. A Muslim man is supposed to pay child support without encouragement. Not him. When Dignity turned two and a half years old, I had still received nothing. The welfare office no longer wanted to support us either. A new law had been enacted that required everyone on assistance to work a certain number of hours.

I could have been devastated. It would be difficult to work and care for Dignity. I would have to depend on Mom or sisters to babysit and I would miss her dearly. Yet, I was happy. Freedom was staring me in the face. My Father and husbands had not permitted me to seek employment. Now the law was telling me I had to leave the house and *work!*

Chapter 16

Freedom at a Cost

Working outside the house would go against everything my family believed. If I wanted a job, I must first convince Father it was necessary. He wouldn't want me leaving his house, and he certainly wouldn't want me to have money of my own. I decided to take advantage of his weakness: greed.

"I need to speak to you about my welfare money," I told him one evening when he returned home after drinking with the men on Dix Avenue.

"What is it?" he growled.

"I just found out today," I said. "Now that Dignity is older, they will not give me assistance if I do not start working."

"Work?" he said in a guttural tone. "Where will you work? You cannot keep a husband. How can you keep a job?"

I put on a fake smile. "There are a lot of jobs I can do."

"Humph!"

"I can type and file in an office."

Father glared, about to say no. And a lot of curses too, judging by his expression.

"I must find a job in one week," I said, "or the welfare checks stop. No more money."

His anger collapsed like a hot air balloon with a big leak.

"Okay," he said. "Look for something in the Yemeni neighborhood. I don't want you working for no Lebanese."

Mom put up more fuss.

"You cannot work." She was hungry for me to get married again and it would be difficult to find a husband for a working woman. In her eyes, I was only safe if I was married. "Who will watch your daughter? I have too much housework."

"Huria will watch Dignity." My sister had nothing to keep her occupied during the day. "I'll give her some money."

"You don't have to pay me," Huria said when I asked her. "I will watch her for free."

That was the first nice thing I had heard from my younger sister in years.

When Father left that afternoon I walked to Dix Avenue, just a few blocks from our house. All the business people were from Yemen, except the doctors. They were educated people from Lebanon or Syria. Father didn't want me working for them because the Arabian community in Dearborn separated itself along ethnic lines. We were all from Arabia, but the Yemenis were considered a lower class by the others.

I ignored Father's order. I would take any job that was available and hold my head high.

"I am looking for work and wondered if you are in need of someone," I asked again and again, trying both retail stores and medical offices. Most said "no." Others asked if I was married, how old I was, or whether Father knew I was looking for work. A few told me to go home. I would not be deterred.

At a dental office with white walls and leather chairs, I approached the reception widow and was greeted by a woman with a light complexion, round face and green eyes.

"May I help you?" Her voice was squeaky like a mouse.

"I am looking for work," I said.

"What experience do you have?"

"No work experience, but I can answer the phones and file or fill out papers."

She eyed me as if trying to see beneath my *balto* and scarf.

"Yemeni?"

"Yes," I said. "I am a good worker and learn fast."

"Education?"

"I graduated from high school."

She seemed surprised by that and called the dentist out to meet me. He was a tall, handsome man with wide shoulders and a nice smile.

"This girl is looking for a job," she said.

"My name is Jasmine," I said. "I am willing to learn."

I was hired that day. At first I was a combination secretary and dental assistant, cleaning teeth, typing bills, making phone calls, and setting appointments. I worked six days per week, from 7:30 in the morning to 6:00 at night and was paid $100.00. I did not have extra money or time for lunch, but felt free for the first time in my life. If I never married again, I would be happy. I liked being my own woman and bringing in money.

Impressed with my work, Dr. Bedwoon asked me to study the tools and equipment in order to make me his assistant. "My wife will take care of the secretary part," he said. "Lena, let Jasmine teach you the billing process."

Eyes narrowed, she said, "I know how to do that already."

I knew then I was in trouble. I was only there to do my job and already I had a jealous wife on my hands. In the days that followed, Lena would pop in on us at different times to see if something was going on. Of course, nothing was. We were with patients most of the time. It wasn't that I looked attractive in my *balto* and scarf. And I certainly wasn't interested in her husband. I had already had two husbands and no plans to add a third to my list.

"Why do you Yemenis wear all black?" she asked one day.

"I do not know why," I said. It was tradition. I wondered what traditions she followed, but dared not ask for fear she would think I was being difficult.

"Why do you look sad all the time?" she said. "If we had enough business we would pay you more money."

She assumed that was why I was unhappy. She wore Clinique makeup and drove a Lexus. It was not that they were poor and couldn't afford to pay more, they were greedy like Father. I didn't care. How could I explain that there were more important things in my life than money?

"So why are you working?" she asked. "Are you in college? Are you married? Yemeni men marry their daughters at such a young age."

"I'm divorced from my second husband," I said, "and I support a two year old." That shut her up for a time. *Be thankful you are an airheaded Lebanese*, I thought. She would never survive in Father's house. Although I deeply respected Lebanese men, I could not stand these backstabbing Lebanese women.

From then on, she interviewed me as if she were Barbara Walters or Oprah. She was interested in my horrid life. I continued to answer her questions even though they were too personal for conversation. At least I was chatting with someone. It was better than being alone.

Sometimes I worked by myself in the office taking care of patients who had no appointment. Most of these patients were Arabic men and being alone with me brought out the worst in them. Old or young, confident or broken, they were all the same.

Sometimes they wanted sex. "Let me kiss you just once on the lips." "Ohhh. You are too beautiful to be from Yemen; you look Lebanese." "Ohhh, my hand is in my pants. I feel I am coming because of you."

I kicked a few out of the office and threatened to call the police more than once.

Even the ones who engaged in respectful conversations wanted me in marriage. "What is your father's name? Give me his number. I will call and ask for your hand tonight."

Sometimes I wished I had a gun. The world would be better without these men. Where was their respect for women? Where was their love for the Qur'an? But then I would hear the call for prayer in the distance and I would feel sorry for them. They had not been taught better.

Many days I returned home upset, the emotions of dealing with all of these lost people bottled up inside. I hated them, but was part of the community. Could nothing be done?

Mom was no help.

"Go change your daughter's diaper!" she snapped when I walked in the door.

"Can I please take my shoes off?"

Dignity was almost three by then. I missed her when I was at work, but couldn't explain that to Mom. She thought I had abandoned my child.

I removed Dignity's diaper and her butt was as red as tomato.

"What the fuck is going on!" I called out. "Mom, did you guys change her at all today?"

"I was too tired," Huria said. "Plus you do not pay me enough for supplies."

"You fucking bitch!" I said, sounding just like Father. "I just paid you $70.00. I only make one hundred dollars a week."

"Get out of here!" Mom shouted. She had shown an evil side since I started to work.

I felt sorry for Dignity. We were outcasts from our own blood and people.

I felt hopeless and sad. There seemed to be no real friend for me in this world. My sisters were out of the question. When I pleaded with Tumasha to open her sisterhood to me, she transformed love into a hurtful pain. I had babysat her children while I was pregnant with Dignity. Now that I needed help, she not only refused, but took me into the bedroom to ask, "Are you fucking my husband?"

Since returning to Father's house, I had caught Asser watching me from across the room. When Tumasha wasn't home he would make conversation, but I had no interest in the man.

"How could you ask such a thing?" I said. Her words cut me like razors. I was her sister. I would never betray her. I cried so long, my eyes hurt. My own sister was jealous and I had done nothing to deserve it.

As usual, I turned to the Qur'an for peace, *tagweeding* the verses aloud. I identified with the story of the Prophet Joseph and how his brothers were jealous of him. One day Joseph went to his father to tell him about a dream.

"I dreamt there were eleven stars bowing to me," he said. Of course, his eleven brothers were eavesdropping.

"Do not share this story with anyone son, even your brothers. They may become jealous and try to harm you."

One of the brothers said "My father loves and favors Joseph. We shall kill him."

"No," said another. "Let us throw him in a well and tell our father a wolf ate him."

They agreed on that plan.

"Oh, Father, let us take Joseph out to play and run with us."

"No," the father said. "I am afraid you will wander and a wolf could eat him. You cannot defend your brother."

"We promise, Father, we will guide him. We are eleven brothers."

He eventually gave in to their request. The eleven brothers did as they planned and came back crying, clutching Joseph's white shirt stained with animal blood.

"The wolf has eaten Joseph!"

His Father cried for many years until he became blind.

In the meantime, a couple found Joseph in the wilderness and sold him to a rich family. His adoptive mother found him handsome and trapped him in a room to seduce him. He felt aroused, but an angel appeared and told him to stop. He tried to run out the door, but she grabbed his shirt and ripped it. When Joseph opened the door, her husband was standing before them.

"Joseph tried to rape me," the woman said. Her husband was outraged.

One of the servants said, "Let us see if the rip on Joseph's shirt is in the front of him, then she is telling the truth. If from behind, she is deceitful."

Joseph was innocent, yet they still put him in jail. While in jail, he translated dreams for a man who spread word of his talent to the King. Joseph was taken to translate the King's dreams. He saved the King's crops and was hired to be in command of marketing them.

Later, Joseph's brothers were shopping for flour in the market where Joseph worked. He recognized them, but they did not recognize him. He grabbed the youngest brother. "I am going to frame you for stealing the gold spoon from the flour," he told the boy.

"Hey, this boy tried stealing," Joseph said.

"Please, let him go," the brothers pleaded, "Our father, will never trust us. We have lost a brother before."

"Have you forgotten what you really did with your brother?" Joseph asked.

"Brother Joseph," they cried.

"Yes! I want you to go to Father and tell him that I hold your brother until you return." He handed them a white shirt to take with them and told them to throw it in their father's face and his sight would return.

They did as he ordered, but before they could throw the fabric the father exclaimed, "I smell Joseph!"

"You are crazy and blind father," they told him.

"Here," Joseph said, stepping out of the shadows and handing his father the shirt. "Run it on your face."

Their father did and suddenly he could see. Joseph reunited with his family, and his brothers bowed on the floor to ask forgiveness.

"Father, my dream has happened," Joseph said.

I wished that one day my family would come together as a real family, but it seemed that would never happen. My job gave me freedom, but my home life was worse. I felt like Joseph in a family of jealous brothers. If they could have thrown me down a well, I think they would have.

Chapter 17

Man of the Month

One day a handsome young man arrived in the office. He was Yemeni, with beautiful dark eyes and a sculptured face. I kept my eye on him from the moment he arrived, but did not actually interact until Dr. Bedwoon called me to take off the patient's bib and show him out. I did not greet him, only removed the bib and stepped back.

"Thank you," he said.

"You're welcome." My cheeks warmed. As I turned to leave, he grabbed my arm and my eyes fell into his.

"Please, take this," he said. It was a twenty dollar bill. My first assumption was that he wanted sex. At least he was willing to pay for it.

"No," I said. "I can't..." I wasn't a prostitute and I wasn't taking his money.

"Please, I insist. For me, take it."

He seemed sincere. Maybe it was a tip. Maybe he felt sorry for me having to work in this Lebanese office. I folded the money into my hand and rushed from the room before something else happened. *Good God, almighty!* Chills had their way with my spine.

The next day the same man came into the office at closing time. I was working behind the counter window filing some forms. When I looked up he smiled through the glass.

"What do you want?" I said. I was alone in the office.

"I just want to talk," he said. "My name's Mohammed."

I figured it did no harm to talk, especially with the office window between us. This was America, not Yemen, and I was tired of all the rules.

"I'm Jasmine." I tried to appear calm, but underneath the *balto*, my heart raced.

"How long have you worked here?" he said.

"A few months. Where do you work?"

"I'm a musician," he said. "I play the Aood and have my own band."

"So, Mohammed, do you play here in Detroit?"

"Yes, and all over," he said.

That day and the days that followed, I asked him many questions about love, family and religion, wanting to preach some wisdom to him at the same time. Mohammed was different than any man I had met, but I didn't trust him completely.

"I will take you to California or Houston or anywhere you want," he told me.

"What do you mean?"

Slowly, he came closer, his nose touching the window. "I feel a special bond between us. I am in love."

"You do not want me, Muhammad. I am divorced and I have a daughter."

"Huh, you are crazy, woman. I'd love to be with you. We can travel. Or you can go to school. I will support anything you want to do."

It made sense that he would like to travel because he was from Aden, Yemen. He was a romantic, but I had been fooled by a romantic before.

"We will explore the whole earth together," he said. "With music." His eyes were tremendous and the rest of him looked good too.

I started to feel my spirit fly. No, it was too good. I was not getting married again. No. No. No.

"Marry me," he said. "I will give your father whatever amount he wants."

His voice was like a song to me. Lord, he was sweet from head to toes.

"No, I cannot," I said. "I am sorry." My mouth said no, but my heart screamed yes. *What are you doing? This man is perfect! He will take care of you. He will take you away from here.*

Muhammad tried over and over to get me to marry him. I told him I wasn't playing hard-to-get. A marriage wasn't happening. I wondered what he saw in me anyway. Did he really love me or were those just words like Habul's words. I couldn't let my fantasies lead to a wrong decision, not this time.

Mohammed eventually gave up and I never saw him again. All I could think of was his charming smile. *Damn this,* I thought. *Dam the timing. Damn my mind. Damn the fears and darkness I live within.*

☪

108

I began to wonder if there was a "marry-me" sign over my head. I tried not to speak much with the patients, but single men rained down all around me. It seemed that once a week someone was talking marriage. One older man spoke fluent Arabic and bragged about owning four gas stations and land in Yemen.

"Well, can I come tomorrow to get acquainted and ask for permission to marry?"

"No," I said, "I'm honored, but I am not available." With all his money he must have five or six wives already.

"Okay," he said.

That was an easy one.

When I got back to Father's house, it was in chaos. The Monster and Mom were in the middle of a fight. With their verbal missiles and grenades falling around me, I almost wished I had said yes to the man.

Battle Ground

Sell me, use me, rape me, beat me
Burn me out of my black gown
Kill me Ohhh! Absolutely!
I plead. Please! Please!
The words have no meaning.
To you.. all of you!.. or me
I and this battle ground were *not* meant to be!

A Moroccan, younger than me by two years, was the next to ask for my hand. He came into the office in a gray gown, leading me to assume he was familiar with the wisdom of the Qur'an. I was right. He wanted to be a sheikh. That intimidated me and no matter how much we talked, I didn't feel comfortable. When the Moroccan asked for my hand, Father refused.

Later, a man named Enad from Palestine came to the office. He was lanky, with a greasy Santa Claus nose and black beard. He was well spoken and polite, but my gaze always pulled to his claw-shaped hand, a disability he had had since childhood. When Enad asked for my hand, I dismissed him immediately. For me, the claw only accentuated his unattractiveness.

As time went on, I learned that Enad taught at the Mosque on Dix Avenue. He became close with my youngest brother, Hissam who spoke of him in glowing terms.

Enad was a patient, persistent man. Each time he came to the office, he would politely ask for my hand. He did not pester me or go to Father. He did not swoon over me or offer gifts he couldn't afford. I began to wonder if an ugly person might love me better than another man. Maybe he would understand my pain. Maybe he would have compassion.

I gave in and told Enad I would marry him. I didn't think Father would agree, but Tumasha's husband, Asser, spoke on Enad's behalf. That made me worry. I didn't understand why he would be anxious for me to marry this ugly man when he seemed to want me for himself. Maybe Tumasha had poisoned him against me.

Father agreed to the marriage and I began to doubt my decision. I should marry for love, not because a man was ugly enough to treat me kindly. It was too late to turn back, though. I tried to convince myself this marriage would work. Enad would be a kind and generous husband and a good father to Dignity. That was what mattered.

A few days later, Uncle Gaban came to the house. We were all sitting in the living room. I had just finished praying. Father greeted him and asked him to join us.

"What brings you here?" he asked.

Gaban did not sit. Instead, he turned to me.

"I just want to say that this man is not for you, Jasmine. You are much prettier than that. This man will not be good for you. How do you feel about canceling this?"

I couldn't believe what I was hearing. Was Uncle Gaban actually concerned for his niece?

"He is from Palestine," Gaban said. "He is not even Yemeni. Say no to this marriage."

Had Allah sent a messenger to warn me? I looked to Father. He had not been overly fond of Enad and seemed to have no objection.

"You are right, Uncle," I said. "I should not marry Enad."

That night when Enad dropped off my brother from the mosque, Father shouted to him, "Enad! Come in to the house. We need to speak with you."

I was upstairs. Jerraf called to me to listen. I sat beside her on the top step.

"Enad, please sit on the couch," Father said. Enad replied something I didn't understand.

"Now, you know that Yemenis do not give their daughters in marriage to men other than those from Yemen."

There was silence.

"You are not from Yemen," Father said.

"No, Father." Enad sounded as if he were crying. "Please. I cannot live without her."

Mom came into the conversation. "Please, Enad, you will find someone better."

"She has been divorced two times," Father said in a kinder tone. "You have not yet married."

"Please." Enad's voice trembled so much I almost felt sorry for him.

"How can you take care of her and her daughter?" Father said.

"Father, I love her and cannot breathe without her. Please, do not do this." Enad was crying at this point. Hissam joined us on the stairs to mock Enad's tearful face.

"Hissam, where are you?" Father shouted. "Get Enad some water."

Hissam slid down the stair rail and went to the kitchen, barely holding back his laughter. Jerraf laughed aloud beside me. Who were these cruel people who could laugh at another's pain?

"It is time you go," Father said gently He was being kinder than I expected. "It is over."

"No," Enad said "I am not leaving."

"He's kneeling and kissing Father's feet," Hissam said as he scrambled up the stairs. He made kissing motions with his lips and laughed.

"Oh, Allah!" I whispered.

Enad sobbed. He begged. He pleaded. After what seemed hours, even Hissam and Jerraf didn't think it was funny anymore. I sat on the stairs wondering where I stood in this drama. Was he worth all this crying?

When Enad finally left, Hissam followed him to Asser's house, two houses from our own. He told me later that Asser was still determined to see us married. I wondered why.

Somehow Asser convinced Father to give Enad a second chance. I did not hear what money would change hands, but I'm sure it was substantial. Father called Enad back to the house and agreed to the marriage.

The next day I would be married for the third time. The mosque woman decided I deserved a party. I did not want one, ashamed at the idea of women cheering for me for the third time. Nothing felt right about this whole process.

Chapter 18

Monsters

Before the wedding party Asser spoke with Mom. "Let Jasmine and Enad live upstairs in our empty apartment. We can give them a low rent and Jasmine will have Tumasha to talk to."

My sister was even excited, but I knew it was for her own benefit. She would expect me to clean and cook for her. I would become a slave to her. Still, it was better to be living in my sister's house than with Father.

The new apartment worked out well at first. Enad was funny and fun. But things changed when Tumasha was admitted to the hospital and diagnosed with bipolar disorder. While Enad was at work, Asser found excuses to talk to me. He stopped by for no reason.

Asser's friendliness made me uneasy. He was my sister's husband, and he should stay downstairs in his own house. I had seen him as a good husband and father. Maybe it was only because Tumasha was away. Loneliness can drive a man away from his normal behavior.

But, no, I could not be so lucky.

"I have to confess," Asser said one morning. "I have been in love with you since you were twelve."

"What?"

"One day I accidently walked into the bedroom at your uncle's house and saw you with your other cousins in the room. You were without your scarf."

"No," I shook my head. Seeing me without my scarf should not cause a man to fall in love. "That's not love."

"It is, Jasmine," he said. "I'm in love with you."

I stood my ground and insisted he leave me alone.

What was with these men? Was there not a single one who had read the Qur'an? Could they not follow the Prophet's laws? Were there no good Muslims in the entire neighborhood?

☪

Enad was plagued by nightmares. He cried sometimes for no reason. Other times, he would wake up and start breaking dishes and throwing pots and pans. The sores on my scalp had nearly gone away after Dignity's birth. Now, they re-emerged as blooming red welts on both my scalp and torso. Could I not have a break, I asked God, just a little time to breathe or heal or clear my head? My life was one continuous disaster, one horrible event after another. Now all the poison in me was seeping through my skin.

When Enad told me he was going to start working midnight shift, worry turned to fear. I didn't want to be left alone at night, especially with Asser wandering about. He did not respect my privacy during the day, what would keep him away at night? I wanted to gather up Dignity and return to Father's house, but that would only bring abuse. I felt trapped yet again.

I couldn't sleep. Every creak sounded like footsteps on the stairs. Every squeak was a door opening. I would watch the bedroom clock, waiting for the hours to pass and the sun to rise. Only then did I feel safe.

My fears were not unfounded. Enad had worked midnight shift barely a month when I heard a knock on our door. It was two in the morning. I knew it was Asser.

"Shit," I whispered. There was no way I was opening that door. I huddled under the blankets, heart pounding so loud I was sure he would hear it through the door.

Everything was quiet. He had gone away, thank Allah.

A sliding, crackling sound broke the silence.

Oh my God! I thought. Someone was opening the window by the door. *Fuck! I can't believe this.*

I tossed the blankets over my head and edged my back to the wall. Floorboards creaked. With squinted eyes, I peeked as a dark shadow crept slowly closer. It felt like an elephant's foot squeezed down on my chest. Sweat drenched my nightclothes.

I played dead. In the faint light from the street I saw blue jeans. I heard the sound of Asser's zipper. A rough hand grabbed mine and forced it onto a penis.

Damn! My mind raced. *What do I do?* I pulled my hand away as if moving in my sleep. *Go away,* I screamed inside. *May Allah strike you dead for what you are doing!*

I felt his penis touch my lips. *I should bite the thing off.* Instead, I turned away from him, and forced my breathing to be steady.

Where was my sister? Was there no other soul awake to scare him away?

His breath came rapid and deep. The edge of the bed pressed down.

God help me!

Please!

Blessed Allah, the phone rang in the apartment below and Asser ran from the room.

"Oh God, thank you."

The phone rang again.

I waited.

Ring.

"Hello," I heard Asser's muffled voice through the floor.

Shaking, I searched in darkness until I found a piece of the table that Enad had broken during one of his fits. I slammed the window shut and jammed the wood into the track to keep it from opening. I slid to the floor near the door, hands trembling with fear and rage.

Monsters. Would I be haunted by monsters my entire life? I thought of Dignity sleeping in her bed and tears poured from my eyes. It was not safe here. We needed to leave. We needed a house where I could sleep without fear.

☪

I couldn't tell anyone about the incident with Asser. I would be blamed for tempting him or not wearing my scarf right or conversing in an incorrect manner. So, the next day, I called upon all my womanly charms to convince Enad to move.

"Maybe that's why you have these bad dreams," I said. "You would feel relaxed in a house of your own. It would be your property." I rubbed his shoulders.

"I don't know," Enad said.

"You have money from renting that semi-truck, and I can start working at Salina School as a paraprofessional. We'll work together." I gave him my most pleasant smile. "Please, Enad, I cannot live here. My sister controls me too much. I cannot deal with her anymore." I summoned tears to support my argument. It was not difficult.

It took many such conversations, but Enad relented and found a place in the Dix Avenue area far enough from Father's and

Asser's houses that I could breathe. It was a large home with a big yard. An elderly American woman owned it. She wanted $85,000.

"It's perfect," I said. "Look how much yard is around the house. Dignity can run around and play. What do you think?"

"If she will sell for $80,000, I will buy it," Enad said.

I called the woman one night after praying harder than ever.

"I can see that you are a good person," I said. "I'm not going to play hard to get. You have been honest, and I will be honest with you. I love the house and I want it. My husband is willing to buy it for $80,000. If you will accept, you are helping two people to live a happy life."

"Well," she said. "That's fine, I accept."

"Great! May God bless you. Thank you. Thank you so much!"

Finally, I was going to have a home. I hoped Enad's bad dreams would stop and we would become the happy family I had dreamed of.

Chapter 19

A New Home

I was on top of the world, thanks to Allah. The house was more than I could ask for. The main floor had a carpeted kitchen, dining room and living room and two bedrooms. A larger master bedroom occupied the second floor. The basement was finished as a recreation room and I set up a punching bag and weights for exercise. The kitchen even had a dishwasher. It all felt so good, I was sure my life would get better. I never thought twice; I did not think, period. Somehow, I had come to believe a beautiful house meant a beautiful relationship. I did not listen to the voice inside telling me to be cautious, to remember my marriage to Habul.

With this gorgeous house and expensive leather furniture, I suddenly became popular with my family. Tumasha called me every day to see what was cooking. I loved to cook and the new kitchen allowed me to make lots of food: hummus, roast lamb with potatoes, Yemeni flat bread, spicy yogurt. Sisters and aunts and cousins came to hang out. Aunt CNN stopped by to catch up on gossip. Even a few of my American friends from school came by.

The company of these women was priceless and the laughter that sprang from their hearts moved my spirit. I began to think I could help them, get them motivated to change things. I could explain how women in our society needed to stand up for ourselves. If we stood together, we could make our lives and the lives of our children better. We didn't need to put up with abusive husbands. We didn't need to be treated like property. We could be real people.

Enad was much better than Habul when it came to my freedom. He was Palestinian and they are more flexible. We had a white Honda that I adored and I would sweet talk him into letting me drop him off at work so that I could have the car. He also allowed me to get a job. Of course, I had to give every penny I earned to him, but that was a small price. I would not even cash my check; it went directly into his hands.

After taking a number of tests and being drug tested, I worked part-time as a teachers' aide in Salina School's pre-school and kindergarten. Mom agreed to babysit Dignity, and I got other jobs in the school as a secretary and helping disabled students. I loved the kids.

And then things began to fall apart. The women stopped coming to my house, busy with their own lives or maybe threatened by their husbands. Enad's nightly behavior escalated from bad dreams and throwing dishes to slapping my face. I convinced myself that I could take a slap or two once in a while, but the thought that he might strike out at any time kept me on edge. I found myself flinching when he came home from work and starting at the sound of his voice.

When Enad was at work and Dignity sleeping, I would sit at the sliding glass door in the dining room and look out at the pine trees encircling our back yard. Was I putting up with Enad's behavior because I had been exposed to dysfunction my entire life? Was I expecting more than I should? Maybe what I had was a normal marriage. Maybe I was dreaming about something that didn't exist. Prince Charming was only a fairytale after all.

At work, some of the teachers recommended I be hired full-time. Unfortunately, favoritism was rampant there just as it was in our community. An American looking in from the outside would see Yemenis, but inside the community we were divided by our family ties. My family was from the Sana'a region, while many of the other women were from Adan. Whether I could be hired full-time or not was based more on family than job performance.

My heart raged at the inequities of life. Jealousy and envy were alive and well in our community. We were so fragile that if anything hurtful, even a small thing, was said we would turn a cold face toward that person. If someone had longer eyelashes it would be a problem. A woman with beautiful hair would be talked about behind her back. We could trust no one, not even family members. But understanding that did not undo the damage jealousy created.

I saw women trapped within a whirlpool of hatred and mistrust. Jealous of my freedom, they condemned me for having a job. I had no idea how far they would go to undermine my life until I lifted the phone receiver and overheard my husband talking to Tumasha.

"... divorced two times," Tumasha said. "She could not keep a husband because they did not trust her. I think you should make her quit her job."

I hung up, shocked. Why would Tumasha be against me? She had lived in California and even worked herself.

"Enad," I called from the kitchen. "Who were you talking to?"

"Nobody," he said from the basement.

"I know it's Tumasha," I said.

Enad walked up from the basement trying to look innocent.

"I know you were talking to Tumasha," I repeated.

Enad walked by me and up to the master bedroom.

"Do you believe her?" I followed him. "Do you trust me to continue to provide for us?"

"I don't know," he said. He closed the door, shutting me out. Sometimes he spent his entire day in the bedroom. It was his sanctuary. I went back to the kitchen and called my sister.

"Tumasha," I said. "I know you were talking to Enad. How can you say those things?"

"What things?" she said.

"You were the first Yemeni girl to work at Salina school," I said. "You helped a lot of Arabic woman open doors to work at the school. Why, Tumasha? Why do you continue to beat me down and bruise my heart?"

Tumasha was quiet.

"You have created a ghost in my soul that keeps stabbing me inside."

Tumasha let out a string of profanities. She told me I was a curse on the family. She said I would never have a happy marriage like hers.

"I don't want to ever talk to you,'" I said. "You're not a sister, you never were." I slammed the receiver down.

I should have told Tumasha everything. I should have told her about Asser's sexual advances. Asser had called me, saying he was sorry for everything. He told me how much he honored me and how beautiful I was. I felt sorry for him. He was as confused as Habul and Enad.

He said he wanted to run away to California. "I am not living with your crazy sister anymore. I will provide for her and my children, but I cannot live in the same house."

I had convinced him to stay and this was what I got in return? She talked behind my back to my husband. Tumasha would be my sister no matter what happened between us, but I saw Father's monster in her. It seems we would never be free of him.

☪

One year into our marriage, I spent my non-working time with Dignity. No one called. No one came to visit except my two American friends, and they did not visit often. Enad had lost interest in me as a wife and I wondered if he might be gay. That was fine, I told myself, I had cable TV to keep me company.

I reminded myself that I must be grateful for what I had. I had more possessions than most of my family. I should be happy. I prayed to Allah to make me happy, but still there was something wrong with *me*, not my situation.

The sores on my skin grew worse. They started in three areas, one patch on my back, one on my shoulder and the rest on my scalp. Thankfully, as a Muslim I was expected to keep myself covered and Enad was not interested in me by then. But I dreaded to see myself turning from a woman with soft skin to a creature with scaly sores all over.

I asked Enad for the car and went to visit an Iraqi dermatologist. He said I had a condition called psoriasis and gave me steroid shots and ultra-violet light treatments. Instead of the sores improving, they seemed to grow worse overnight. I wondered if the doctor knew what he was doing. Doctors had almost killed Mom when they treated her lupus.

When I picked up Dignity after work, Mom noticed a difference. "What have you been doing? Why are you so dark?"

I told her about the psoriasis. "The UV treatments are making my skin darker."

"That is not right," Mom said. "Let me see you."

I took off my scarf. Flakes of skin fell to the floor.

"Praise, Allah!" she said. "Where else are they?"

I lifted my dress to show her my back.

"It's the evil eye," Mom whispered. "Someone has cursed you."

She insisted I remove my dress. She called my brothers in to look at me stripped almost naked. I was embarrassed and angry.

"What the hell is that?" Mouzi said.

"Psoriasis," I said.

"The evil eye!" Mom said.

After that day, my brothers stopped by every day. They were concerned that I was doing something wrong. They had some idea that my psoriasis was caused by my own doing.

"Fuck this!" I said after Mouzi interrogated me one evening. He believed I was sneaking men into my house or something crazy like that.

☪

Enad's strange behavior continued. One night he came home early. I woke to find hands on my throat, pressing hard, strangling me. Instinctively, I brought my leg up and kicked his chest. His hands loosened and he fell backward to the floor.

"What are you doing?" I screamed. My throat hurt. Memories of Habul's abuse came flashing back. What had happened to the man who wailed and cried that he loved me so much?

Enad sat up and stared. I had wrestled my brothers before and was used to fighting a man. As men went, Enad was not particularly big.

"What has come over you, Enad?" I said.

"Huh," he said. His breathing was loud as if he had been running. "You are the one acting strange. You did not answer the phone."

"The phone? I was probably sleeping. Were you calling?"

He looked away and I realized that Enad had been eating something besides my cooking. My brothers had been filling his head with stories. He probably suspected I was inviting men into the house while he was away.

He stood and walked to the door as if nothing had happened.

"Where are you going?" I said. "Talk to me."

"I have to go back to work. I came on my break."

Break? You came home on your break to kill your wife? Thoughts pounded in my head like thunder. This man was capable of killing me at any time.

After that, I could not sleep. While Dignity slept in her room with her Barbie sheets and matching furniture and lamp, I prowled the house. *All of this means nothing*, I thought as I paced in the darkness, listening to every sound, fearing the door would open. This leather furniture, the dishwasher, the big kitchen, did not define me. This was not who I was. I was not about "stuff". All these years I had been searching for love in any form. No one would ever replace Gais. A new house or a car or fancy sheets meant nothing next to that.

☪

A few weeks later, I went to the emergency room because my menstrual bleeding had been going on for a month and I was feeling weak. Mom said she could not watch Dignity, so I had to leave her with Enad. I dreaded the six hours I spent in the hospital, wishing they would hurry, but the doctors and nurses took their time. When I finally arrived home, I found Dignity playing in her room. The entire side of her face was bruised. Her ear was black like a prune.

"What happened?" I sobbed, holding her. I felt as though whatever kept my ribs and heart in place had collapsed.

"I fell from the bed," Dignity said in her little girl voice. "I was jumping."

"You never jump on the bed. Are you sure that's what happened?"

She nodded, but I didn't believe her. Days went by and I questioned her several times. She continued to say she fell from the bed. My intuition told me otherwise. She was covering for Enad. She didn't want to provoke a fight between us. She didn't want me to get hurt.

It was finally Enad who confirmed my suspicions. A few days later while I was working in the kitchen, I heard keys jingling, then a slap. I ran to the living room. Dignity stood next to Enad with her hand on her cheek. Enad's face was purple with rage.

"You motherfucker!" I walked to Enad and kicked him in the balls, hard. He fell to the ground moaning.

"You bitch," he mumbled.

"Come on, Dignity," I said, pulling her away. I put a cartoon on the TV for her and went back to the kitchen. My heart thumped in my chest. I did not want her to grow up in a house of fighting, but it was already too late. She had seen everything.

I washed dishes, trying to calm my anger. What kind of life was this for her? A step-father who hit her and tried to kill her mother. A father who did not support her. She had no good role models and no normal kids to play with. I pulled a butcher knife from the drawer and stared at the large blade. I could end it, free us both from this life of misery.

Holding the knife, I peered around the corner. The coward was sitting in a chair with his back to me. It would be easy to kill him. He would never hit my daughter again. He would never hurt any woman. The thought of it energized me. For those seconds I was a killer lioness ready to defend my cub.

The urge passed. It was not the thought of jail blunted my rage; I had been in jail my entire life. What I worried about was losing custody of Dignity to her father. As crazy as Enad was, he was not as crazy as Habul. I put the knife away.

When Enad went to work that night, I went to the basement, turned the music on loud and did my kickboxing and punching bag. I hit the bag with all my strength.

"I am not crazy!" I yelled. With each punch I heard the voice of someone who had threatened me. Father's voice insulted me. *Punch!* Mouzi's voice degraded me. *Pow!* Mom's voice denied me. *Bam!*

At the end of this process, I broke down and cried, transformed from this huge strong rock to a worthless baby who craved love more than ever.

Chapter 20

Damage Revealed

Enad never talked about his family, so I was surprised when we received a call from his mother. She lived in California and had decided to visit us. I spent the week before her visit cleaning the house until it sparkled. The last thing I wanted was another family member unhappy with me.

I expected Enad's mother to cover herself in black, but she did not even wear a headscarf. I later found she was Christian, something Enad had not mentioned. I welcomed her and helped carry her bags to our spare bedroom.

"I hope this bed is comfortable enough for you," I said. "There are towels in the bathroom and hot tea and cookies in the kitchen."

His mother smiled softly. "Look Jasmine, do not feel because I am your mother-in-law you have to serve me. Please, be yourself."

I was shocked. Did she mean that, or was it a way to trick me so that she could complain to her son? After Gais' mother, my radar was up.

In the days that followed, we had woman to woman talks when Enad was not there. His mother was a bright light in my life. We shared philosophical views and agreed on so many things. If only I could speak with my own mother and sisters this way, my life would be happier.

His mother asked often about our relationship.

"How are you and Enad doing? Is he being a good husband?"

"Everything is just fine," I lied.

"Are you sure?"

"Really, we are fine."

One morning, she found me in the kitchen looking tired.

"Is something wrong?" she asked. I was still afraid to mention Enad's strange behavior.

"Look, Jasmine," she said, "I have a Masters in psychology and I understand that a person who stays awake all night is not okay."

I poured us some tea and we sat at the table.

"I need to share a little bit with you about Enad," she said. She told me about the time when he fell from a five story building in

Kuwait. He was only five years old at the time. "In that incident he cracked his head open and broke many bones. He had steel pins put in his hip. Bones heal, but ever since, he has had mental issues."

"How do you mean?" I asked.

"Well, we thought he recovered, but as he grew older he became aggressive. He would attack his sister with knives and beat her badly."

I remembered hands on my throat.

"I know my son. You can tell me anything."

I still hesitated to tell her. It was so difficult to break out of custom. A Yemeni woman does not defile her husband's reputation.

"You are a beautiful young girl," she said. "Enad should be kissing the back of his hands for what God has given him."

"There have been some things happen," I admitted. Little by little I told her the chaotic things he had done.

She smiled gently. "Good, Jasmine. It's important you trust me. I want you to be aware. I want you to be safe." She confided to me how she had been divorced from Enad's father for a long time because he beat her badly.

Another beaten woman, I thought. If this intelligent woman with a Masters degree had been beaten, was any woman safe? Did we all have to live in fear?

Enad's mother stayed two weeks. It was wonderful having her around, but when she left, I felt even more alone than before. Oh Allah, if Enad's mother feared her son, I *really* had to watch out. I was married to a dangerous man.

☪

I spent sleepless nights wondering what to do with my life. I could run back to my family, but what good would that do? Finding no answers within myself, I turned to prayer.

Each day I did my ablutions and prayed on my sacred rug. As I bowed and my tears fell, I felt Allah wiping sorrow away inside me. His love was so deep and unlimited that it sealed my wounds. Confidence and hope grew within me.

Yet, nothing changed in my marriage. I considered suggesting that Enad see a psychiatrist, but what would they do for him, give him drugs to numb his mind? We are human; we are supposed to *feel*. It seemed that modern medicine could put Band-Aids on the symptoms of mental illness, but could not cure the mind, that dark mystery of life.

One day blended into the next. I found myself smoking three packs of cigarettes a day and staying up all night guarding Dignity. She was a bright moon to me, my hope and my reason for staying alive. I had fantasies of a life where smiling people handed out love as a glass of pure clear water. I envisioned changing our community, reading and translating the Qur'an verse by verse, women and men coming together to follow the truth revealed in the Qur'an by our beloved sacred prophet, Mohammed. All would be happy and equal in my world.

☪

Enad became more withdrawn after his mother's visit. He spent more time away from home. "Doing errands," he would say. Another man might have been seeing a woman on the side, but I didn't think that was the case with Enad. He didn't seem to have much interest in women. But he was certainly up to something.

After seeing him sneak papers from his briefcase under the bed, I became curious. When he was at work, I opened the briefcase and found our mortgage papers. I wondered why he was concerned about them. We were not planning on selling the house. As I read through the papers, though, I realized what was going on. My name had been removed from the mortgage.

I put everything back the way as I had found it. Was he planning to sell the house? Did he want a divorce? I brought my hands to my head. No, it must be something else. I needed to talk to him. There must be some explanation.

That night I sat with him after dinner and told him about finding the mortgage papers while I was cleaning. "Why, Sweetie?" I asked. "Why did you have the papers changed?"

He became soft and humble. "I was married before in Kuwait."

This was a shock. He had never mentioned being married. Tears came to his eyes and I couldn't help feeling sorry for him.

"I bought her a big house," he said, "and it was so beautiful. One day I came home and she was gone and every little thing in that house was gone too."

"That's terrible," I said. Obviously, he thought I would do the same thing to him.

He wiped his eyes. *Poor miserable man*, I thought.

"I would never betray you," I said. "You know that don't you?"

"Can you believe it, Jasmine? She even took the fancy light switch pads from the walls." He chuckled, trying to laugh it off, but I could see he was hurting.

I laughed with him. "But I am not her, Enad, I promise. Life is too short. I want to live in peace with you."

He smiled. "I am sorry I listened to your sister. I will never believe her again."

"It's okay," I said.

Tumasha! I should have figured she had a hand in this. Why was she determined to destroy my marriage? If she spent more time on her own marriage Asser wouldn't be trying to get me into bed with him.

"You are a good wife," Enad said.

I did not ask him to have the mortgage papers changed, but assumed he would add my name again.

☪

Not long afterward, I came down with a bad flu. I could barely get out of bed. Too sick to drive, I went to Tumasha and begged her to take me to a doctor. After I offered to buy gas, she took me to see an Arabic doctor in the neighborhood. I returned home with a dozen little brown bottles of white liquid antibiotics. I was so sick, I went straight to bed. The little bottles of samples sat on a marble lamp table.

One night I saw a shadow walking slowly to my lamp table. It was Enad. I pretended to be asleep. When he reached the bed, he stood silently, staring at me, for a long time. I didn't move. Finally, he turned to the table and opened one of my antibiotic bottles.

He added something to the liquid. My heart sped. Was he trying to poison me? He slowly closed the bottle and replaced it on the table with the others. I lay still until he left the room.

Shaky from sickness, my soul shattered beneath the weight of this horrible deceit. It surrounded me like giant black wings, stopping my breath, squeezing my heart. I could not force my legs from the bed. When I slipped into delirious sleep, I thought I would never wake again.

In the light of the next morning, I forced myself out of bed and went down to the living room couch. If Enad would poison me, Dignity was not safe either.

I called Mom. "We have to take these bottles to the doctor," I said. "We need to know what Enad put in the medicine."

"I am sure it is nothing," Mom said. "Maybe you were dreaming."

"I wasn't. I saw him with my own eyes."

"Now don't be crazy, Jasmine."

"I'm not crazy!"

"You were sick, Jasmine. Sick people sometimes see things that are not there."

"I know what I saw."

"Okay, okay. Bring me these bottles and I will go tomorrow to see the doctor."

I walked them to Father's house that afternoon.

The next day I called again. "What did the doctor say about my medicines?"

Mom didn't answer.

"Mom?"

"Do not bring this up again," she said. "I threw the medicines away."

"Why, Mom? Now I'll never know. Have you forgotten the other things he's done?"

"I do not care, Jasmine. You are dirty blood to this family and a disgrace to Islam." She hung up on me.

Tears

Ohhhh
Tears, tears, tears, tears
My head spinning
Confused, hurt
Tears, tears, tears,
Ohhhh

I had to discover the truth. When Enad returned from work, I would begin a conversation about the mortgage papers. Then I would bring up other issues, force him to admit he beat Dignity, confront him about his violent behavior and his trying to strangle me. If I could get him to own up to that, it would be a short step to the pills.

When I asked about the mortgage, Enad admitted he had not changed the papers back to my name. After some time, he confessed to hitting Dignity.

"How did you bruise the whole side of her face?" I said. "Her ear was black. Did you repeatedly slap her face or what?"

"No." He shook his head. "She pulled the toilet paper roll on the floor in the bathroom and I slapped her hard once."

I knew he was lying, but remained calm. For once in my life I was in charge. Enad had no power over me. He was a little boy cowering before me. I was the confident parent. I kept probing and he acknowledged most of his strange and violent behavior.

"I'm done," I said finally. "I want a divorce. You can have everything we own. I will not fight you."

"No, Jasmine I love you. You taught me what love is about. I have never had anyone last this long in my lifetime." He went to his knees and cried.

"I've seen this begging before," I said firmly. "It's not going to work."

"Let's go out," he said, smiling suddenly. "I will treat you."

"Fine," I said. Let him think I might change my mind. In the meantime, I would make plans to get the hell out of there. Enad's trying to poison me was the last straw. Mom's throwing away the pills was the last straw. Dignity's blackened ear was the last straw. I would get out. Out of this marriage, out of this house, out of Dearborn, out of Michigan if need be. I did not want to be near anybody Arabic. I hated the hypocrisy of this culture.

Enad took me to an expensive restaurant at the Renaissance Center in downtown Detroit, and actually wanted to have intercourse afterward. It was laughable. I let him have his way with me, all the while making plans. I would hide my checks from Enad. Then, when I got my tax refund in a couple of months I would quit my job, making some excuse about not having a babysitter. That would give me enough money to leave.

It was difficult not to see all Arab men as cruel and greedy, but then I remembered my grandfather, Ameen Musleh. I did not know him, but felt like I did thanks to Mom's stories. He always kept his door open for anyone. He always had candy to hand out to children when they came by. He was always there to help. Thinking about him gave me butterflies in my stomach. Grandfather was a man I could respect, a man of wisdom and understanding. None of my family's men were anything like him. Gais was the only one who came close and he was out of my life forever.

The next few weeks, I was a spy in my own house, careful of every word I said, watching Enad's comings and goings. I convinced him to let me have the car and drove to the Dearborn library to look up shelters. I found one in Tucson, Arizona, clear across the country from Michigan. Maybe that would be far enough. I bought a phone card so that no one could trace my calls after I left. If Enad suspected my plans, he did not show it. I was careful. Arab men are not smart, but they can smell a fox in the hen house.

Chapter 21

Flight

The only people I told about my escape were Gena and Lisa, the two American friends who had converted to Islam. I invited them to the house a few days before my departure.

"What if they catch you?" Gena asked. "Where will you go? What if you run out of money?"

"Don't worry about me," I said. "I have Allah with me." I couldn't tell them where I was going. I didn't think my family would question them, but it was better if they didn't know.

"Can we help you with anything?" Lisa asked. Tears fell from her eyes. I had no more tears to share, but ached at the thought of missing these precious two friends. Of the women who had come to my new house to eat my food, they were the only true friends. For the rest, visiting had been a social occasion, like attending a wedding.

"Take anything you want from the house," I told them.

"We can't do that," Lisa said.

"Yes you can. I don't need it anymore. Take something. Anything."

They finally took a couple of small things, but I had to push hard. Why should Enad end up with everything?

"Gena," I said, handing her a small box, "I want to give you my set of gold jewelry. Please hold it in safety. If I ever need money, I will call you to send it to me."

"Sure, Jasmine."

"Please, don't call here anymore," I said. "I don't want my family to harass you guys."

They nodded.

"You must go now," I said. "I have things to do." I didn't want them caught in the middle of this. If Enad caught me running away, I could only imagine the rage that would erupt from him. I remembered the bruise on Dignity's face. If he could do that to a child, what would he do to Gina and Lisa?

That night I called an airline with my calling card. "I need two tickets from Detroit to Arizona." They wanted $700.00 for Dignity and me.

"Please," I begged, "I'm trying to run from my abusive husband. I don't have that much money."

"One moment." The woman put me on hold and it was all I could do not to hang up. I imagined her calling my family and telling them I was trying to leave Detroit. I feared Enad would storm through the door at any moment.

"Ma'am?"

"Yes," I said too loud.

"I can sell you the tickets for $300.00."

"Thank you, thank you so much." The flight was a few days later.

"And your name?"

"Please," I said. "Do not put my name in the computer."

"Yes, ma'am," she said. "I will give you a reservation number to get your tickets."

"Thank you," I said. I would leave Monday morning at 4 A.M. when most people would be sleeping and Enad was at work.

Sunday night, I packed a suitcase with a few clothes along with my prayer rug and Qur'an. I didn't pack scarves or *baltos*. It seemed unnatural, not having a garment to cover myself, but I had to become invisible. In America, that meant going without Arabic clothing.

At about 11 P.M. I got a call from Gena. She and Lisa wanted to come over to say good bye. "Is it okay? Is anybody there?"

"No," I said. "The coast is clear." I shouldn't have let them come over. It was too dangerous. But I was getting nervous about such a big move and longed to see them one last time.

A few minutes later, a car drove up in front of the house. *Please let this be the girls*, I thought. If Enad came home early and saw I had packed a suitcase, he would surely beat me. Or worse. My heart clenched tight like a fist.

There was a light rap at the door and relief washed through me. Enad would never knock and my brothers would be much louder.

I opened the door and motioned the women inside. The street was empty of traffic.

"Oh, Jasmine," Gena said. "We had to see you one more time. Are you okay?"

"Yes," I said. We hugged, but I kept listening for car doors.

"Call us if you need anything," Lisa said.

"I will." We hugged again.

"We'll pray for you."

"Thank you," I said. "I'm so glad you came." It had only been five minutes, but it meant a lot to see them. Checking the street for cars, I let them out. They ran to their cars.

I sighed and closed the door. Dignity was sleeping on the couch. I checked to make sure her shoes were on, zipped up my suitcase and placed it near the door.

The doorbell rang.

Oh my God! Who would come here now? I ignored the ringing for about five minutes, but the visitor would not leave. Finally, I gave in.

Asser stood on the front step. I opened the door.

"What are you doing here this time of night?" I said, trying to look irritated. Inside, I was a quivering bowl of Jello.

Asser smiled. "I just came to give you some cigarettes, that's all."

"Cigarettes? It couldn't wait until morning?"

He shoved the box through the gap in the door.

"Thanks," I said. "I'm going to sleep now. I'm really tired." I hoped my voice didn't give away my fear.

"Why are you wearing a sweat outfit?" he said.

"I just finished working out." It sounded like a good reason. "I'm going to take a shower and go to sleep. Good night."

Asser shrugged and left.

I shut the door. My knees were shaking. *Help me, Allah*, I prayed.

At 11:30, the phone rang. *Oh, no,* I thought.

"Hello?"

"What are you doing?" Mom said. She never called this late. It was probably her intuition. She always knew when something was up. The night that Asser broke into our apartment, it had been Mom calling on the phone that chased him from my room.

"Nothing," I said.

"Well, your father and Tunfakh are on their way." Tunfakh was my third brother, a couple years older than Hissam. I got along with him better than the others.

"Why?" I said. "I'm getting ready for bed." *Oh Allah, don't tell me that Asser saw the suitcase.* He must have said something.

"They are coming over to check on you. I wanted to let you know."

"Thanks, Mom." We hung up.

A minute later, Father and my brother were at the door.

"What are you doing?" Father said. "Your mom said to come visit. She feels something is going wrong with you."

"I'm fine," I said. "I was working out. I'm going to bed now." I felt like my knees were going to give way. They didn't have the time of day for me when I was sick, but now that I didn't want them here, they were all over me.

"What is this?" Father said, spotting the suitcase. "Why is it in out here?"

"I was putting some clothes away," I said. It wasn't really a lie. I did put clothes in it. "Winter clothes. I'm packing them away for the summer."

That seemed to satisfy him. "All right," he said, "Take care of your husband and be a good woman."

"I will," I said. Tunfakh gave me with a knowing look. He never said anything, but I'm sure he suspected. He was the only one in the family who might understand.

The moment they left, I lit up a cigarette. Maybe this wasn't the time to leave. Would Mom call Enad at work and tell him to come home? Father might be convinced by my story, but I wasn't sure she would be. By then I was shaking so much, I felt I couldn't even walk from the house without collapsing.

It's now or never, I told myself. But how was I going to leave? It was too late to take the bus and I didn't dare call a taxi now.

I called Gena.

"Gena! Can you come and pick up Dignity and me? Tonight is crazy. People keep popping up at my door. I'm afraid to leave."

"Okay," she said. "Just stay calm. My husband comes home from work at 12:30. I'll come over after that."

"Okay," I whispered. I lit another cigarette.

"Hang in there."

"I will." I hung by a thread for the next hour, pacing the living room, checking on Dignity, peering out to the street. I jumped whenever a car drove by. I imagined Mom and Mouzi coming next, then Enad with a clenched fist.

Finally, Gena arrived. Shaking like a drug addict, I carried Dignity out to the back seat of her car and put my suitcase in the trunk. My heart beat so loud I was sure Mom would hear it and come running.

Once I had my butt on that car seat and it moved two blocks away, I was much calmer. Gena lived in the heart of Detroit. There were no Arabs there. I would be safe. I took deep breaths over and over again, trying to relax.

Sensing my anxiety, Gena talked about the good times we had had and the prayers I had taught her. I was able to laugh with her. For a few moments, I left my fears behind and felt good.

When we reached her house, I insisted on sleeping on the couch in my clothes. Even in the American part of town, I did not feel entirely safe. I wanted to be ready if someone came to the door.

If I slept at all, I don't remember. When the clock reached 3 A.M. I went to Gena's room and touched her shoulder.

"Gena, wake up, it is time to go to the airport."

"Already?"

"I want to get there early, so that I will have the first seat on the plane."

"Okay," she said, climbing out of bed.

We picked up Lisa on the way. By the time we reached the airport, I felt like I was swimming in thick water. Even this early, the terminal was crowded. Voices rumbled around me and my vision seemed to blur. I held Dignity tight, keeping her close to me.

"Have a safe flight," Gena said when we reached the gate. She and Lisa hugged me again and again.

"Let us know when you get there," Lisa said. "At least send us a postcard or something."

"Call collect," Gena said.

"Sure," I said. It was like being on a rollercoaster, riding so fast I couldn't see anything clearly. Every man's voice sounded like Father's. I expected them to appear at any moment and pull me out. It seemed to take forever for the boarding call to sound.

At the boarding gate, I gave our tickets to a young woman. She smiled and told me to have a nice trip. I couldn't respond to her. My tongue was frozen in my mouth. I put Dignity down and we walked the long, shaky corridor toward the plane.

"Come on, Dignity," I said, pulling her by the arm. Her three-year-old legs could only walk so fast.

"Bye bye," she said.

"Yes. We are going on a big plane."

The stewardesses welcomed us, but I could only think of escaping to safety. Finally, when we were seated, I began to feel more relaxed. My family wouldn't find us now. The rest of the passengers took their seats and the engines rumbled. *Thank Allah,* I thought.

I prayed the entire way down the runway. When the jet took flight, I sobbed. We were free.

Chapter 22

Tucson

At the Phoenix airport, I picked up my suitcase at baggage claim and dragged it outside into a blazing hot day. I expected a taxi, but after waiting ten minutes, none came. People walked to and from the parking area across the street. Busses whooshed by, but I didn't see one taxi. I finally found the courage to talk to a man.

"Excuse me," I said. "Are there any taxis?"

"No, ma'am," he said. "Where are you going?"

"I am trying to get to Tucson?"

"Oh, you still have about three hours to go. You don't want a taxi, it will be too expensive. You should take a shuttle."

He pointed me to the shuttle station and the small bus to Tucson. There were no other passengers and I was nervous. Fortunately, the driver was a plump woman with bleached blond hair. I wouldn't trust being alone with a man.

"Come on," I said to Dignity. We climbed on and walked to the back. The seats squeaked when we sat. Dignity looked out the window. I stretched my legs and wished for sleep. It had been over a day since I had slept. I was exhausted, but could not stop worrying.

The shuttle rumbled from the airport service road onto a highway. We were on the outskirts of a city, but not for long. I looked left. I looked right. Desert as far as I could see.

I had never been exposed to such wide open spaces. I watched for a gas station or a market, some sign of civilization. What if we got a flat tire? What if this woman was a murderer? No one would ever find us.

"So, ma'am," I said, "Do you live in Tucson?"

"No. I live out in this desert." She had a rough voice. "Where you from?"

I almost said Detroit, but caught myself. This woman would probably never speak with my family, but I couldn't take that chance.

"I'm from the east," I said.

"I can tell that from the way you talk." In the mirror I saw that she had no front teeth. "What state?"

"Indiana," I lied.

"Never been to Indiana," she said. Now that she had started talking, she wouldn't shut up. She told me about her kids and horses and the old house she lived in. I didn't really listen after a while, but the sound of her voice kept me from thinking about my troubles. Dignity fell asleep. I turned my attention to the roadside, watching for snakes and scorpions in the coarse sand.

Hours later we reached the Tucson a shuttle station, a small cabin.

"Come on, Dignity," I said, waking her. I paid the woman and got off, pulling my daughter with one hand and lugging a suitcase with the other. Inside, a very fat man sat behind the counter, clothes so soaked he looked as if he had been out in the rain. There was no rain; it was hot and dry.

"Can I help you ma'am?" His face was all cheeks and chins, glistening with sweat.

"I am trying to get to this place," I said, showing the shelter address on a piece of paper.

"You'll need a taxi," he said. "It's about an hour from here."

My head swam. My psoriasis itched like a thousand ants crawling over me.

"Mommy, I'm hungry," Dignity said.

"I know, Honey, so am I." It was afternoon and we hadn't eaten since the plane. I was so parched and hungry my stomach rumbled aloud.

"Sir, can you tell me, where is the nearest McDonald's here?"

"There ain't no McDonald's," he said.

"Okay. I need to call a taxi then. Can I borrow your yellow pages?" The man slapped the book onto the counter, looking irritated.

I called for a taxi, but it didn't arrive for an hour. Dignity kept complaining she was hungry. I assured her we would get something soon, all the while hearing Father's curse words in my mind. Bitch! Whore! Fucker!

Finally the taxi pulled up to the building.

"Where to ma'am?" the driver asked.

I showed him the address.

"I can't take you that far, but I can get you a half-hour closer."

What kind of a place was this? Would I never get to my destination? I thought about giving up and going home, but that wasn't an option.

"Okay." I nodded. "Take us as far as you can."

We ended up in a larger town with lots of restaurants.

"Yeah!" I said, smiling for my daughter. "Dignity look, food! What do you want? Mama will buy you anything you want."

The afternoon sun was bright and heat rose from the pavement. Summers were hot in Michigan, but not like this. This was dry desert heat. I felt comfortable in it. I didn't remember Yemen, but imagined it would be like this.

I saw a McDonalds down the road. Suitcase in one hand, Dignity in the other, I walked. Cool air hit us as we entered the colorful building and the smell of burgers made my mouth water.

"What do you want to eat?" I asked Dignity. "A happy meal and some ice cream?"

"I want water," Dignity said.

Tears formed in my eyes. "Okay," I said. "You can have all the water you want." Suddenly, I had no appetite.

I ordered a happy meal and soda pop for Dignity. It was more than she wanted, but I was glad to see her eat. I tried to keep up my spirits and act as if everything was normal for her sake. This escape from Enad was more for her benefit than mine. I couldn't let her live in a culture where she would be beaten and maybe killed. Things were difficult now, but the future would be better. I wouldn't let her be scarred as I had been.

After our meal, we went outside and I had a cigarette. With each exhale, I released some of the tension pent up inside me. I wished the journey was over. At least Dignity looked refreshed.

"Are we there?" she said.

"Almost." I called another taxi. This time the driver knew where the place was.

"I wish I would have met you a long time ago," I said to myself. I wondered what the shelter would be like. Only women, thank Allah. We would be safe. We would have fun, hang out and talk with American women. Maybe my psoriasis would go away.

We drove through town, passing many houses of creamy adobe. Now that the sun was sinking they resembled beautiful glowing stones growing from the ground, much different from the ugly wood houses in Detroit.

"Are we in Mexico?" I asked the driver.

He laughed. "No," he said, turning onto a long road. "But we're almost to your shelter."

He stopped at a pink single-story adobe building surrounded by a fence with wide steel gates painted black.

"Here you are," the driver said.

"Thanks." I paid him the twenty dollar fee and he helped me get the suitcase from the car.

The gate was closed, so I pushed a buzzer at the side.

"Can I help you," a woman's voice screeched over the intercom.

"Yeah," I said. "I am the woman from Michigan."

"What is your name?"

"Jasmine Sharif."

A buzzer sounded and the gate unlocked. As I pushed it opened, I felt some sense of relief. We had finally reached the end of our long journey.

With my very last drop of energy, I dragged the suitcase along a wide sidewalk surrounded by open yard. No one greeted me, but women stared and talked among themselves. I couldn't blame them. I suppose they wondered where this Arabic woman with long black hair had come from. Certainly not Arizona.

I passed through a set of green doors. Inside, the building was laid out in one long row. The smooth yellow walls were bright and cheerful. I walked to the office, a small room with a heavyset American woman behind a desk. I took a seat. She didn't seem too happy to see me.

"Name?"

"Jasmine Sharif."

She asked me a series of questions without so much as a smile. *What kind of a place was this?* I thought shelters helped women. This lady acted as if she would rather be someplace else. *Do not judge others*, I reminded myself. Maybe she was having a bad day. Still, I could not get the feeling of unease to go away. I hoped I hadn't made a mistake. I hoped this wasn't my punishment for leaving home. I pushed back the guilt that tried to surface.

After completing the paperwork, she walked us down the hall. We passed a room with washers and dryers, then two bedrooms, and the bathrooms. Our room was narrow, with a single window, dresser and bunk beds along one side.

"This is it." The woman turned and left.

"Thanks." I closed the door.

"This is our new place," I told Dignity. She looked as tired as I felt. "Let's get your pajamas on. It's been a long day."

"Okay, Mom." I changed her clothes and tucked her beneath clean sheets. She was soon asleep on the bottom bunk.

My psoriasis, now the size of saucers in several places, burned and itched. My scalp felt like a steel helmet. The sores did not show through my thick hair, but I could not help scratching madly, leaving flakes on the bed and floor.

I dozed off for a few minutes, but couldn't stay asleep. Wanting to be free of the burning, I went to the bathroom. There was a huge bathtub. I was tempted to throw my body into soaking hot water, but wasn't sure how clean the tub was. Besides, I would leave behind all my flaking. It would be disgusting. I opted for a shower instead.

When hot water hit my hair and skin, it felt like a shower of natural rain flushing away my worries and refreshing my strength. We were going to be just fine. We would start a new life here in the Arizona desert.

After putting lotion on my sores and brushing my hair, I checked on Dignity. She was sleeping soundly. I walked outside to a picnic table near the apartment door. The sun had set and stars shown in the night sky, brighter than any I had seen in my life.

I remembered my honeymoon night with Gais. *You should see these stars*, I thought. Only Allah could have made something so beautiful.

Chapter 23

Sister, Saint, Sinner

The sun's rays streamed into our window. I woke Dignity and decided to give her a bath. We played in the water for a while; the smile on her face crisp and clean.

During breakfast, we joined a group of women chatting and eating in the shade of a covered patio. I felt a little awkward, but forced myself to sit at one of the picnic tables.

"Good morning," I said.

"Hi," a Hispanic woman said. Another woman with a red-headed boy about Dignity's age nodded. A black woman waved.

"I'm Sabrina," the red-headed woman said.

"I'm Sara," I said. "This is my daughter Dignity." It felt funny using an alias, but the shelter had suggested it for my safety.

Sabrina nodded, looking concerned. "So Sara, what happened to you?"

"Oh, it's a long story," I said. "I don't feel like talking about it right now."

"I understand. We've all been through a lot."

Most of the women were easy going and cool. Dignity and I made many friends. I was not alone in the world. I learned that abuse was not only a problem in my Arabic community; but throughout the country, permeating every ethnic and racial group. My spirit lifted as these woman became my new family of sisters. I felt free to bloom into a colorful flower. Sabrina, in particular, was someone I could trust. We were one and the same, mothers looking for a safe place to raise our child.

☪

Of course, there were a variety of women at the shelter. Maria, a Hispanic girl, would do anything for cash. She worked as a stripper.

"Why do you do such a thing?" I asked one day as we sat with a group outside. I couldn't imagine a more degrading job. Here I thought going without a scarf was exposing my body. This woman took off *everything*.

"What choice do I have?" she said.

"You're in America," I said. "Nothing is impossible." If only they knew the world I came from, they might value their freedom to choose.

"The money is good," she said. "I can earn in one night what would take a week working in fast food." She looked me up and down. "You should think about it, Sara. You have such beautiful bedroom eyes. You would make a lot of tips."

"Sure," I said. I started dancing around one of the patio roof poles. Everyone laughed.

"Go Sara! Go!" Women clapped and yelled.

"No. No way," I said, returning to the table. "I was just kidding. There is no way in hell I would be a stripper."

"It's easy money," Maria said.

"I don't care. My dignity is priceless. Besides, stripping gives men the wrong idea about women."

A black girl leaned toward me. "I never heard truer words," she said. "I was a model for a company and my boyfriend still fucked around. He ended up breaking my leg and my hip bone. He didn't give me no respect."

"Son of a bitch," I said. "All men that hurt women should die!"

"Cheers to that!" some of the women said.

Later that day, Sabrina and I went to the food stamp office in Tucson. That was one of many trips in the hot dry sun. We walked miles and miles. I would carry Dignity on my shoulders and we would laugh and play. I loved the sunshine and the heat. I dreamed of traveling to Yemen to see the desert where my family was from.

C‍

One afternoon, Sabrina looked into our room through the open door.

"Hi Sara," she said. "Jim and I are going out tonight. Do you want to go with us?"

I trusted Sabrina, but I was still nervous about being around men.

"Come on," she said. "It'll be fun."

"I don't know Jim."

"You'll like him. He's very respectful. He would do anything for me."

"What about Dignity?"

"Anna can babysit."

I finally agreed. Anna said it would be no problem to watch Dignity. I didn't have many clothes, so I picked out the best of the donated items I had. After dabbing on a little makeup I was ready.

We left around 5 P.M. and ended up at the house of one of Sabrina's friends. Since this was after Desert Storm and our short war with Sadam Hussein, everyone was interested in Arabia. They asked me lots of questions about Islam and what people were like in Yemen. I told them general things, but nothing specific about my family. As I talked about our traditions, I missed home, missed Yemeni tea in the morning and the comfort of my own bed. Mostly, I missed Mom. She must be disappointed in me. I had disgraced the family in a big way.

Someone brought out some weed to smoke. I had never tried the stuff, but it smelled so sweet I couldn't resist. I took a drag. I thought it might be like chewing khat, but it was different. It relaxed me more, eased my guilt and I felt like giggling.

We left around eight to get back to the shelter early. When I returned to my room, I felt bad about having a little fun and leaving Dignity behind. I was also guilty about smoking the weed. I was going to hell for sure. Allah gives me this chance to escape my family's abuse and I repay Him by going out to party?

☪

A week later, a councilor called me to her office.

"Jasmine," she said. "We have many rules here and we don't tolerate rule breakers."

"What are you saying?"

"We're evicting you. You have to be out by Friday."

"For what? What rule did I break?"

"I think you know."

"No, I don't."

"We suspect you are taking drugs," she said.

"Drugs?" *Oh my God!* I just had a little weed at one party, I wasn't bringing drugs into the shelter. I had only done it once. Several other girls who were doing drugs all the time.

"No excuses Jasmine," she said.

"But…"

"You have to be out Friday morning."

I can't believe this, I thought as I walked out of the office. The blue Arizona sky became the grayest of grays and seemed so chilly that it crawled under my skin and into my bones. I was scared. I had no resources and wasn't in the mental condition to find another shelter.

I paced the hall, wondering if it might be something other than drugs. Did someone not like me because I was Arabic? Did they think I was the enemy? I went to Sabrina.

"What's the matter?" she asked the minute she saw me.

"They're kicking me out."

"What?"

"They think I'm taking drugs."

"Oh, no!"

"I shouldn't have gone to your friend's the other night."

"It's my fault," Sabrina said. "Jim will take you and Dignity in. I know he will."

"I cannot do that," I said. "Thank you though."

"Where will you go?"

"I don't know."

That night I sat alone at one of the picnic tables. The sky was bright with stars and the moon full. To me, it looked like white scars dotting black tissue, a memory of all the misery of my life. This week I would add another scar. As I silently sobbed, Juliet joined me. She was a Jewish girl who had been there for several weeks.

"I'm leaving the shelter Friday," she said. "You can move in with me."

"Really?"

"Sure," she said. "I have enough room."

We made plans to meet at her apartment three days later.

☾

Friday morning as I was packing my suitcase I discovered that my citizenship papers had been stolen. I complained at the office. They suspected the cleaning lady because she had stolen from others before, but she didn't speak English. I never did find my papers before it was time to leave.

It was long walk to the apartment complex, probably fifteen city blocks. By the time I dragged the suitcase all that way, both Dignity and I were tired.

"I'm hungry," Dignity said.

"Hold on, Dignity, love," I said. "Juliet said she would be here and take us out to eat."

We sat in the hot sun, waiting and waiting.

"I'm thirsty," Dignity said. Sweat beaded on her forehead. I knew she needed water, but I couldn't just leave my suitcase and run to a store. Juliet could arrive any time.

Minutes turned to hours and I started getting anxiety attacks, fearing every person who walked by, every face that looked at me. The sun started to set and I realized Juliet wasn't coming. I started to cry.

"Mom, why are you crying?" Dignity wiped a tear from my face.

"I'm just tired, so I cry. I love you, Dignity. Everything is okay." My ribs squeezed in on my heart. The women I thought were friends were my enemies. I could trust no one.

An elderly man walked from the apartment building and asked if I was okay.

"I'm waiting for a friend," I told him.

"You've been here for hours," he said kindly. "Come on in off the street. It isn't safe for you and your girl."

Desperate, I followed him into his small apartment and sat on his couch. He said he didn't have water, but offered me wine and Dignity some ice cream.

"You can stay here 'til your friend comes," he said. "My name's Richard, by the way."

"I'm Sara. This is Dignity." I drank the wine without guilt. Dignity ate ice cream and entertained herself on the floor, playing with his two cats. As I watched her, I fell asleep.

The next thing I knew, I heard Dignity. "Wake up, Mom. Juliet is here."

I jumped. "She's here?"

Dignity nodded. I got up and went to the screen door. "That's her!"

"Thank you, Richard, for having us."

We left quickly. When we reached Juliet, there was a man with her. She had not mentioned a boyfriend.

"Hi Sara," she said. "This is John."

I nodded. John looked at me longer than I liked. I tried to ignore him.

"We've been waiting a long time," I said.

She didn't seem concerned and invited us into her apartment. That night I was happy to have a roof over my head, but I didn't think this living situation was going to work. I didn't like the idea of sharing the place with a man.

Over the next few days, we hung out at the apartment and talked. I cooked and cleaned for everyone. Her boyfriend seemed to be flirting with me right in front of her, which made me nervous. I didn't want trouble. I just wanted a safe place to live.

Without warning, Juliet decided I couldn't stay anymore.

"Why?" I asked.

She shrugged. "It's just not working out."

I was so upset I didn't know which way to turn. Was she jealous that John was paying attention to me? Maybe it was because I was Arabic and she was Jewish.

That afternoon I wrote her a letter.

Dear Juliet,

I cannot believe you are throwing my daughter and me out for no fucking reason! You are just like the rest of ignorant people in the world. If you want to be a Jew who hates, well I am a Muslim who cannot hate you in return, yet I hate you for what you have done to me. Women will never win this domestic violence crap because WOMEN are BITCHES and CATISH towards each other! While men still stick like glue to each other. Your bad intentions about life are wrong and you will never have a good life. Remember this for the rest of your life.

Sara!

I left the letter on the table, grabbed the suitcase and Dignity and headed for the street. Before I got to the end of the parking lot, I realized I had no phone numbers for anybody, even the women in the shelter. The Earth spun faster than a merry go round.

"Where are we going?" Dignity asked.

I don't know. Tears pooled in my eyes until I could barely see. Where could we go? I didn't know anyone, except Juliet and the old man.

"Let's go see Richard," I said.

Richard took pity on me once again and put us up for a few nights. When I talked of getting a job, he said he had a lady friend who needed someone to clean her house.

"Stella can give you a place to live until you get your things together," he said.

I thanked him for his kindness.

☾٭

The trip to Stella's house included several bus rides and a long walk down an isolated dirt road. Was everything here so far apart? Richard led us without slowing. I struggled through the heat with Dignity on my shoulders. It must have been ten miles from the road to a clump of trailers and old houses. A mangy dog wandered nearby. I hoped it wasn't dangerous.

"I'm thirsty," Dignity said as Richard pointed out a small brick one-story house. At least Stella didn't live in one of those stuffy trailers.

"We're almost there," I said. I put Dignity on the ground and took her hand. "Come on."

Richard knocked hard on the front door and we were soon greeted by a short, stout woman with flaming orange hair and thick glasses.

"What is it?" she said.

"It's me, Richard," he said.

"Oh for God's sake, Richard. Come in." We stepped inside and I was overwhelmed by the sour smell of the cramped room. "And who is this?"

"You said you needed someone to clean your house."

"Oh yes. Yes I did. Come in."

I couldn't identify the sour smell, but it looked more like a garbage dump than a home. There were piles of paper and clothing and dishes and trash all over the place. I could barely see the furniture. The floors were sticky as if someone had spilled honey to make it shine. She did look like a nice lady though, strange, but nice.

"This is Sara and her daughter Dignity," Richard said.

While the two of them talked I decided to get started with the cleaning. I went to the kitchen, but hardly knew where to begin. There wasn't a clean spot in that room. I picked a counter that hadn't been washed in months and began at one edge. Some of the dishes must have been sitting there for years. Jars of spices and boxes of coffee and tea were strewn all over. This woman didn't need someone to clean her house; she needed to have it bulldozed.

151

Richard left. I tried my best to make the kitchen livable. I organized cabinets to make room for spice jars. I scrubbed and scraped and washed and scrubbed again. It took four hours, and by the time I finished my fingernails were black. My throat was drier than the desert by this time, but I didn't know if I dared drink the water. How could anyone live like this? I had been depressed, but never so bad that I would let my house get this dirty.

Stella gave Dignity treats and drinks while I worked. She seemed happy with my progress. That night Dignity went to sleep in our small room with no problem. I was itching from cleaning fluids and dust and took a long shower, scrubbing deep and hard to get off the bacteria I knew must be there. Exhausted, I finally fell asleep next in the bed to Dignity.

A rooster woke me to a "new" day. Stella asked if we wanted breakfast, but I insisted on cooking. It was the only way I could be sure the food was safe. Dignity wanted French toast and I fixed eggs for Stella and myself.

That afternoon, I called Gena to ask her to sell one of my pieces of gold and send the money through Western Union.

Later that day, I discovered that Stella had a tenant when a skinny young guy walked out of a bedroom off the living room. He smiled and I saw he had no teeth. It seemed that many people in Arizona had lost their teeth. Maybe they had no dentists. I remembered my days working for Dr. Bedwoon and earning my own money. I would need to get a real job to support myself and Dignity. But where?

Stella's daughter, Mary, came to visit later that day. She was in her mid-twenties, just a few years older than me, and had bleached blond hair and a loud voice. When I told her my family was from Yemen, her eyes lit up.

"My husband was in the Desert Storm," she said excitedly.

We got into a conversation about Iraq. "War talk" was not my favorite subject, but I had to make friends somehow.

"You're nice, Sara," Mary said. "I like you. Do you want to go out this weekend?"

"I don't know." My last night out had gotten me evicted from the woman's shelter. "I don't have anyone to babysit."

"Mom'll watch your cute daughter. She likes kids."

"Sure, I can watch her," Stella jumped into the conversation. "You need a break."

I tried to think of another excuse, but my mind went blank. "Okay," I said, feeling awkward. Maybe it would be good to have a night out.

By the time Saturday came I had forgotten about going out. I had just finished washing the dishes when I heard a car pull up, loud bass vibrating its windows. A few seconds later the back door slammed. I jumped, thinking of Father.

"Sara?" Mary called out. I dried my hands. Mary strolled into the kitchen in high heels. She wore short shorts and a blouse that exposed much of her breasts. Her makeup reminded me of the Yemeni women at weddings. "Come on Sara, aren't you ready?"

"Sorry," I said. "It won't take me long."

"Here," she said, handing me a bag. "I bought this outfit for you."

The black and gold outfit wasn't as skimpy as hers, but still made me uncomfortable. My psoriasis had not gotten any better since leaving Michigan and it nearly showed beneath this outfit. I would have to be careful how I moved.

"We're going to have so much fun!" Mary was so excited she freaked me out. I was not used to this stuff.

I was even more shocked when we arrived at a night club. Just seeing the women in their skimpy clothes was embarrassing. I pretended I enjoyed the place, but the music was too loud and the men vulgar. I spent the evening missing Dignity and having second thoughts about Arizona. What was I doing here? Watching women flaunt their bodies at a club was not how I had imagined my new life would be.

We got back to the house at midnight. Stella opened the door to let us in and the first thing I heard was Dignity crying.

"What happened?" I said.

"Your daughter was very bad," Stella said.

My heart fell to the ground. I rushed to our room. Dignity was sobbing uncontrollably.

"It's okay," I said, taking her in my arms. "I am so sorry." *I regret my actions*, I said to God. *I will never do this again.* I held Dignity close, rocking her until she calmed down. When she finally went to sleep, I returned to the living room.

Stella said, "I can't take this anymore. You're living here without paying rent."

"What about all the cooking and cleaning I do? And the food I bought." I didn't have much money, but I had bought some groceries when the money from Gena arrived.

"I want you out tomorrow morning," Stella said.

Battlefield

She screams and she screams
For what, oh God, for what!
I scream too
Inside my head from the fears and terrors of life!
The bloodshed from all the bull
The wars that leave cuts and arrows of poison shot into me
This destructive home is killing me
Fighting, yet I fail
I am losing; I and Dignity in me.
Wars, alone I fight
Thrown into this
Help! Please help me!
White, black, brown, yellow
I don't hate you
So can you just rescue me?
From this battlefield!

Chapter 24

Angels From Allah

I woke to another sunny, hot day only to discover that Stella wasn't home. It didn't take me long to get packed. I am not a thief by nature, but I took some food. I was out of money again, and who knew if we were going to find a place to sleep.

"Dignity," I called. "Time to get up."

"Where are we going?" Dignity asked when she saw the packed suitcase.

"A new place." I would call Gena for more cash, but who knew when that would arrive. In the meantime, I planned to stay in Tucson.

It seemed like an endless journey back to the main road. My psoriasis was screaming by the time we reached a bus stop. I imagined myself traveling the sands of Yemen alone, lost in the wilderness, looking for Allah. In these last few weeks I had been caught up in events and hadn't taken time to pray as I should. Now, I prayed with all my heart, thanking God for everything he had given me and asking him to protect our journey that day.

A bus squealed to a stop, tossing up orange dust. I had just enough change to pay our fare into town.

I sat on the cool vinyl seats and noticed blood seeping through my shirt. My psoriasis was so bad the sores had cracked and bled. If only I could bleed this disease out of me. If only I could find some peace in this world, I would set my life to a purpose. No woman should have to go through what I had. Was there no place to help a woman on the run?

Just when my hope was lowest, Allah sent an angel. A young Moroccan man with a square face and athletic body moved to the seat next to us and started up a conversation. I did not tell him much about myself, but he gave me some money and his phone number. I had no reason to call him, but thanked him and recited a prayer in Arabic.

"May Allah bless you," I said.

"Maybe you can come to my soccer game," he said. "You and your daughter." I smiled, but going to a soccer game was the last thing I was interested in. He was a nice young man, though, and I treated him politely.

When we reached town, I found a small restaurant named Sinbad. We ate like we hadn't eaten in weeks. I was thankful to the young man for giving us money, but we couldn't rely on the generosity of strangers for everything. Somehow, I had to find a place to stay.

While we rested at the table, I asked the waiter if they had the Yellow Pages. He gave the book to me and I looked for a Mosque. Nothing. I looked up churches and there it was, Mosque Yousuf. I went back to the counter.

"Do you know where this street is?

"Oh, it's only a block away."

"Thank Allah."

When we went outside, Dignity abruptly said, "Mom, I miss Grandma. I want to go home." My heart broke. I could not blame her. I was feeling the same way, but I could not go back. I had disgraced the family by running away. If I was worth nothing to them before I left, what was I worth now?

We found the mosque's white bricks and golden dome without problem. I had not prayed *salat* since we moved into that old lady's house. Her house had been too filthy for prayer, but that was no excuse. Allah was not a perfectionist. He would hear prayer from any place. It was what was inside a person's heart that mattered.

The moment I reached for the Mosque's door handle, I felt victorious. I felt at home. My heart beat fast, but my mind was calm. Allah was with us. We found the door to the woman's section and removed our shoes. The red carpeting felt smooth against my aching feet.

"Where are we, Mama?"

"A safe place." I took some clothes from the suitcase and made a pad for her to lie on. "It's your nap time. Try to get some sleep."

"I'm not sleepy."

"I'll lie beside you." I curled next to my daughter. "Everything will be okay." *Please*, I prayed to Allah, *please help us.*

A woman with dark eyes and thin cheeks entered the prayer room. I turned my face from her so that she would not see me crying, but it was too late.

"What's wrong?" she asked.

"Nothing."

She sat near us. "You can talk to me."

I wiped tears from my eyes.

"I do not recognize you," she said. "Where are you from?" She put her hand on my shoulder. I pulled away. This woman was a stranger. Maybe she was planning to steal from me.

"My name is Soria," she said. "I am from Libya. What is your name?"

Jasmine, I thought. *No. Sara.* I didn't know who I was anymore.

"Did someone hurt you?"

A sob shook my throat. My eyes burned as if they had been cut by shards of glass. The verbal abuse, the beatings, the mind games of my brothers, husbands, and Father weighed heavy on me. I remembered the Monster climbing from his hole to brutally beat my mother. I remembered being unable to fight back, unable to escape.

Soria noticed psoriasis sores on my forehead and arms. I must have looked like a monster myself, but all I saw was compassion in her eyes.

"I... I am from the city of Sana'a," I sobbed. "From Yemen and my name is... Sara."

"It is okay, *habeebti.* I can help you. Trust me."

I took a deep breath and dried my tears.

"Who hurt you?"

I told her a small part of my story and how I had run to Arizona to escape my husband. "Now, we have no place to stay"

"I know someone you can stay with," Soria said. "They are good Muslims from Sana'a. I'll call right now." She went to a pay phone near the door. I watched her dial and made sure I could hear what she was saying.

After their hellos and some small talk, Soria turned to me and extended the receiver. "Come here, Sara. Talk to Nagat. She wants to talk to you."

"Hello," I said, half expecting Mom to answer me.

"*Salam Alaikum,*" Nagat said. Her voice was soft and rhythmic. "Do not fear anything, okay?"

After talking on the phone for some time, I felt comfortable enough to allow Nagat's husband, Jamal, to pick us up at the mosque. While we waited, Soria reassured me.

"I have known Nagat since college. She is my best friend, and will care for you as if you are her sister." Hearing that these women were college educated was empowering. I was thrilled to meet open minded women from our closed society.

Jamal arrived and greeted us outside the mosque. He had a sandy tan and dressed meticulously in a suit and tie. He seemed friendly, but while he carried my suitcase to his trunk, I purposefully sat in the back seat with Dignity.

Jamal looked at us via the rearview mirror and smiled. "Do not be afraid. You are safe now. I have four children, two boys and two girls. Your daughter can play with them. She will never be bored." His eyes sparkled and he laughed in a cheerful way.

I liked this guy and admired his openness. He was not afraid to talk to an Arabic woman, even a runaway. I could not wait to meet his wife.

Before I could get out of the car, I saw Nagat standing outside a large one story adobe house. She looked like an angel with smooth skin, delicate facial features and silky black hair. I had never met a Sana'a woman in real life. It is true what they say, they look and sound like doves. Very unique is their beauty. Their voices are delicate and seductive.

I only hoped she was as beautiful on the inside as she was from the outside.

"*Salam Alaikum*," she said, welcoming me with open arms and a smile. "Come in."

She introduced me to her beautiful children. The girls possessed their mother's delicate features while the boys more resembled their father. They were all older than Dignity, but welcomed her with open arms. They were well mannered and charming and very clean.

"Are you hungry or thirsty?" Nagat said.

"No." I should have been hungry, but my stomach had been so filled with anxiety all day it did not want food.

She took me to the living room. Unlike Stella's house, this room was spacious and uncluttered. Wide windows faced the street, letting in the afternoon sun. Leather sofas took up much of the room.

"Please sit." Nagat turned to her older daughter. "Sana, go get our guest a glass of water."

"Yes, Mom."

"Now, what is your name, my sweet friend?" She asked so kindly my heart wanted to confess the truth, but my mind won out.

"Sara," I said. I started to feel very comfortable and just wanted to fall asleep, but the sun was still high in the sky. I imagined flying in those blue skies and feeling no worries.

"So, do you want to talk about how you got here?" Nagat asked. "You do not have to tell us anything. We just want you to feel safe and comfortable."

I nodded.

"Remember this, Sara. You are my sister and I mean what I say from my heart."

How sweet, I thought. But I wasn't ready to tell my story, not yet.

Nagat and I made small talk while Dignity swam in their pool. As night came, I was given a room for myself and Dignity. Dignity was tired from playing. It didn't take her long to fall asleep. I felt relieved and laid next to her, sleeping for about a half hour.

When I awoke, I knew I must pray. I got up and changed, did my ablution and took my prayer rug and Qur'an to the living room. Everyone had gone to bed. I went to my knees and bowed, asking for forgiveness and feeling God again in my veins and my bones. After prayer, I opened the Qur'an and read.

At three in the morning, I saw a shadow in the doorway.

"Who's there?"

Nagat stepped into the light. "I heard you crying."

I closed the Qur'an.

"Sara," she said. "Why are you crying? Come here to my arms."

Like a child, I went to her and curled into her arms.

"You are pure and you are beautiful," she said. "Allah is with you."

She held me for a long time. No one had held me that long, not even Mom. In fact, I couldn't remember when I last did get a hug from Mom. As I pulled myself politely from her warmth, I saw tears sliding from her almond-shaped eyes.

The first thing I thought was that maybe *she* was going through abuse. Thank Allah, I was wrong about that. Actually, she was the boss over her husband completely. He was fine with it, and well, that was maybe how it should be.

☪

In the days that followed, I became comfortable enough to cook for the family.

"This is delicious lamb!" Nagat said. "Where did you learn to cook?"

I shrugged. "I cooked a lot at home. I like doing it."

"You should be a chef."

"From now on, Nagat, I am your cook. I don't want you to cook and ruin your beautiful self."

Nagat broke out in bursts of pleasant laughter. "You are too funny for me," she said.

I was so funny that she got a video camera and taped me mimicking my family members and even her. Those were the best days ever. I had finally found a real sister of Islam, a true woman with an open mind. Allah had truly sent me an angel this time.

I opened up about my family and Nagat told me of hers.

"Actually, *habeebti*, I come from a huge family. My dad works as the ambassador for our President of Yemen."

"What are you doing here?" I said. I would have expected a man like her father to control his daughter more tightly than most, yet she was freer than any Arabic woman I had known.

"My parents let me marry an ordinary man," she said. "Mom said if I care for him and get to know him and we love each other, it will be better than marrying an egoistic rich man."

"What about egoistic *poor* men?" I said with a grin.

"I guess all men are egoistic in some way," she said. "That's just the way they are."

"Well," I said. "All men need to tie their dicks and carry them over shoulders."

Nagat burst into laughter.

"Speaking of men, let me show you a picture of my brother," she said. "He has bad luck with woman."

She left the room and came back with a photo of a man with smooth brown skin and dark, straight hair wearing a *foutah* with a tank top and sandals.

Damn, he is too fine, I thought, then quickly reminded myself that I was a married woman on my *third* marriage. The last thing I needed was to meet another man.

I cleared my throat. "Th...tha...that is your brother?"

Nagat chuckled. "He's single."

"I am going to go and cook something *hot*," I said.

Eventually, I confessed my real name to Nagat and spilled the poisoned snakes and demons from of my system. She continued to hold me in her arms and tell me positive things. I loved that wonderful sister and felt blessed to meet such a family. Yet, I couldn't rid myself of guilt. I kept thinking about Mom. How could I be happy when I knew she was still trapped? No matter how I tried, I could not get Dearborn out of my blood.

☾

Jamal asked me to help him drive some new cars to his dealership. He said I could work for him as a driver and he would give me a car on his name with insurance and gas. Wow! This was too good to be true. "I have seen you staring at the gold Acura with the sunroof," he said. "It can be yours in a few weeks."

Later, Jamal sat me down in the living room with Nagat. They were such a cute couple. They talked to me, and said they would pay rent for an apartment until I got welfare. If I wanted to go to college, they would babysit Dignity. I could not believe what I was hearing.

The next day, Jamal took me to a nice apartment complex across from their house. It had a swimming pool and roomy apartments with dishwashers and microwaves.

"I paid for this apartment and you will be moving in three weeks," he said. I wanted to kiss him on the forehead and thank him and praise him, but I was too speechless and a little ashamed from all their generosity. I did not feel I deserved it.

Nightmares began to wake me, eating at my heart, haunting my emotions and blocking the vessels to my brain. As wonderful and as normal as everything was here, I was not normal. This was too good to be true; something bad would happen soon. Guilt ridiculed me. What if Mom died? God was going to take me straight to hell. God was going to punish me forever.

"We want to get you some furniture for your apartment," Nagat said the following day after breakfast.

My heart sank. I knew I had to tell them I couldn't stay.

"Maybe not," I said.

"What do you mean?"

They had been so kind to me, I couldn't get the words to come out of my mouth.

"What is it, Jasmine?"

"I can't take the apartment."

"It's all right. We want you to have a place of your own."

"It's not that," I said. "I have to go back home."

"Why?" Nagat said. "You were not happy there. Your husband abused you."

"You have been more than kind to me," I said. "But I can't stay." I could not share my guilt about running away, my sorrow for leaving Mom behind, my terror that I would be punished for taking all these generous gifts while abandoning my family. It was too complicated. I wasn't sure that I even understood.

"You are safe with us," Nagat said.

"I know," I said.

"Then stay. Think of your daughter."

Nothing she said, not even that, could convince me. It was like a compulsion deep inside me I could no longer deny.

☪

Jamal called Father. "Your daughter is with us, she is safe and she has done nothing wrong. She went to Mosque, so I want you to vow in Allah's name that you will not harm her in any way."

I could only imagine what Father was saying on the other end. No doubt he was playing the concerned Father, looking for his lost daughter. But Jamal knew better.

"I have your address and your name," he said. "If anything happens to my sister, I will make sure you go to jail."

As he spoke, I realized how much these people truly cared about me. They gave me their undivided attention; they heard me when I spoke, they saw me as a person to trust and *respect*. I would always hear Nagat's gentle voice in my mind and know the meaning of good life and laughter.

I'm going to miss all this terribly, I thought as Jamal hung up the phone. I wanted to cancel going back to my family, but it was too late.

Chapter 25

Not Expecting Reconciliation

When Father and Mouzi arrived at Nagat's house, the Monster was disguised as a normal man, but I could see the fire burning behind his eyes. I was not expecting any kind of reconciliation or restoration; it was not necessary. Still, I felt something die deep inside when I saw them. It was not my heart or my soul, but something that had tried to grow from a root or seed toward blossom. Now there was a hollow space.

Nagat welcomed them inside.

"Will you stay for tea?" she said.

"Take the suitcase out to the car," Father barked at Mouzi. Mouzi was a follower, doing Father's bidding, unquestioning and dense. "We have to go," he said to his hosts.

"So soon?" Nagat said. I think she wanted him to stay, hoping I would change my mind now that he stood before me.

"You too," Father said to me. "In the car."

"Just one minute," Nagat said. "I have something for her."

I followed Nagat to her bedroom.

"Are you certain you want to return?" she said. "It's not too late to change your mind."

But it was. It always had been. Guilt would eventually pull me back there as sure as the sun rose and set.

She touched my hand. "I can't," I said. "I can't stay even though I want to."

"I understand," she said softly, though I didn't see how she could. She lifted a beautiful gold necklace from her dresser. On the chain dangled an ornate box containing a tiny Holy Qur'an. She put it around my neck and kissed me.

"I want you to keep this on you and never take it off." She took me into her arms and held me tight. "I wish you were not going."

"I love you so much, Nagat," I said. "One day we will see each other again. All right? It will be okay, Nagat."

"Yallah!" Father yelled from the living room. "Jasmine, we've got to go."

I gave Nagat one last hug and obeyed Father's command as I had done so many times. We got to the car and my skin broke out in goose bumps. My legs were heavy and shaking, even my mouth was suddenly dry. The psoriasis sores began to burn.

Dignity was quiet, but I could feel her disapproval. She had had a taste of normal family life with brothers and sisters who played rather than hitting and sang rather than shouting. A sob built up in my throat. *Where is home?* I thought. To me, home was where Mom was, but as long as she stayed with Father it would be a living hell.

☪

When we got back to Michigan, Father and my brothers gave me the silent treatment, which was fine with me. I would rather they say nothing than abuse me with words. I found Mom and my sisters in the kitchen. I kissed and hugged Mom, but felt no response in return. The hollowness inside me expanded.

By then my psoriasis was itching so badly I couldn't wait to take a shower. When I opened the suitcase, Mom noticed my prayer rug and the Holy Qur'an on top of everything. I saw a spark of admiration in her eyes. Of all her children, I was the one who read and respected the words sent down personally from Allah. Islam was sacred to me as it was to her. We had that much, at least.

The shower was as painful as it was cleansing. My psoriasis sores were inflamed and peeling. I put cream on them afterward, but nothing seemed to help. I thought back to the hot sands of Arizona and wondered if going to my homeland might be what I needed to heal my disease and myself. Maybe the sands of Yemen would cure me.

When I finished dressing everyone was sleeping except Mom. I heard the *irgeelah* gurgling in the living room. Father's rumbling snores echoed from his lair in the basement. Wrapping a robe tightly around me, I went and sat by Mom.

"I'm so sorry," I said to her in the semi-darkness. "I'm sorry for the troubles I have given you in life. I do not mean to hurt you in any way."

I waited, anticipating a bit of understanding.

"You are forgiven," she said, sucking on the pipe, "but it is not forgotten." Even now, when we were alone, she would not show compassion. This only intensified my desperation for love and threw me into a sea of despair. I felt as if I were drowning, trying to hold my breath. Could she feel me trying to survive at that moment? *Allah*, I prayed, *please transform me into a dolphin or some animal that can survive this deep water between us.*

"I'll take Dignity upstairs," I said.

"Leave her down here." Mom said. "She can sleep in my bed. She missed her grandmother. I will make sure she's safe."

I headed upstairs to lie on my old bed, shutting down my feelings step by step. By the top of the stairs I was a robot.

☾

In the days that followed, I was so sick that my body started to eat me from the inside out. I thought I had a stomach flu. Tumasha took me to the doctor.

"Are you depressed," he said. "I will prescribe some medicine." Was it the medicine to solve my problems or grant me life again? I didn't think so, but I went with the doctor's suggestion. I picked up the Zoloft at the pharmacy and tried one pill. Whoa! Reality became a numb illusion.

I heard Father and Mouzi talking in the kitchen about divorcing me from Enad. They wanted to make him to sign the house over to them. I walked straight to them like a soldier, fearless because of my wonder drug. I leaned against the table.

"What are you saying?" My voice was not my own.

"None of your business," Mouzi said.

"I heard you," I said. "You and I will not be getting the house from Enad." I shook my index finger in their faces, feeling sorry for poor Enad. His first wife had taken enough from him. I didn't want to be married to him, but that didn't mean I wanted to steal his money. "No. No. No," I said. "Okay?"

Father stared at me. "Are you okay? Have you really lost your mind?

"No," I said. "Not me. Never will I lose my mind." I walked upstairs, feeling as if my body had separated from my brain. *I will never touch those pills again*, I thought. But it sure felt good to face the Monster without fear.

I paid for my outburst later. My brothers surrounded me in the kitchen like pit bulls ready to tear off my flesh. They spat on me and beat me.

☾

A strange thing happened. One afternoon we got a call from Omar, a cousin who worked on boats that transported cargo to and from America. He was coming to visit because of my return from Arizona. *Why would my return have anything to do with him?* I hoped Father did not have another marriage on his mind. I wasn't yet divorced from Enad.

A few hours later, we got a call from an uncle on Father's side, Mukanath. He was also coming to visit. All of the sudden these hidden relatives wanted to be part of solving my problems. I had not even met these men.

We welcomed Mukanath into our house two days later. He was a very tall middle-sized man in good shape. His hair was cut so short he almost looked bald; he had big eyes and a black mustache that hung down to his chin on each side, giving him a Mexican look.

He stayed in the bedroom in the basement next to the Monster's lair. I could hear his husky voice echoing up the stairs as he talked to Father. A meeting was planned at my Uncle Gaban's house. I assumed they were going to discuss my divorce from Enad and what they wanted me to do next. Undoubtedly, Father would want to marry me off again.

"Let's go," Father said the day of the meeting.

"Where?"

"Gaban's. You and your mother are coming."

They were taking me? A woman was never in allowed at such meetings.

At Gaban's, Mom and I sat on a couch in the far of a corner of the long living room. Uncle Gaban and Omar were to our left. Omar was this skinny man with the most fantastic silky hair swaying from side to side when he moved. Mukanath was not there. Father did not sit, but paced the perimeter of the living room with his usual limp. We all watched him, waiting for someone to start a conversation.

"All right," Uncle Gabon said. "Everyone praise the Prophet before we start."

We all mumbled prayers and the discussion began. I watched the men talk without hearing word they said. My mind was numb. This meeting would only bring more suffering. What was the point? I didn't want to be part of their decision on how to handle the divorce. I should have listened to Nagat and stayed in Arizona.

"What the fuck!" Father screamed, snapping my attention awake. He spat in Omar's face. "You have no right making decisions for me." He towered over Omar until I was sure he was inches away from punching the man.

Omar did not recoil. "You cannot keep arranging marriages for your daughter."

"You son of a whore!" Father said.

"I'm willing to take her to Yemen, provide for her and give her what she needs."

"Bastard!" Father's body became twisted and misshapen. His face turned red and puffy. I thought he would transform into an actual monster.

"I am willing with my honor," Omar said.

"Pork eating bastard!"

Uncle Gaban looked uncomfortable, but did not have the balls to say anything. All he did was sit there looking pretty. It disgusted me. His actions disgraced my grandfather, Ameen Musleh, the real and only legend in our family.

"Fuckin' bastard!" Father said, clomping back and forth before Omar. "Who the hell do you think you are? Swine!"

"Stop!" I screamed, covering my ears. Omar was married and his intentions were good. I honored him for stepping up to Father. "Stop it! Please!"

Mom did not react.

"Stop," I whimpered. "I do not want to hear any more hate and denigration. I *want* to go to Yemen. I want to live with my cousin Omar."

Everyone was speechless. The door opened and Mukanath sauntered into the room.

"So what has happened?" he asked, looking from Father to Omar and back again.

Uncle Gaban spoke at last. "Everything is solved and done."

"Let's go home," Father said. He waved for me to stand. I followed him to the car, confused. It didn't seem like any decision had been made.

"Am I to go to Yemen?" I asked.

"No," he said.

"Why not?"

"Why not? You do not know Yemen. You will not like it."

How could Yemen be worse than here? I ground my teeth like he usually did and imagined chewing him up. At that moment it would have been *hallal* to have his life taken. I climbed into the backseat. Mom crawled in beside me.

"I want to know my family overseas," I said. "I want to know my roots and my grandparents."

"They are all dead!" He sat in the driver's seat and started the car.

What he said was not true and I knew it. My grandparents were still alive and lived with some of my aunts and uncles. What really concerned Father was fear of losing control over me. He was hungry for more marriage money. If I went to Yemen, he might never get me back.

"I have the right to go to my country," I said. "The country I am really from."

We drove by our house and I wondered what he was up to. Mom remained silent.

"With what will you go," he said, eyes fixed on the road. "You have no money."

"With the money Enad has promised for the divorce. Three thousand dollars." We had agreed in writing that I did not want my possessions and no part of the house, in exchange for money. Father paused as he mulled the idea over.

"Will you take your daughter? She is too young. She will get sick there."

"I'll buy her medicine," I said.

"Okay," he said. "Tomorrow we will go and get you and your daughter's passports and I will pay for it. *We* will go to Yemen."

I was surprised. Why had he agreed so quickly? Had he come up with a plan to take my money once we got to Yemen? There was no end to my father's scheming. I was happy he would let me go, but worried that another surprise was down the road.

Chapter 26

Honey for the Wound

I don't know what was happened to Father, but he seemed to keeping his promise to take me to Yemen. Just as he had said, he took us out the next morning to get the paperwork completed for the journey. He even took Dignity and me to Big Boy for breakfast. It was difficult to believe. I remembered when I was a kid he would tell me to cut the grass for two dollars, but he never gave me anything. Like an idiot, I would believe him every time.

A few days after receiving our passports, I discovered Mom wearing one of her better dresses in the living room.

"Are you going somewhere?" I asked.

"I am going to visit Fiazah," she said. "I want to see her new baby."

I didn't think anything about it. I was sure she would be back before Father and Mouzi got home. They were the ones who didn't like her leaving the house.

Uncle Mukanath was still staying with us. When we entered the kitchen, he noticed Mom was dressed to go out. "Why are you dressed?" he asked. "Are you going somewhere?"

"No, I just took a shower," she lied.

"Well, I am going to visit my boys," he said, "and take them to get some paperwork for their jobs."

"What time will you be back?" She eyed him suspiciously.

"Maybe around seven tonight."

"Okay," she said, looking relieved.

She waited an hour before making a move. While she waited, she prayed and read the Qur'an. Finally she put her shoes on and her *balto*.

"Take care of the house and do not let anyone in," she said. Apparently, she suspected something fishy was going on. I figured it was her mistrust of me. Did she think I would sneak a man into the house while she was gone?

I took the opportunity to sit and watch the Cosby Show and other cable shows. I made Yemeni tea and had some of Mom's cookies. I was enjoying my peace of mind when the door bell rang. *Shit*, I thought. Who could it be?

I opened the inner door. It was Mukanath. I hesitated, standing inside the screen door. It was too late to pretend I wasn't home.

"What do you want?" I asked.

"I live here, remember?" he said.

He was right. He was my cousin and Father would be angry if I kept him out. I opened the door and Mukanath strolled by me to the kitchen. I returned to watching TV.

"Auntie, Auntie, Auntie," I heard him calling.

He looked into to the living room. "Where is my Aunt?"

"She went to a lady's house to see a new baby."

"Oh," he said. "Come here. I want to talk to you about Arizona. Come to the kitchen."

I had little choice but to comply. I joined him at the table.

"Now tell me what happened," he said. "I want to know the whole story."

Thinking he was truly interested in my life, I spilled out the horrid story of my marriages and running away from crazy Enad.

"You need someone to take care of you," he said. "Someone to treat you like a queen. I see by your eyes you need a man who can give you so much in bed you will have to say stop."

Oh, no, I thought. *Not again.* Were men only interested in one thing? He stood from his chair and I quickly stood also, looking for escape. He went to his knees and grabbed my legs.

"Stop," I said, trying to back away. He held me tight.

"I can be the man that pleases you," he said.

"No!" I pushed at his shoulders. Pain arched through my upper leg. "Fuck!" I screamed. He had bit me.

I shoved his head away and ran for the door. He came from behind and tore the *balto* off, which pulled me back toward him.

"Stop this!" I shouted.

He grabbed my breasts and held them so tight I felt they would pop like balloons.

"No!" I pushed his big hands off.

"I love you," he said. "I have wanted you since you were 10 years of age, but your parents said no."

My thoughts sped round and round. I barely knew this man. How could he love me? He twirled me to face him and pressed me into the wall.

"Look, look at it," he said, motioning to his penis. "It is so aroused by you."

I looked to the ceiling and prayed to God for protection. *Allah, break him from this evil Satan taking him over.* I glared straight into his face. "You should be ashamed of yourself! My parents trusted you in their house."

Mukanath released his hold. He bowed down.

"I am sorry," he said. "Please forgive me." Sweat covered his body. God was there again for me. He never failed me. Now he protected me from losing my dignity to this man.

I ran to the living room, letting the door close between us. Why did this keep happening? Was it something inside me? Something I did or said? I had never flirted with Mukanath. I was too scared for such childish doings. Tears fell from my eyes. I couldn't help feeling dirty even though nothing happened.

After a time, a door banged and I looked into the kitchen. Mukanath had left by the back door. I should have felt relief, but did not. This man was still living in Father's house and I would have to see him every day. Should I tell Mom? Pain lanced my upper leg and I remembered the bite he had given me. What would she say about that? Would she blame me for being home alone with the man? Would she take his side?

I went the bathroom and pulled down my pants. His teeth marks, both the top and bottom, were already black. I feared I could have a disease or maybe AIDS. I did not know where his mouth had been. I put some lemon juice and honey on the wound to kill any infection, but nothing could salve my inner torment.

I went upstairs and changed my clothes, which smelled of him. I did my ablution and prayed to Allah. As I bowed down, I trembled with rage. I was sick of Muslim men getting away with cruel behavior and blaming women.

☪

That night I was expected to cook food that Mukanath had bought earlier. I'm usually an excellent cook and pride myself in the dishes I make, but that evening I cooked with the fire in my heart. When Mukanath sat at the table with the rest of the family I slammed burned food in front of him, hoping he would choke.

"What is this?" Mom said.

I glared at Mukanath.

"What is wrong with you?" Mom asked.

"Come and eat with us," Mukanath said with a sweet smile. "Family should eat together."

"I'm not hungry." I was ready for a Zoloft, but my daughter needed me. I went upstairs and tended to her, ignoring the anxiety tensing my whole body.

The next day, Mukanath commanded me to make him coffee as if I were his slave wife. I put the coffee on to cook and washed dishes while he and Mom had a long conversation. As I washed each pot and pan I thought about putting rat poison in his cup. Enough to make him sick. Enough to make him roll on the ground in pain. Enough to kill him.

When the coffee was ready, I took a cup to the table. Mukanath grasped my hand.

"You have hurt my heart," he said. "You do not deserve this and I am mad at you for running to Arizona. You could have gone to the house of a family member."

"I suppose you would have welcomed me to your home," I said.

"Of course I would," he said with a smile that made me wish I had followed through on the rat poison plan.

Rage boiled inside me. How dare he act concerned. How dare he sit there and talk to my mother as if nothing had happened. I wanted to expose my bite wound and ask if that was how he cared for his family. I wanted to show Mom what he had done. But of course, I did not. I turned away and started cleaning the counter.

That night Mom surprised me with some *khat* during our regular smoking time. We chewed and smoked. Once the mood settled into a comfortable buzz, I started talking.

"Mom, I love you and I have never told you but you are my best friend. I want to never hide anything from you, no matter what."

"What is wrong?" she asked.

"I want to share my pain. I have never told you how men have acted towards me. I have bottled it inside for so long. I need to tell someone. I trust you with my life."

"What is it?"

"That day you left me alone at the house," I said. "The day Mukanath said he would be gone. He returned. He tried to rape me." She did not react, but only sat and listened as I told the entire story.

When I finished, she spoke softly. "Mukanath wanted you since you were a little girl. He has asked for your hand every year since you were ten years old."

"Isn't he my Uncle?"

"No, he is your father's nephew." She drew another breath of smoke and released it into the air. "I can never trust anybody. This is why I overprotect you even when you are married."

I could see in her face wrinkles of despair and discouragement. There was no one in the house she could complain to. The men would turn everything on me and say I was the reason for Mukanath's behavior. They would call me a liar. She knew that and I knew it.

"Jasmine," she said. "*Mahbooba men thakar, wa mushnia men al nisa,*" You are too loved by men and so envied by women.

I did not know if I should I take her words as a compliment or a curse. I only wanted a normal life. Was that too much?

Chapter 27

Spectacular Glow of the Mountains

Knowing I was about to leave for Yemen, Mukanath tried several times to convince me to stay. I discouraged him as strongly as I could. If only he had known how repelled I was by him, he might have given up. As it was, I didn't have to wait long to be away from him.

All I could think of was my family roots. I would learn more about Grandfather Ameen Musleh and the Musleh family, which was more a part of me than Father's side. It would be a great journey. Dignity would get to meet many new cousins and see the deserts of our heritage, not the barren sands of Arizona.

One week before the trip, Mom pulled me aside.

"I must talk to you," she said. She looked so concerned I thought the plan had been cancelled.

"What's wrong?" I said.

"I don't want you taking Dignity to Yemen."

"Why?"

"Things will be difficult for you there. It will not be a good time to have her with you."

"She went to Arizona with me," I said. "She's my daughter."

"You must think of her safety," Mom said. "Yemen is not America."

"But, we'll be with family."

"You have not been to Yemen since you were a child. You do not know what it is like."

"I'll keep her safe."

"How?"

I sighed. Why did she have to make everything difficult?

"I tell you what," she said. "If you get there and find you like it, we will send Dignity."

"But how will she get there?"

"We will send her with family," she said. "Don't worry. Everything will be fine."

Maybe Mom was right. It would be difficult leaving Dignity in America, but I didn't really know what I was getting myself into. I would have to trust that Mom knew what was best.

When the day came to leave, tension was a rock sitting on my chest. No one cried as my father packed the car with our bags. I couldn't bear the thought that it would be months before I saw Dignity again, but what was I to do? This was my one chance to go to Yemen.

Dignity waved as the car pulled away from the house. I cried all the way to the airport, tears of sadness and tears of joy.

☪

The flight to Yemen was longer than I imagined. Hour after hour I sat so close to my father I could hear his heavy breathing. This was the closest we had ever been, but still we were strangers. We could never talk to each other. He would always be the Monster and I the disobedient daughter.

When we finally reached Sana'a Airport, I was surprised by the look of it. It seemed more like a messy warehouse with low ceilings and dim lights reflecting off dull yellow walls. The place was crowded with people, mostly men wearing *foutahs* and dress shirts. The women were totally covered and the few children present hung close by their mothers.

"Where is Omar?" Father said. "He is supposed to meet us here."

I looked through the crowd. I didn't see how he could find us in all the commotion. The men inspecting our luggage rummaged through the contents, stealing some of the gifts we had brought. Father did not complain. I dared not say anything.

At the exit doors, we were greeted by poorly dressed children hustling for money by offering to carry our luggage. We found Omar waiting near a sturdy SUV. He seemed a different man here in his own country, paler and less thin.

"Welcome!" His face lit with a wide smile. He shook Father's hand and gave him a hug. To me, he nodded respect. He tossed our bags into the back. Inside, I discovered the vehicle dash was covered in a rainbow of colored material.

"How was your flight?" Omar asked. "Not too long, I hope."

"Miserable," Father said.

Omar drove the dusty road from the airport to Sana'a. I bounced in the back seat. Father stretched his legs and put his arm on the open window ledge. The land didn't look much different from Arizona, with scrubby growth and distant mountains, but I could already tell by the smell I was in my home county. The air was delicately scented with cumin and mint.

"Keep your uncovered face from the window," Omar said, glancing in the mirror. I sat back as we passed smaller cars, donkeys pulling carts, people on bicycles and pedestrians, all making their way toward the city.

In many ways, downtown Sana'a was no different from a modern American city. There were paved roads, congested traffic, tall hotels and apartment buildings. But in between, two- and three-story red stone buildings had withstood the test of time. White domes and minaret's of local mosques rose above the skyline. Narrow streets wound through neighborhoods that had existed in the same place for hundreds of years.

"Let us stop at a store for Jasmine," Omar said. "We will get a proper veil and *balto.*" Every woman I saw was covered in black from head to toe. I wanted to be covered too. I didn't want to feel different. Also, I did not want to be overexposed. I had already experienced what Yemeni men did in America. I did not want to encourage trouble here.

"Never mind that," Father said. "Let's go buy some *thieab* and *khat* and fresh tobacco."

Omar left the main road and stopped near a crowded market. The market street was lined with booths displaying everything from clothing, fresh fruit and meat to jewelry and makeup. The aroma of roasting lamb and fresh bread was strong. Everywhere I looked, colorful goods were displayed in random fashion, men bargained over prices, and people snaked through the street to get a better view. I felt naked without my face covered. Maybe there would be a vendor with veils and *baltos.*

I followed at Omar's heals. Sweet aromas of fresh mango and oranges wafted from fruit stands and I realized I was hungry. We pushed farther into the crowd until we reached a booth crammed with women's clothing.

"Pick out what you want," Omar said.

I nodded gladly. This reminded me of the first time Gais had taken me to the mall. For a moment, I wished Gais had been there as my husband. How wonderful it would have been to share this experience with him.

The booth had some elegant outerwear. I picked a *balto* with black and brown leather in the center and a black silk veil with tassels.

"I like this one," I told Omar and he spent the next ten minutes haggling over the price. It was nothing like America. I couldn't imagine bargaining for a price at the mall.

Father focused on himself as usual, buying new shirts and tobacco, never asking if I needed anything. I could have caused a fuss. It was my divorce money he was spending, but I chose to remain silent. This was my first day in Yemen. I didn't want to mar it by getting into a fight. Besides, Omar was treating me with kindness and respect.

We returned to the SUV. Being covered, I was now free to stare out the window as much as I wanted. Each intersection seemed to have both a traffic light and a cop directing traffic. No one seemed to be paying attention to either one. A mass of cars, busses, bicycles and pedestrians all made their way through in a haphazard way. When cars stopped children would run into the traffic to sell things. I closed my eyes, hoping no one would be injured.

Cars were packed with people who did not seem to mind being crammed together. Male pedestrians held hands. I knew in my head that this was normal in Yemen where hand holding expressed deep brotherhood. Still, it took me a while to get used to the sight.

Sana'a offered so many new sights, but I was curious to see my home village, Juban. Thus, I was happy when we left the city for fields of the greenest grass and distant, barren hills. The air was so clear that I did not need my glasses. Yemen was not the simple desert I had imagined, but a mix of sand and lush vegetation.

I had thought Juban was close to the city, but when morning turned to midday we were still on the road. The farther we traveled the rougher the roads became. Omar named every village we passed: Mabar, Dhamar, Yarim. We stopped at a restaurant in one town. It had only a few tables, but each was supplied with a sheet hanging on a line that could be pulled across. This allowed women to remove their veils and eat without being seen.

Omar ordered for us and we were served soup, rice and lamb in bowls. The food was not bad. I was starving and ate quickly, something I'd learned to do in our household, where we shared food from the same plates.

Afterward, we followed curving roads deeper into the mountains. The stones around us glowed orange and red in the afternoon sun. The scenery was spectacular. I fell in love with this country and hoped my family would accept me here. Did they know I had run away to Arizona? Would they respect me?

Come on, Jasmine, I told myself. *Just be yourself. No one will hurt you.* I needed to stay positive and move forward, but I couldn't help but worry. So far in life, when I expected the best something bad always seemed to follow. Not this time, though.

"We are near Juban," Omar said. "It will not be long now."

"It is always too long," Father grumbled. "Damn roads."

I suddenly felt a shortness of breath. I needed a cigarette. How would I smoke here? Women were not allowed to smoke cigarettes, only the *irgeelah*. I did not like the water pipe much, I needed a *real* cigarette. If only I could sneak one from Father.

We rounded a bend and I saw Juban below us, nestled in a green valley between red rock mountains. Two- and three-story houses with flat roofs lined the streets. The houses were made of the same stone as the mountains, some trimmed in brick and others painted. Near the center, a white mosque rose above everything.

"Praise, Allah," I whispered. *Thank you for bringing me to my home.* This was where I belonged, not the snowy streets of Detroit. I breathed deep, inhaling crisp air. I would call Mom and tell her to send Dignity as soon as possible. We would make a good life here with our own people, away from my Dearborn family's abusive ways.

Omar turned again and again until we stopped before a three-story building. It looked like a small castle with a huge wooden gate and short arched bridge leading to it. The setting sun made the red stones glow like fire.

"We have arrived," Omar announced. My grandmother, Hayla, and the wives of two of Father's brothers and their children rushed to the bridge to greet us. The house was Father's but Omar and several family members lived here. Father sent money to them several times a year.

"Welcome! Welcome!" relatives called out as Father opened his door. Before my feet touched ground the women had me surrounded. They took me by the hand and guided me as if I were a long lost princess.

"I hope you had a nice trip."

"You must be tired."

"Would you like some tea?"

We entered through the wooden gate, walking first on natural sand and then long stones that made the main floor. Turning right, we reached an opening to cement stairs that circled up three floors.

It was dark since there was no electricity and I bumped my head on the low entrance. On the second floor, the women showed me to a large bedroom with two beds.

"Come sit with us and have tea," my aunt said. I needed a bath, but would have to meet everyone first out of respect. I followed them to a large hall on the third floor. Fresh white paint brightened the walls and a burgundy and gold *jalsa,* a set of matching floor cushions divided in sections, lined the sitting area. I was impressed by the ornate beauty of the place.

"Please, sit," Hayla insisted. My grandmother was thin and stood with a very straight posture. She had small eyes and a wide nose and mouth. She wore a *mahasha,* a red and yellow cloth wrapped at the waist, which accentuated her figure. It was a piece of clothing we no longer wore in America.

Still stiff from sitting, I strolled across the room and inspected a photograph on the wall.

"That is your father."

I looked more closely. I couldn't believe how young he looked. I had to admit he was very handsome in those days. No wonder Mom had married him.

My aunts served hot food on silver trays. We had *aseed,* lamb soup, and rice with Arabic sauce. Unlike in America, where everyone has their own plate and utensils, we crowded around serving dishes and ate from them with our hands. It seemed inappropriate to me, but I joined in.

Hayla must have noticed the look on my face. I didn't see her leave the room, but she returned with a spoon. "Here," she said. "You want a spoon?"

"No," I said. "I want to eat like everyone else. But thank you for your kindness."

"You are sure?"

"The food tastes better this way." I smiled. She nodded and seemed satisfied.

The food was extremely good. I don't know if it was the way they cooked over an open fire, the spices they added, or their natural methods of growing ingredients, but everything was heavenly. No wonder people lived longer here. The food was healthy and fresh.

After we ate, the women had a thousand questions for me. How was my mother? Who was married? Who was having children? Why didn't I bring Dignity? Would others be coming to visit? How long was I going to stay?

After an hour of this, I was exhausted and asked to go to my room. They agreed. I did not even wash because they had no hot water available. I collapsed onto one of the beds and thanked Allah for getting me here safely and asked him to keep watch over Dignity.

The evening call to prayer echoed through the house. It was so loud it felt as if it came from upstairs. I lay with my eyes closed and let the caller's amplified prayers wash through me. They reverberated in my head and bones; they refreshed my system and restored my life. This was the Muslim heritage I belonged to. This was my land and people.

Another caller's voice from a distant mosque overlapped with the first. I floated in a sea of the names of Allah, a sea of serenity. I felt secure and at home in this strange old house my father had built years before. I was suddenly proud of his house and proud of his presence. I was thankful to Mom for teaching me the Qur'an.

Inspired, I climbed from bed and did my ablution. I took the Qur'an from my suitcase and read it aloud, feeling free to recite the words as loudly as I wished. No one would disturb me in this big house. I read until tears fell from my eyes, so moved was I by the verses. When it was time to pray the third prayer, Asr, I prayed and kissed the Qur'an. "I am Muslim," I said, over and over again. "I am Muslim and I thank you, Allah, for the knowledge of Islam. Guide me to more and do not let me go astray. Amen."

After evening prayer I heard a light rap on the door. It was my grandmother, Hayla.

"Jasmine, you want to come and chew *khat*? There are women here to see you."

"Sure," I said. "I'll be there."

I changed into a clean skirt set and put on some makeup. I noticed my hands were shaking. I was anxious at the thought of a full sitting place among the women. How should I speak to everyone? Should I greet some women before others? Should I ask questions or let them do the asking? I did not know the correct ways and hoped these guests would realize that.

"Mom, I will not fail you," I said, looking into a handheld makeup mirror.

I met the women in the third floor hall. They seemed as curious about me as I was fearful of them. Soon I realized that they were just regular women. They had come to meet me, not judge. The *khat* relieved my anxiety too, but I didn't feel quite free to open up yet. When they brought up children, I remembered Dignity and sadness roosted inside me. I hoped she was doing okay.

I was very tired, but didn't know how to excuse myself. When Father came to get me at 10 P.M., I got rid of the *khat* in my mouth and followed him downstairs. I was uneasy at first, staying in the same room with him. For a long time I lay awake. When his snoring told me he was deeply asleep, I finally closed my eyes and embraced the darkness.

Chapter 28

Here in My Country

I kept my distance from people at first, feeling at home, but also a stranger in my father's house. Maybe it was the long flight. Maybe it was my exhaustion or that I missed Dignity. I was not my usual self and my psoriasis was hurting again. I kept covered, afraid that someone would see sores on my arms and think something was wrong with me.

As days passed, I found that life in the house followed a routine. Most people in the village tended gardens, but there were none at Father's house. They didn't need to grow food because he sent them money for support. They bought fresh milk from a neighbor and picked peaches from a tree in the yard.

We spent a great deal of time in the morning preparing food. Then we did chores, ate at noon, and chewed *khat* until sunset. I interrupted my chewing for prayers, but the other women did not pray daily. That surprised me.

My aunts recited poetry when they cooked or cleaned. It was fascinating that they could make up verses on the spur of the moment. Their poems spoke mainly of pain and suffering. Art flowed from their tongues and was lost to the air. Soon enough, I found the poetry of my father's father starting to come out of me also.

Father's aunts and uncles dropped by to visit. I enjoyed meeting the women. I even found myself laughing and doing impressions of Father. The women enjoyed my sense of humor, but I never felt entirely free to speak my mind. Father's presence always loomed in that house. Whatever I said seriously would find its way to him.

A couple of weeks after our arrival, Father called me to the third floor after sunset. He told me we were leaving to go back to America. He could not stay longer.

"Why?" I said.

"Because my bones hurt and I am too old to sit on the floor," he said.

"I can't go now," I said.

"I cannot leave you here alone."

"I won't be alone. I'm with your family. I have grandmother and aunts to watch over me."

"It is time to go back."

"I'm staying here in *my* country," I said. I don't know what gave me the courage to stand up to him. Maybe it was the *khat* I was chewing. Before he could recover, I returned to the second floor to sit with the women. This was definitely my home; this was who I was.

☾

Father invited me to sit with him and Uncle Kalb on the third floor. They had been talking about Father's plans to return home. My uncle asked me what I wanted to do.

"I want to stay here," I said.

"How long do you expect to last?" Father said. "There are no flush toilets or running water."

"That doesn't bother me," I said.

Father continued with a long list of reasons for me to return with him. I countered each, determined not to go back to Dearborn.

"She is welcome to remain," Uncle Kalb said.

"What about your daughter?" Father said.

"Send her here," I said. "She can travel with the next person who comes to visit."

He didn't mention the issue again.

Father left later that week. At the airport, I cried when he hugged me. I would never miss him, but felt sorry that he must always battle the demons that plagued him. There were moments in our relationship where I felt the glow of genuine concern, but then the greed or the hate would resurface and the Monster was back. In some ways his veils were darker than mine.

When I arrived back at the house with Uncle Kalb, I was a changed woman. My body was energized. After eating I took my shower and dressed up to look my best. My previous visits with the women had been a blur of conversation. Now I felt at ease to laugh and fully answer their questions. I felt an urge to express myself creatively. My mind opened like a book. I created poetry, singing about missing Dignity, singing away the ache in my heart. I told the women of my love of for these mountains and the clear Yemeni sky. I composed poems about my long lost love, but never mentioned his name.

Unfortunately, I also started itching for cigarettes. Even here in the land of my ancestors, I couldn't go without them. I got to know which children I could trust.

"Ahmed," I said. "Here is 100 riyals. Buy me a carton of *Karman*, will you? You can keep the change." His eyes grew round and he smiled. He needed new shoes, but would probably spend the extra money on candy.

"I will get them for you *fast*," he said. In a blink, he was across the yard and on his way to a shop in town. In Yemen there were no restrictions on selling tobacco to children. No one would question him and my aunts would never know I bought them.

I was in the middle of hanging clothes to dry when Ahmed returned.

"This is the best brand," he said, panting. He must have run the entire distance. "I have tried it before."

That made me realize I was being a bad influence on him. The children looked up to me as an adult and an American. I couldn't have him thinking that I thought smoking was a good thing. I cupped his chin in my hand and said, "Son, smoking is not good for you. Do not do things that will hurt you for the rest of your life. You understand?" Ahmed nodded.

I wondered what else was going on in the lives of these poor children. What kind of attention were they getting? What was expected of them? I began to watch their interactions with adults and each other. They were treated like grownups and mimicked adults in many ways. There was no expectation of education or improving their lives. It was the same with women.

It hurt me to see this and I withdrew into myself, praying to Allah for an answer. How could I help these women and children? There seemed to be so much need and too little help. I began to refuse invitations to feasts at other women's homes.

"What is the problem, Jasmine?" Hayla asked, sitting beside me on my bed one night. "The women are worried. Are you sick?"

"No, *geda*," I said.

"Then what?"

"Things could be so much better here."

"We all wish things could be better, Dear."

"But I want to speak out. I want to tell the women to take charge of their lives. I want children to get an education and make something of themselves."

Hayla chuckled. "You *do* sound like an American."

"That's what I mean," I said. "These women will think I'm crazy."

"There is no shame in thinking as you do." She put her arm around my shoulder. "Maybe you are right. It would be good for some things to change."

"Do you think the women would accept my ideas?"

"Go to these feasts," Hayla said. "The women will see you are sincere. You cannot hide in this room for the rest of your life."

I couldn't help but smile. Hayla was right. I had come to Yemen to be with my people. I would have to take a chance that they would accept my message of change, because I could not talk with them without my views coming out. Later, I wandered outside to smoke and gaze into the most beautiful star-filled sky. I vowed to climb out of my shell.

The next day, I was invited to the house of my father's sister, Hanaka. She sent one of her children to guide me there. Covered in my black *balto*, I walked streets of ancient stones worn smooth. How many generations of women had walked these same stones? How many women had lived and loved and birthed children in this town? How much joy and suffering had these stones witnessed? I felt a oneness with those women who had come before me. I wanted to remove my shoes and let loose sand run between my toes. If I did, would the land talk to me?

Hanaka's house was old and small compared to others on the street. We entered through an open front door into a small living room lined with worn pillows. Six women joined us and we ate a meal of soup, lamb and rice. While they discussed husbands, upcoming marriages, and local town gossip, I mostly sat and listened.

After the meal, Aunt Hanaka and I sat alone and she offered me *khat*.

"Your father is a brave man," she said. "Going all the way to America."

It was difficult to think of Father as being brave when he spent most of his time in his basement lair.

"Without his support," Hanaka said, "we would have nothing, not even the house over our heads."

"You are family," I said, not knowing what else to say. I guess I knew Father was sending money to them. I didn't know it was their only income.

"We are very thankful," she said.

I nodded. There was some good in Father, I had to admit, but that didn't excuse his abusive behavior. That didn't give him the right to become the Monster.

"You don't believe me?"

"No," I said. "It's not that, just--" I didn't know how to explain my feelings for Father.

"I remember when your parents were married. We all lived together in your father's house. Your mother worked so hard to make him happy." She paused. "One day she served him breakfast and he took the tray and threw it across the room. Before we knew, he was out in the middle of the street yelling and complaining about nothing important."

"That's the man I know," I said quietly.

She told a few more stories, but I think I did not want to hear. I already knew more than she could imagine. Would she be shocked if I told her about Father waiting for Mom with his gun? I decided it was best not to. The Monster was her brother after all.

As sunset approached, I excused myself. It was best to get back to the house while it was still safe for a woman to be on the streets.

"I am so happy you came to visit," Hanaka said. She held me and cried. "You are such a beautiful girl. I pray someday a good man will be found to make you happy."

"Thank you," I said. "May Allah bless you and your family."

I left feeling a little sad. When I got home, I prayed for forgiveness for my father.

☪

It was difficult to find an open line to call the United States and expensive if one did manage. Instead of calling, I recorded messages on cassettes and sent them with travelers from Juban going to America. I told Mom I was ready for Dignity to come to the village and that I was pleased with my country. I had the freedom to go to the mosques and pray with women, and hearing the prayers was magnetic to me.

I heard nothing in return. I didn't know if they were not getting the tapes or if they weren't answering. Maybe Father was angry at me for not returning with him.

One day, I finally received a phone call from my parents. They never said they missed me or asked how I was, but only insisted I come home. When I asked about sending Dignity to Yemen, they would not answer. By the end of the call, I was furious. In effect they were holding Dignity hostage to force me to return.

"Why are you so angry?" Hayla asked. "Was it not good to talk to your parents?"

"No," I said. "They want me to come home."

"They should be proud that you came here from America. They should be happy you love your country."

"I just want my daughter," I said, tears forming. "They promised they would send her to me. They lied! I trusted Mom."

"Can you get her any other way?"

I shook my head. I didn't have money to fly Dignity to Yemen. Hayla nodded. "Pray to Allah. He will find a way."

I thought I could be strong enough to outlast my parents. Eventually they would give in and send Dignity to me. I continued to visit women's feasts, but found myself chewing more and more *khat*. My senses dulled, but my stomach was always tight.

Over time, more and more women gathered at these feasts. By then, I didn't care if my opinions offended them. I felt free to speak my mind and that is just what I did. I would sit with my back against the wall to face everyone and they would ask me about America.

"America is the not the only solution to your problems," I would say. "It does not rain money there. You have to work hard wherever you are. Yemen is a poor country, but everyone has a gift, and you can make a difference for yourselves without worrying about taxes taken from you, or working for someone else who controls you. You can make *this* country so much better."

Many asked me to marry their sons.

"Your sons don't need wives; they need to educate themselves as much as possible. Education is their path to success."

"You are still a virgin and beautiful," one woman said. "It would be ideal for you to find someone to make you happy."

I laughed. "Do you think marriage is the solution to everything?"

"Yes," someone else said.

"Well, I am no virgin. I have a four year old daughter and have had three marriages."

Many women looked shocked.

"Now tell me," I said. "Did marriage solve my problems or give my daughter a better future?"

They had no answer.

"Wake your minds to Islam," I said. "Look at what the prophet taught us. Did he tell us to be slaves? Did he tell us to live in ignorance? Did he tell us marriage would solve our problems? Did he tell us to let men walk all over us? No, he did not. We will not succeed in life by waiting for a husband to protect us. We must do it ourselves."

Women nodded in agreement, but actual change was slow. I had to repeat my words many times before the ideas sank in and I saw results. The Beni Musleh were the first to put my words into action. It was small things at first, cleaning the village a little, teaching themselves not to say negative things to their children. They spoke without cutting someone off in the middle of conversation. They cut back on gossip, not judging the old lady who begged for money or claiming she was a hex thrower, not calling an old man crazy who talked to himself about music. They curbed their jealousy and began to feel empathy for others.

I made it my daily job to gather good news and encourage the positive aspects of their lives. I gave the poor as much as I could afford, and gave children treats every chance I could. I shared canned food with everyone in the house. I tried to instill hope in their lives and show that nothing is impossible for God.

One afternoon, as I *tagweeded* the Qur'an aloud, I heard a knock at my bedroom door. It was Bahiya from Beni Musleh.

"Please, come in," I said.

A large breasted woman with smooth brown skin and a wide face, she walked cautiously into the room. "Wow, you have the most beautiful voice. *Ma sha, Allah*, Jasmine." Other women followed her into my room.

"We came to ask you a big favor," Bahiya said.

"Anything, anytime, if I can. What is it?"

"We wanted to ask if you can be our teacher for the moms in the Arabic school? We have had no one to teach us for a long time. We quit trying. But now you are here, you can teach us."

I was so honored, God had not brought Dignity to me yet, but He had answered my other prayers. "Of course," I said, smiling.

"We will pay 20,000 riyals each month."

"That's fine," I said. The money was good, but I was not interested so much in payment. Teachers were well respected in the community. The position they offered was priceless.

Chapter 29

Meaning Behind the Words

I had never taught before, so I stayed up all night preparing. I planned each word over and over in my mind. I pictured the ideal teacher and how I could influence these women to change their lives for the better.

The next morning, I was so excited I didn't feel tired. The walk to the simple block school building in the middle of town invigorated me even more. I entered to find ten women sitting patiently on the carpeted floor. At one end of the room was a blackboard and desk. *This is it*, I thought, taking a deep breath. *This is my first class.*

"Salam," I said. Holding my head high, I walked to the desk. The women responded with such warm smiles and excited looks I thought I was in a class of six-year-olds. My heart giggled with joy. After taking attendance, I asked them to open to the lesson they had stopped at in their previous class. They weren't very far along in the book and I needed to find out how much Arabic they remembered.

"Nasra, please come to the board and write a couple of words in Arabic," I said.

Nasra hesitated then scrawled a couple of partial words. The others showed similar results.

"I see most of you have trouble writing," I said. "We will start from the beginning and review." That brought a sigh of relief from the class. I was glad. I wanted to instill confidence in them that they would pass on to their children, not fear. They had enough fear in their lives.

The next day I gave a spelling test. They women grouped close and obviously cheated, but I let them continue. When they turned in their tests, I asked for them to get up and do their ablution; we were going to pray the *duhr*.

"Can you lead us in the prayer," Behiya asked.

My joy and inspiration, I couldn't refuse her. I chose to read the *Pen*, a chapter describing education as light. I read the verses slowly and carefully allowing the women have time to understand the meaning behind these words. I hoped to start them on a quest to read more of the Qur'an on their own.

At the end of class, I told the women to be ready for a surprise the next day. Maybe they thought I was going to bring cookies. What I had in mind was a true test of their knowledge.

☪

"We are having another test," I told them.

"We just had a test yesterday, teacher."

"Everyone get a piece of paper." I pointed to Behiya. "I want you to the corner."

She followed my instruction without question or complaint. I didn't know whether to be happy or sad about that. I sent a woman to each of the other three corners as well.

"And the rest of you in the middle, leaning on each other's backs."

They giggled with embarrassment.

"Do you know why I am doing this?"

They didn't answer.

"You all passed the test of following directions perfectly, so now I want to see how smart you are *without* cheating, shall we?"

As I expected, they failed. When I handed the papers back, no one looked me in the face.

"Look at your tests," I said. "You failed, but that does not mean life is over. This is a new beginning for you. With all my heart I will teach you and love you. I will make sure you know every word in every story. This is why you are here, right?"

"No one cares for us or teaches us like you," Behiya said. "We love and honor you so much."

"I love you too," I said. "Make me proud."

In just a few weeks, the women made big progress. I cannot explain the joy these women brought to me. I learned from them that if you put your mind to something and take risks, you will succeed.

☪

My relationship with students did not stop at the classroom door. They came to the house in the evenings to pray. As I instilled confidence in them they lifted me up. I was a daughter to them as well as a leader. They looked to me for everything as if I were the queen bee spreading sweet honey to my hive.

We shared many loving and close moments, but it was their stories that broke my heart. I learned that a sixty-year-old man could buy a thirteen-year-old in Yemen, that a twelve-year old girl could be forced to submit to her husband under threat from her uncle's rifle. The new husband forced himself inside her as she bled and screamed. Another woman was driven insane from her husband's brutal beatings. When he took a second wife, she took his rifle and shot the new wife and then herself. Everywhere there was darkness. So little light. I tried to remain a source of inspiration. Together we would support each other and improve our world.

Even the men began to speak about me when they gathered. Some called me "the wisdom woman." Men started appearing at the house to ask for my hand in marriage. I had to remind the women that I wasn't looking for a husband; they must let their husbands and brothers know this.

One evening, I was invited to a feast with the Sarhan family. They possessed a gorgeous house and seemed to be doing well, but their son Theab, whose name means "wolves", was out of control. He stole his father's money and stole from the village market.

"We don't know what to do with the boy," his mother said.

"Does he steal because you do not buy him what he needs?" I asked the father.

"I give him the world," he said. "Ask him."

The parents were certainly not too poor to support their son. He had to be stealing for another reason. "Theab," I called as the adults sat in the living room chewing *khat*. The boy came in. He was ten years old, but very small in stature.

I motioned him to sit beside me and put my arm around his shoulder. "How is school?"

"Good, Teacher."

"Do you get good grades?"

He shrugged, but seemed pleased from the warmth of my hug.

"It is important to do well in school," I said.

"Yes, Teacher."

I got him to sit with me for about ten minutes before sending him off with 200 riyals to buy candy. "I think I know what his problem is," I told his parents. "If you don't mind, I'd like to see him after school."

"Anything," his mother said. I knew exactly what was missing; it was love he wanted.

C⋆

As a first step, I had Theab sit with me and read some lessons. I asked him to teach me what some of the concepts meant. He swelled with pride at the opportunity. After that, Theab stopped by every day after school and we read the Qur'an. I grew close to him as if he were my own son.

His parents saw a change in him and thanked me. His father offered money, but I refused it. One does not pay for love. It is a gift that goes both ways.

There was a dark side to this, however. The experience with Theab intensified my own anguish for Dignity. If she could be here with me, I would be the happiest woman on Earth. I vowed to fight for her.

Arguing with my parents was like hitting my head against a stone wall. Even after weeks of me insisting they send Dignity, they continued to refuse. My days were filled with teaching, but at night my heart called out for my daughter. I lined my room with pictures of her smiling and sleeping and posing in pretty dresses. One by one, I would touch them and asked Allah to help me. A daughter should not be separated from her mother.

One night, exhausted from work and wide awake from chewing *khat*, my agony exploded like a grenade. I picked up a pencil and paper and wrote poems. They were fluid and quick. I went with it. I wanted it. All my emotions ran across the page in black ink, my despair, my craving for my daughter, my fear of losing the one I truly loved. I wrote of my mother, my marriages, my loves and my fears. Words streamed from my mouth, repeating what I had written. And when I was done, I felt cleansed of some of my anxiety, but not all. How could I ever be free from missing my daughter?

I shared the poems with the women at our usual gatherings. One poem had to do with marriages and selling and my mother. When I finished reading, I looked up and saw women crying. There must be some reason for their tears; my poem had dipped into their personal wells of torment. *God please help me to help them.* As I prayed, I realized it was I who needed help. I felt helpless about my missing daughter, depressed for this downtrodden village. I could not go on, and stopped reading even though I had brought other poems.

I cried nights. I smoked more. Psoriasis spread across my skin, a vine of ugly red flowers.

Oh Yemen

When I learned to in lie in your arms
When I learned the blood of me was Yemen
When my existence was comforted by your presence
When even I rose from being dead
When wisdom embraced me and my love for you bled
When I soaked my soul in your sand
When I finally reached you by the hand
When I lit candles of harmony, long to stand.
When I favored you over my beloved America instead!
When furious groups tore me and left me for gone
When I broke loose, striving on the road of the sun.
When I learned alone to love and hate
When my destiny faded and I arrived too late.
When suffering grew inside out, my soul easy bait!
When I lived with no home, my existence in debate.
When I had no power, but from Him, love in me to create!
When I asked God to keep my hope and give a solution
When it broke down again to see life's big illusion.
When I held tighter amid the toughest confusion.
When my body's existence was lost from division
When my tears became blood,
I screamed, I AM NOT MADE FROM METAL.
I knew God would take over and things would be settled.

Chapter 30

A Matter of Dignity

Uncle Omar was out at sea. Uncle Kalb promised many times he would take me to Sana'a to find a good doctor for my psoriasis, but he never did. My skin became so red and cracked, I resembled a lobster. I gave up. I wanted to hide away, but the Beni Musleh women made sure I visited them at their houses. They knew I should not be alone.

On my last day of teaching, I was invited to a feast. After eating and chewing too much *khat,* the women gathered around me to read poetry. Psoriasis covered my arms and could be seen on my forehead around the edges of my scarf.

After reading one poem, I broke down and cried. The women joined me with their tears and I saw that they understood my pain. Until now, I had thought I knew their pain, but they could not really know mine. I needed this understanding, their ears, their hearts. We were related through our stories. Too bad they were so filled with despair.

Behiya pushed through the crowd and sat on the floor, tear tracks shining on her face. "I swear, Jasmine, I will not let you go home to your uncle. I will call the men from Beni Musleh and get them to force Kalb to take you to Sana'a. If not, we will take you ourselves. If we have to give up our last dollar and give up eating, we are willing."

She held me in her arms while sobs shook my body.

I stayed that night at one of the Musleh houses. After sunset Uncle Kalb came looking. I heard his voice insisting I come home.

One of the younger men yelled out, "You will not take my cousin anywhere unless it is to Sana'a to heal her skin condition."

"I will take her," I heard him say.

"Really? Take her tonight."

That shut my uncle up and he left. He did not return until the following morning at 7 A.M.. Hayla was in the car with him.

"Get in," he said. "We are going to Sana'a."

And so, we drove the long, bumpy roads to Sana'a, my uncle's mouth running the entire time. He had nothing but insults for the Beni Musleh.

First, he complained about Mom. "She milks my brother in America. That is why he will not bring you all back here."

Uncle Kalb knew nothing of the situation in America. My father was the Monster, not Mom. I held my tongue, but it was difficult even with the veil to remind me. I knew, for example, that Uncle Kalb had been selling crops from Father's land to make money for himself while telling others the household could not make ends meet.

The Qur'an says, *Woe unto the defrauders, those who when they take the measure from mankind demand it full, but if they measure unto them or weigh them, they cause them loss. Lo! Those who devour the wealth of orphans wrongfully, they do but swallow fire into their bellies, and they will be exposed to burning flame.* Surely my uncle would face that fire.

Uncle Kalb had much more to say, of course, but I tuned him out, watching the landscape through my window, or concentrating on not scratching the terrible sores beneath my scarf.

We reached a hotel in Sana'a late in the day. I had time enough for evening prayer, but fell asleep soon after that. In the morning, Uncle Kalb took me to a doctor from Iraq. He recognized my condition immediately and seemed shocked by the extent of its spread.

"Did you lose someone in death or has something tragic happened?"

My mind bulged with examples, but I could not discuss my many abuses, my marriages, the absence of my daughter. These were things to be left unsaid to a stranger.

"No," I said.

He frowned. "Stress is usually a trigger for this condition."

I shrugged and looked away.

"I'll give you some herbs and ointments," he said. "Avoid stress as much as possible and I want to see you again in a week."

"Thank you, Doctor."

Hayla and I stayed in the hotel room all day while Uncle Kalb enjoyed himself in Sana'a. I felt cramped in the little room, but it gave me time to relax and take the herbs the doctor prescribed. By the third day, my psoriasis was starting to heal. On that day, I also received a surprise phone call.

"Hello?"

"Hi, Sweet Love, it is me." Habul. Dignity's father. How could this be? I went to the hotel windows, trying to see if he was in Yemen.

"Why are you calling me, Habul?"

"I know everything," he said. "I'm coming to bring you home and remarry you." *Oh no!* I screamed in my head. He was from the Beni Musleh and I did not need a catastrophe on that side of the family too. If he came to Yemen there was no escape.

"There's no reason to come here," I said. "I will not marry you."

"If we remarry," he said, "Dignity will have both parents. She needs a father as well as a mother."

"Forget it, Habul. There will be no marriage." I hung up, but couldn't stop my hands from shaking. My parents had probably promised Habul we could remarry if he convinced me to go back.

"Who was that?" Hayla asked.

"No one," I said. So much for avoiding stress.

My uncle decided he was not going to take me back to the doctor. He had to return to Juban right away. *Asshole*, I thought.

When we returned to the house, I spent my days reading poetry and chewing *khat*, yearning to see Dignity. I had lost hope again.

Without an appetite, I lost weight. Soon, I was 110 pounds and none of my clothes fit. Beni Musleh women donated their teenage daughters' clothes so that I had something to wear. Bahiya tried to feed me every day, but I remained in my bedroom world. I did nothing but write and chew *khat*. One of my aunts came in and told me how her father went crazy and died from writing too much. I enjoyed her company, which offered nutrition for my soul, but was not suitable for my body. I continued to decline.

☪

By this time I preferred to die in Yemen rather than go back to my parents. They would not give up, though. Like psoriasis, they kept coming back. In the midst of my depression, they called with some news.

"You must come home, Jasmine," Mom said. "Welfare is going to stop sending checks for Dignity. You have to come back and sign some papers."

"Send her here," I said. Maybe now that they couldn't make money off my daughter they would send her to me.

"We cannot afford to do that," Mom said.

She was lying. They didn't really need welfare money for Dignity either. She was a small girl and didn't eat much.

"We need you here," Mom said. "We cannot take care of Dignity if we do not get this money."

Mom never said the words, but implied they would give Dignity to her father if I did not return. I was now certain that *my* father was behind Habul's phone call. He had made promises to Habul. If I came home, we would remarry. If I did not, he would get my daughter. The situation was becoming too complicated for my depleted mind to sort out. The only thing I knew for sure was that, after what Habul had done to me, I would not let him have Dignity.

Defeated, I gave in and promised to return home.

Chapter 31

Caged Again

Of course, the welfare papers were just a ruse to get me home. Now that I was back in Michigan, I could do nothing without my father's permission. For an entire year, I tried to convince my family to let me return to Yemen. They always had some excuse. There was not enough money. There was no one to take me. It was the wrong time of year.

I saved a little bit of each welfare check to by plane tickets. When I heard that Asser's brother was traveling to Yemen, I asked if I could travel with him. He was willing. All I needed was Father's permission. Gathering my courage, I crept downstairs to his basement room.

"What do you want," he grumbled, looking up from the TV.

For a moment, my tongue did not move.

"Well?"

"I want to return to Yemen," I said.

He did not look at me. "I can't afford to send you."

"I have money for the tickets. I'll pay my own way."

Father looked surprised, but not yet angry.

"And how do you think you will survive?"

"I was a teacher and I was earning good money."

"Yemen is a poor country, Jasmine! I don't know why you want to go back."

"I lived rich there. I don't want money. I just want to live. Please."

"And what about Dignity? Your mother--"

"I will take Dignity with me this time."

He scowled.

"You will not have to support us," I said, hoping to hook his greed.

He ignored me.

"As a teacher I can help support *geda*...and the rest of the family."

Father watched TV as if he hadn't heard. Then he waved his hand in the air as if chasing a pesky fly. "Okay," he said.

I rushed upstairs before he could change his mind.

Mom was not as accepting. She stormed around the house.

"You can't stay in one place. You are not controlled or disciplined. I hate you the most of my children. You hurt me!"

Her words stabbed like cold knives, but I endured them. This was my chance to break free. With Dignity at my side, they couldn't control me. I would return to teaching and make a living for the both of us.

☪

I bought supplies from Sam's Club, including medicine for Dignity and clothes. A week passed and Asser's brother called.

"If you need money or clothes, please let me know," he said. I couldn't understand why I was so highly respected by a man I had never met.

"Thank you," I said, "but we have everything we need. Bless you."

Two days before we were to leave for Yemen, women came to the house to say good-bye. Mom made a complete fool of herself, cursing me and asking God to give me every disability she could think of. She even wished me dead. The women tried to calm her. She cried and told them to convince me to not go.

I reminded myself that I was the mother now. I must think of what was best for my daughter. Dignity would become fluent in Arabic and learn the roots of her family. I would be able to save money as a teacher. Once Dignity was seven years of age, we could come back to America. By then, I hoped to have a book of Arabic poetry completed. I would be like my grandfather, a poet who cared for others and kept his door open to everyone.

☪

The night I was to leave for Yemen, Father called me to the basement. When I entered his room, I saw my brothers, Mouzi, Munsee, Tunfakh, and Hissam, and my brother-in-law, Asser, standing around him like body guards. The room was so hot, sweat beaded on my forehead. It smelled of alcohol and spoiled meat.

"What the hell is going on?" I said.

"Shut up," Mouzi said. His mouth curled into a hard smile and I knew I was in trouble.

"Father, she is not your boss," Asser said. "You need to straighten her out."

Who was he to say anything? He was the one who required a beating. It took all my strength not to spit out what Asser had tried to do to me. My tongue was afire wanting to expose him. But I thought of my sister and remained silent.

"She thinks she is in control," Mouzi said. "No women should demand."

Munsee joined in. "Show the bitch who is boss."

Mouzi shoved me. "Who do you think you are? You're no teacher. Learn your place *gabha*!"

"Yeah," Tunfakh agreed. His presence here hurt me the most.

Asser smiled. I imagined taking a knife and cutting off that penis he had dangled in front of my face.

"You are *not* going to Yemen," Father growled.

"What? Why?"

"Because you're a fucking whore," Mouzi said.

"Please," I begged Father. "I've paid for the tickets. It will cost you nothing."

Mouzi laughed. "You heard what he said."

I tried logic. "Why do you want me here if I'm such a disgrace? Wouldn't it be better to put me out of sight?"

"I have decided," Father said. Asser's smile grew teeth. Munsee spat on the floor. Only Tunfakh looked hesitant.

I stumbled upstairs to my room and threw myself onto the bed. How could they do this? Petty little men. Why was it they could only define themselves by how many women they made suffer?

I sat up and stared out the window, imaging a fall to the ground, glass shards slicing my skin, blood splattering the sidewalk. I did not care. I did not care. I did not care. In that moment I hated God. I would rather die than live in this house one more minute. *Throw me into the fires of hell*, I prayed. Even that would be better than this world.

For days after, I did not talk. I washed dishes and walls. I scrubbed the carpet with my bare hands just to keep from standing still. I fasted for two months in a row, not eating several days of the week. I prayed for God to forgive me. I prayed for him to show me my way. When Mom offered me the *irgeelah* or *khat*, I ignored her. Instead, I mopped and waxed the kitchen on my hands and knees. I washed thick blankets with my hands and feet, like women did in Yemen.

I tried to write poetry, but it faded quickly. I was too distracted, too unfocused. My psoriasis worsened again. I even thought about letting Asser fuck me. I would get pregnant as proof of his infidelity and let him destroy himself and my family. Thankfully, I thought better of it later. I turned to God, hoping he could rid my heart of the hatred I bore for my family.

☪

Two years passed. It seemed I would grow old in Father's house.

I thought he had given up on marrying me again. Then, one day, he spoke of a man from a village in Hajaj. My grandfather had a saying about people from Hajaj. *Hajaj, Hajaj, Ya Rumat-idahash, Omyan , Suran, kam An-nidadi.* Hajaj Hajaj, those who are stunning in beauty are blind and deaf. How much can we guide?

"He is rich," Father said. "He is Yemeni, working in Qatar. He will make you happy."

I knew a couple who were related to the man. I didn't like them. We had argued and disagreed. No way was I was marrying one of their relatives.

Mom was not so eager to marry me off this time either. "I heard from women in the village that he is already married," she said. "He wants American citizenship."

"Who said I want him?" I said. "If you had just let me stay in Yemen, I would not have to deal with another marriage proposition."

Museebah, a lady who was related to this man, kept calling and pushing me to get married. I couldn't think of any other way to discourage her, so I asked her to come to the house.

"I want to show you something," I said.

When she came to visit, I took her in the bathroom and showed her my psoriasis. By then, it covered a good deal of my torso and arms. In some places it was cracked and bleeding.

"I do not want marriage," I said, "because I have been through enough. He needs to know my condition so he does not feel cheated and bad talk me afterward."

She inspected the sores. "This is definitely the evil eye. You need a lizard to cure this problem."

"I'm not even allowed to go to the doctor. How will I find a lizard in Michigan?" If Museebah was not offended by the sight of me, then she was desperate to find a wife for this man. I imagined him as old, ugly and deformed, someone no other woman would want.

"I will ask Khabeeth to take you wherever you need to go to heal this," she said.

I did not believe her.

"I am being sincere. Khabeeth will do this." Museebah paused. "He will care for you better than your family. He is an honorable man."

"My other marriages did not work," I said.

"Do you want to live here the rest of your days?"

Museebah seemed to understand my condition. She saw that living in my father's house was not where I should be. I had to admit, getting married looked better than remaining with my parents. This man was from Yemen. Maybe he would take Dignity and me back with him.

"I'll consider the marriage," I said. "As long as he is aware of my condition."

Museebah promised to call me later. I didn't know whether to be happy or sad. I didn't really want to marry again, but I couldn't see any other escape. How bad could a fourth marriage be? How could Khabeeth be any worse than paranoid Habul or crazy Enad?

Museebah called two days later. "Khabeeth is willing to take care of your condition," she said. "He also asked if you were beautiful. I told him that your eyes are beautiful enough to shoot cupid with his own arrow of love."

The compliment meant nothing to me, knowing how I used to look and how awful I appeared by then. I was covered over fifty-percent of my body with red puffy sores. How could any man desire me? I think deep down I had wanted Khabeeth to abandon his proposal. When he didn't, I decided to turn it down. Dignity was only five years old. What would happen if this Khabeeth was abusive? Would I see black and blue marks on her pretty face? I didn't want to go through that again.

In the end, it was not my decision. Father decided for me. I was informed that I would meet my future husband on Sunday. This traditional meeting is arranged so that the woman can see whether she likes the potential husband. With her input, the father then decides. I'm sure it would make no difference to Father whether I liked the man or not, as long as he got his money.

☪

I made sure to look my worst on the day of our meeting. I did not wear makeup. I dressed in a plain scarf and *balto*. I made no effort to hide my skin condition where it might peek through.

I was relieved to discover Khabeeth was not an old or deformed man. He was slightly built, with skin that seemed too light for a Yemeni man. He had a balding head and neatly trimmed goatee. Despite his acceptable appearance, I refused to smile or look interested in any way. Maybe he would think me ugly and give up on this marriage idea.

Unfortunately, Khabeeth must have seen something he liked in me, even without makeup. He stared during our introduction and turned back for a final glance as the men retreated to the living room to discuss money.

Upstairs, I waited for them to leave. As it turned out, Father had already made plans for the sheikh to meet with them and sanction the marriage. By this time, I didn't care. There was nothing I could do to stop things. Khabeeth and I were married and that was that.

The following weekend Museebah's daughters wanted to throw a party at Beit Hanina. I refused, having no desire to celebrate a wedding I didn't want to a man I didn't know. They went on with their plans anyway. I ended up wearing a crème skirt set. Khabeeth wore a black tuxedo. In some insane quest for revenge, I laughed and danced with my new husband as if he was my long lost love. Inside myself, I played Satan, daring God to make this the worst marriage ever. I wanted my parents to suffer. I wanted to suffer.

Chapter 32

A Distant Fourth

My latest marriage did not get off to a good start. At the wedding party Khabeeth's cousins told me that Khabeeth did indeed have a wife and two kids in Yemen. I knew first-hand how difficult it was to deal with a mother-in-law. I could only hope that another wife would not be as bad. At least she was thousands of miles away.

On the wedding night, Khabeeth wasn't stopped by my psoriasis, but he was no lover. This night of love making ended in less than a minute. Khabeeth turned from me in bed, leaving me alone the rest of the night.

Father found us an apartment one block from his house where he could stop in to check on me whenever he wanted. We had no money and lived mainly on bread and beans while Khabeeth searched for a job. Of course, he had no money for a doctor to treat my psoriasis. So much for Museebah's promises. I tried to make the best of my situation.

"We will be laughing next month about living on beans," I said. He did not see the humor in my comment, but became more talkative after he found a job at Technicolor Video.

A few months passed and Khabeeth seemed happy. He complimented me on my cooking and cleaning and told me how beautiful I was. He bragged to his family about me. I began to feel I was safe with this man, but he remained a stranger. We never talked deeply about anything.

Dignity tried to charm her way into Khabeeth's heart by doing little things for him, like washing his ashtray. He would not be moved to thank her. I worried that his rejection of Dignity meant he might take his anger out on her someday. I was careful to watch his every move.

I had no problem with Khabeeth having another wife as long as he remembered his duty here was to Dignity and me. After a time I wondered if his distant behavior was because he wanted to be back in Yemen with her. Others assured me that Khabeeth's wife in Yemen was neither beautiful nor a good cook. That made me curious. Was she a woman with special wiles? Was he as distant with her as he was with me? I asked if I could talk to her. He kept telling me yes, but never followed through.

Finally, after he sent our wedding party pictures to his mother and family, he called them. I heard him arguing and went to the kitchen to clean and cook so as to avoid hearing the conversation and being accused of spying.

"Jasmine," Khabeeth called. "I want you to talk to someone."

I walked into the room and took the phone from his hand.

"It is my wife," he said.

"Salam," I said nervously.

She did not respond.

"I hope you and your family are well. How are your children?"

Again, she said nothing. I didn't know what else to say so I kept quiet.

Finally, she said, "What is wrong? Do you not have a tongue to speak?"

"I am speaking, sister. I was waiting for your answer." It was such a strange conversation I didn't know what else to say. "Here, talk to Khabeeth. It was nice meeting you."

Not even two minutes later, he hung up and called to me.

"You will never do that again," he said.

"It's okay," I said. "It was a bad connection or something."

"It's your fault she is angry."

Just like a man, I thought. *Always blame the woman.* It didn't matter to me whether his wife wanted to speak to me. I would never meet her.

☪

Five months into this marriage, I had a miscarriage. Khabeeth never said anything directly to me, but I knew he blamed me for losing the baby. He would make snide remarks under his breath. I was sick and depressed and looked terrible. My psoriasis was worse than ever and there was no discussion about getting me any help.

I hadn't recovered from the miscarriage, when Mom called me to tell me Father was sick.

"You must come," she said. "He wants to see all his children." She sounded serious and I thought my father was dying. In that case, I could not refuse to visit him. No matter how bad the Monster was, he was my flesh and blood.

It was a cold and snowy day. I rushed along the sidewalk and tried to think of what I would say. I wanted to tell him I forgave him for everything, but wondered how he would take that. Father didn't believe he had done a thing wrong. I wasn't even certain I would cry for him when he died, but I had to see him a final time if he was that sick.

When Mom opened the door, I saw Father in the kitchen, dressed and smoking the *irgeelah*. Mom was washing dishes and none of my brothers and sisters was there. I paused, wondering what was up. Father did not look sick at all.

"Why did you call me?" I asked mom.

She turned to Father. "Tell her, Amag."

He did not look at me. "No, you tell her."

"What's the matter?" I said. "What has happened?" I couldn't imagine what could be so horrible that my father refused to speak? Usually, nothing kept him quiet.

Father finally exhaled his smoke and said, "Your grandma Hayla died."

My head swam. I felt faint.

"It was your brother, Mathloom."

"Mathloom?" I hadn't seen Mathloom since Father threw him out of the house years ago. I'd heard he been diagnosed schizophrenic, but had no idea he went to Yemen. My stomach tightened. "What did Mathloom have to do with this?"

"He shot her."

Shot her. The words echoed in my head. *Hayla died. Shot her.* Dead.

Everything went black.

☪

I opened my eyes and found myself flat on the kitchen floor. Father knelt next to me, patting my face and calling my name. Mom stood next to him, crying.

"*Geda* dead?" I said weakly. "How can it be?" *It's the Monster's fault*, I thought. His abuse broke Mathloom's mind. That must be it. My parents wouldn't let me return to Yemen, and yet Mathloom was free to travel where he pleased. If only I had gone to the village instead of Mathloom, Hayla would be alive.

"Mathloom is cursed," Mom said. She helped me to a chair. Father retreated downstairs.

"Why would he do such a thing?" I said.

"Mathloom has imagined your father's death for a long time," she said. "You probably don't remember the knife fight."

"I do remember," I said.

"Satan convinced him your *geda* was your father. He shot her. When he awoke to the reality of what he had done, he shot himself. But Mathloom lived. He is jailed in Sana'a."

For days, women visited Father to give their condolences. I stayed in the apartment and grieved alone, remembering my grandma's smile, her gentle words and her support. *I can never return to Yemen*, I thought. *I must erase it from my mind.* If I went back now, I would only feel the pain of her absence.

☪

Six months later, we were forced to move from our apartment because the owner's son wanted the place for his wife who was coming from Yemen. I didn't like the idea of moving, but it did give us a chance to live farther from Father and the Yemeni neighborhood.

We moved to Warren. Lebanon Town, I called it. The people there were Arabic, but much more opened minded. They respected women and owned successful businesses. I could learn something from their example. I decided to sell perfume to make extra money.

Our new apartment was larger than the old one and our landlords were very kind. When Khabeeth went to work, the old lady would sit on the porch with her sons and invite me to visit with them. I was not used to sitting with men and worried that if my husband saw me he would make a terrible scene.

"Maybe later," I said at first. "Thank you, I am honored."

As time went on, Khabeeth became even more distant, spending little time at home. I found the nerve to join our neighbors. They enjoyed my company and were glad to see I was not as backward as many Yemeni people they knew. Over time, I opened up to them about my arranged marriages and the Yemeni community.

A few months later I discovered I was pregnant. I thought Khabeeth would be happy, but he only withdrew further into his shell. When he spoke, it was to degrade me or complain he couldn't afford food on his income. Then he would turn around and invite ten or twenty men to the house for dinner. I was expected to cook and make fresh bread. I liked to cook, but as I grew larger

I barely had energy to care for one man, let alone twenty. It was as if Khabeeth was trying to make things more difficult for me. I sometimes wondered if he wanted another miscarriage.

Even when I learned I carried a boy, it did not stop Khabeeth's behavior. One day, while Tunfakh was visiting, he thought it funny to make degrading comments about my size.

"You look like the sumo wrestlers," he said. My brother laughed.

I gave Tunfakh a dirty look and Khabeeth threw the phone at me, hitting my foot. Pain spiked up my leg.

"Go serve us food," Khabeeth said. "Have respect for your brother."

He probably broke a bone in my foot, for it hurt even after giving birth, but I did not complain. It would do no good. Khabeeth was my husband only on paper. I was his cook and prostitute and nothing more.

At night, I cried in bed while Khabeeth lounged on the couch making phone calls. I didn't learn until we started to receive pornographic magazines in the mail that these calls were to sex hotlines. I continued selling perfumes and used my money to buy baby supplies, like diapers and a crib. Khabeeth spent his money on perverted things.

☪

The morning of September 11, 2001, I sat on the couch and clicked the TV remote. What I saw would forever be burned in my mind. The twin towers in New York City billowed smoke into the blue sky.

"Oh my, God!" Who? Why? What? Was the world coming to an end? I stared without blinking until tears streamed down my face. I felt contractions from such fear and pain.

When Khabeeth came home he watched the towers fall over and over again, turning up the volume until it hurt my ears. After two days of this I asked him, "Why do you watch this again and again."

He glared. "I hope it was Bin Ladin or some Muslim who did this to the bastard Americans. Yeah!" This sudden emotion repulsed me. I'd heard anti-American sentiment in our community before, but seldom like this.

"Why are you here, Khabeeth? Go back to Yemen and see how easily you pursue your dreams there. Why bother finding a wife here? Why become a citizen in a country you hate?"

He didn't answer.

After that, America was no longer the land of the free. Muslim women did not walk the streets for fear they would be shot or raped. All Muslims were seen as terrorists, even those who had lived in the United States their entire lives. These were dark days. When I should have been happy to be giving birth to a son, I feared for my life. Even in Yemen I never felt so much fear. Now I must worry that someone would shoot me because I wore a scarf over my head, because of the color of my skin.

Police were everywhere. People became angry and I couldn't blame them, but yelling obscenities out car windows or telling me to go back to my own country helped no one. America was my country too. It pained me to see such blind rage. We were people just like them.

Dear Racist

I am writing you words that come from my aching heart
I met you and we stood looking at each other
We had bodies and we were the shape of humans!
We spoke English; we even loved flowers and the sun
So when can you love my skin, I ask?
Do you wear clothes of the color brown or black, or white?
Is that enough to say you cannot hate me for who I am!
Because, my lost friend, I bet you love a song that I love.
Yes! The word *love* is shared between us since birth
You and I share this bubble called Earth
Wherever you turn you see God's colors
But close your heart to the truth, like clogged pipes and shutters.

Why not climb the tall mountain built of our fathers' wrong hate?
Like I climb, exhausted, holding tight with hope and fate
I am almost at the top, planting the white flag of surrender
I wave my hands for you to join and share peace, here to render

You struggle half way and I see your wound
HOLD ON! DAMN IT!
I come to help, hurting too, that a little of my color is
ruined
My strength is to save you with love that is tuned.
I can see your shouting eyes!
Pleading of your despair, from the inside it flies
You turn away before me and I see your hand in shadow
Did you not win the war created in your damage mind?
Was it your family that programmed the hate that was fed
Through your eyes in that second that they bloomed into red?

You lost this climb
Why did you let go,
Give in to your weakness with no good story?
I can only respond that I am utterly sorry!
I wanted to make you feel better, to smile and be open
With the inks in the world, no words can end with a pen.
If no one had love for you my lost friend,
I am here with open arms
Please, hold my hand to stop the pain and harm!
Can't you see Satan hates and takes away fortune?
When God only gives peace and love, it is the only solution!
I am so glad I found you on this road to understanding
Shall we share this world to spite our family commanding?

Chapter 33

Mohamed and Solomon

I named my beautiful boy Mohamed after the prophet. Khabeeth called once, but never visited me at the hospital. I was thankful to the women who brought presents, including baby clothes. If I had waited for Khabeeth to pay for clothing, my son would have gone naked. It didn't matter. Mohamed was such a wonderful gift I couldn't help but to be happy.

When I returned home, Khabeeth wanted nothing to do with his son. If the baby woke up crying, he would complain and threaten me. "Shut him up or I will throw him out the window." "Get that screaming thing out of the room." He never even offered to hold his child.

The third day after my return, Khabeeth waited until the baby was sleeping and grabbed my arm. "I want you to be a wife again," he said. "Let me stick it inside you."

"I'm still bleeding," I said. "I have stitches. You have to wait."

"No," he said. He dragged me to the bed and threw me down. "Please, Khabeeth," I pleaded.

He ripped off my underwear and jammed himself into me. I could feel my skin tearing, searing hot pain. I screamed so loud, Mohamed heard me and started to cry. *I am sorry, my son*, I thought as Khabeeth huffed and puffed on top of me. Thankfully, he took less than a minute to relieve himself in me.

He stood, my blood covering his limp penis, a sign of his sin. Afterward, he sat in the living room and smoked. I lay bleeding, milk gushing from my breasts. Forcing myself across the bed, I reached my son in his crib and pulled him toward me.

"It's okay," I said. "I am here for you." I let him feed at my breast. While he suckled, I fed the pillow with tears and filled the sheets with my blood.

☪

I was soon pregnant with my second beautiful son, Soloman. The new pregnancy along with caring for Dignity and Mohammad and cooking and cleaning for my husband wore me out to the point I could no longer sell perfume. When I quit, Khabeeth beat me. I started thinking about Arabic women and women in general. We were not possessions to buy and sell, but people with living, breathing souls. One day I would get out of this abusive marriage and help other women going through this pain. *Please God, let this happen one day for me*, I prayed every day.

Khabeeth's interest in pornography continued and I started to fear for Dignity. Mom convinced me to let her live with them and visit me after school. She didn't trust Khabeeth with Dignity either. As for me, she only lectured on how I should be a good wife to my husband.

Khabeeth continued to complain about having no money. How could I be a good mother when I could not afford to buy my children what they needed? Thankfully, our Lebanese neighbors gave supplies and even clothes for my boys. If it hadn't been for them, we would have gone days without diapers and baby food.

Anxiety inflamed my psoriasis. I was in pain every second of the day, literally on fire. But fire only burns; psoriasis is more than that. The pain dug through my muscles to my joints and cartilage. My skin crumbled, leaving flakes all over the house. I found pieces of myself in the bed, on the sofa and on the floor. No matter how much I cleaned there was always a trail behind me.

Finally, I couldn't stand it any longer and went to Father. I couldn't ask for a divorce, but he might be able to help in some way. I was taking care of his grandsons after all.

"I need you to help my husband," I told Father. "He doesn't pray. He gives me no money to buy food and diapers for the boys."

"What am I supposed to do?" he said.

"If we move to a less expensive apartment, Khabeeth might have money for us to buy the things we need."

Father seemed almost too glad to help us. We moved to an apartment above Uncle Gaban, a few blocks from my father's house. It had two very small bedrooms and was so tiny we could hardly move without running into each other. I didn't care. I wanted to prove that Khabeeth was making excuses. If he still complained of having no money, hopefully my father would ask him where the money was going.

☪

One day during Ramadan, Dignity came home, bursting with joy. She had made the honor roll in school and told me over and over how well she had done. When I sold perfume, I usually had extra money to buy her something as a reward for good grades. She had done more fantastic than ever, but I had no money to spend. I couldn't even buy her a piece of gum.

I felt guilty and decided to take my children to Target. When we got there, I looked at Dignity and said, "When we go in, I want you not to ask me questions, no matter what."

She looked worried.

"No questions," I said.

She nodded.

We walked inside and I pushed a cart up and down the aisles until I found a backpack in the school section.

"I want you to pick out everything you want," I told Dignity.

She frowned. "How will you pay for this?"

"Just do it," I said. "Stuff it in the backpack."

I got diapers for the boys and clothes and bottles for Solomon and candies for them all. We were in the store for three hours, wandering through every aisle. I looked at some things three and four times, trying to convince myself that everything would be fine. I would walk out with the backpack and no one would notice it was full.

God, I prayed, *if you let me get away with this, I will never do it again.* My heart beat loudly as we moved to the front of the store. All I had to do was push the cart out the door pretending the backpack was mine. No one would notice.

I wheeled the cart by the registers. *A few more steps,* I thought.

"Are we going home?" Dignity said. She knew that stealing was wrong.

"Shh!" I said.

Solomon whimpered and suddenly someone grabbed my elbow.

"Where do you think you're going, ma'am?" a tall man in a suit asked. A woman joined him and they took me by the arms.

Dignity looked horrified. Tears came to her eyes.

"We need to ask you some questions," the woman said. Her blue eyes glared. She lifted the backpack and opened the zipper. "I don't suppose you planned on paying for this."

Mohamed began to cry; Solomon soon followed.

"I'm sorry," I said. I saw myself in a mirror, a lady in a long dress and scarf, *stealing*. The worst part was that this was Ramadan, the most important month for Muslims.

We walked to an office where television monitors scanned the entire store. They had probably been watching me for hours.

"Please, don't take me to jail," I begged. "My husband and family will kill me."

The two guards lifted my sleeves and saw the severe condition on my arms.

"What's this?"

"It's a skin disease," I said. "It's not contagious." I was shivering from fear. My children were crying. "My kids did not know anything, I swear to you. Please." They handcuffed me and made me sit in a chair while they counted the merchandise.

"Is this the first time you ever stole?" the woman said.

"Yes."

"You're pretty good. You have four hundred dollars worth of merchandise in there. Why did you do it?"

"My kids have nothing. I wanted to make them happy. I have no record of any crime. Please!"

We were taken in a police car to the police station. My children sat outside while I was in custody. They gave me one phone call, so I called a Yemeni man I knew to bail me out before my husband came home. I promised to pay him back the two hundred dollars. He came immediately and took me and my poor children home.

Too ashamed to tell my family about my shoplifting, I went to court alone and they told me I had to do community service for two months. I nodded agreement. At least I wasn't going to jail. But how was I going to fulfill the court ruling? I couldn't just leave the house. I would have to tell Khabeeth where I was going and was afraid what he might do.

I prayed and prayed to Allah to show me a way out of my situation. I'm sure he thought I deserved what I got. I shouldn't have been stealing. That was a sin. With no help coming from God, I came up with a lie.

"Khabeeth," I said nervously after he had eaten and was relaxing in the living room. "Salina Elementary needs a substitute for a week. I thought maybe I could work for them."

He frowned, but said nothing.

"Maybe if I work part-time now they will hire me full-time later. We would make lots of money and I will give you my checks."

That brought a smile to his face and he agreed.

I chose an indoor job at the dog shelter so that some Arabic person or my family would not see me working. When I saw my probation officer, I told her about my life and the danger I was in if anyone found out about me being arrested. She understood and let me work only that one week.

I managed to avoid trouble with my family, but Khabeeth did not forget to ask about my paycheck. I had to come up with another lie. I told him I had misunderstood the people at the school. It had been volunteer work. He was so upset, I thought he would beat me then and there.

My Sons

Mohamed my sun, Solomon my moon
Beauties from an ugly goon.
I will try to make you a good life with honor
If it takes my whole life, I will be your only donor
I see you as men, one on each side as my guards
Amid eruptions of chaos, we will survive the pain of darts.
You both have changed my life, the truth from my lips
Your smiles are my sanctuary from the darkest of mists.
You will both grow to never use angry fists
Never will your father have a chance at your wrists!
I hope to take your pain and fears with my every true kiss
And hope it is I you grow old with and miss.
My precious boys
I will try to raise you as the strongest warriors of your decades
To fight with your wisdom, not with guns and never with blades!
But only the work of warriors of faith to help those in need
Two lives of me, I pray you are the purest of my new seed
With a duty to your sister, she is yours to protect
Do not ignore her, or estimate her, let her speak her mind and never reject
And above all do good to others, least your God you do not forget.
For now
My love for you is incredible

Like hugging the fluffy clouds, pleasing and untouchable.
Wanting to protect you when ill winds blow your way
Making the toughest moments go smoothly away
Bringing out the sun to shine for days and days.

Chapter 34

Bury It Deep

One day, Anita, my old Arabic teacher, stopped by to see if I had any perfume. I still had a few samples. While I was busy showing her the selection, she noticed psoriasis at the edge of my head scarf and near my wrists.

"What happened to you? Did you get burned?"

"No," I said. "It's a long story, Teacher."

"Tell me, is your husband hurting you?"

"It's a skin condition," I said. "I'm going through a lot of strain which makes it worse. My family will do nothing to help. They keep marrying me to people I do not want and refuse to take me to a doctor."

"I know an Iraqi woman who might be able to help," she said.

"Who?" I was willing to do anything by then. My skin was so bad that my clothes stuck to the seeping wounds and I was in pain most of the time.

"She will look into your past," Anita said, "to solve your problems."

"No." I said. "Magic is forbidden in the Qur'an."

"She does not use sorcery. She opens her session with the Qur'an."

"We'll have to go when Khabeeth is at work," I said. "No one must know."

Two days later, we went to the woman's house on the other side of Dix Avenue. It was sparsely furnished and pictures of her relatives hung on the wall. The old Iraqi woman sat at her kitchen table and placed the Qur'an between us. She did not ask what my problem was. Instead, she told me to put my hand on the closed Qur'an and ask it for answers.

I hesitantly put my hand on the Holy Book, but asked no questions. I had doubts this woman could help and feared God would punish me if this was some sort of witchcraft. I blocked out everything and let my hand sit there. After a few seconds, she had me remove my hand, opened the book, and gasped.

"You have envious eyes on you," she said. "After all these years you still sleep on your first love's heart."

221

"Gais," I whispered. How could she know? Maybe this woman did have some sort of power. I started to cry. "What does this mean?" I said. And how would it cure psoriasis?

"It means, Sweetie, he still thinks about you and loves you."

It had been more than 15 years since our divorce. He had a wife and children. There was no chance that Gais and I could be together. If that was what I needed to cure my psoriasis, I would never be free of it.

"How can I make things better?" I said.

She asked for a picture of me. When I gave her one, she put some herbs on it and pushed it into a sewed sack.

"I want you to go to a graveyard and find seven stones in a row. Bury this deep in the middle of them."

"What do these graves have to do with my condition?" I had not mentioned the psoriasis and didn't know how going to a graveyard could help.

"Honey, you have been dead a few times," she said. I didn't understand what she meant, but her words chilled me to the bone.

"Okay," I said meekly. If this would free me from psoriasis, I was willing to try.

☾

I was scared of going into a cemetery alone so I told Mom about my visit to the woman. She hesitated, but finally agreed to go with me.

It was a cold day, but the ground was free from snow. The cemetery gates were locked.

"We can't get in," Mom said.

I stared through the bars. Even in this cold, my psoriasis burned. I had to do something.

"I'll climb the fence," I said. I had climbed enough trees as a girl to know how.

"No."

"It's not that high," I said. Even in my *balto*, I could climb it, no problem.

"What if someone sees us?"

"I'll be quick," I said.

Mom peered down the street then at the mosque. "Okay," she said. "Be careful."

I climbed the cold metal and felt its pressure squeezing blood from the sores on my arms and legs.

"Hurry," Mom said. "I cannot believe we are doing this."

I jumped down and landed hard on my back. From the ground, I saw the cloudy sky overhead and I felt like staying there forever, my place of rest. *You have been dead a few times*, I remembered the woman telling me.

Mom's crying brought me to my senses. She must have thought I was dead. I forced myself to my feet and sprinted into the graveyard.

"Seven stones in a row," I said to myself. It didn't take long to locate a spot in the middle of seven graves. Burying the bag would supposedly free me of my feeling for Gais and also my psoriasis. Part of me did want to be free of him, but another part of me clung to the happy memories. Gais was the only man I had ever loved. The psoriasis even now dripping blood down my arms and legs was a powerful argument in the other direction.

I had not brought anything for digging. I found sticks, but it was winter and the soil was as hard as cement. Frustrated, I dug at the ground with my shoe and managed to open a small depression. I buried the bag as best I could.

When the psoriasis did not get better, I figured it was because the woman had told me to bury the bag deep. My graveyard adventure had been for nothing.

☪

Two of my Yemeni cousins came to visit one Friday as they normally did while Khabeeth was at work. By now, I could barely stand to have clothes touch my skin. I let them see the psoriasis one day. They were so shocked they started to cry.

"We... how...we thought you are happy. You look beautiful, your face is clear. What happened to you? Won't your family help you?"

"No," I said. "My father tells me I should never show my arms. He says Moses possessed the arm of light. For me, my arms are a curse for my sins. My brothers tell me Khabeeth should divorce me, I'm too disgusting to be married to him. They tell me I look like shit."

"Can nothing be done for your condition?"

"Khabeeth is too cheap to buy food; he would never pay for a doctor. I've tried everything, even a healer at the recommendation of one of my perfume customers." I shivered at the memory.

"We know a place you can try," one of the cousins said.

☪

I went to the man's house thinking he was a Yemeni doctor, but he was more of a healer than a real doctor. On the first visit he examined me and told me to come back in a week.

On the second visit he told me to go into the bathroom and followed me in. I shouldn't have put myself in such a situation, being alone with a man in his house, but I was desperate. The room smelled of vinegar. He was running hot water into a tub and proceeded to add pounds of lamb fat to it. What a mess.

"Strip your clothes and go in," he said sharply.

"What! You have to leave the bathroom."

"No, I have to scrub your sores and read something loudly."

To my eternal shame, I did what he said. He stared at me from head to toe, looking amazed. I wondered if he could not believe the extent of the psoriasis or if he liked what he saw beneath the sores. Either way, I didn't like it.

I got into the bath and the cider vinegar burned me like acid. I cried out and clenched my fists. Water and fat splashed onto the floor.

"Lean forward," he said. He scrubbed my back with slimy hands.

Afterward, I got dressed and paid him what I could. He asked me to come the next week and he would mix some things for me to use at home.

The next visit I expected another bath, but he asked me to sit in the living room and share some fresh *khat* with him. I thought this might be part of his treatment. All of the sudden, he straddled my lap and started kissing me and gazing into my eyes.

I struggled. "Please, I need to go home, please get off of me, please!"

"Do not be afraid," he said.

I arched my aching body, nearly throwing him into the air. He slid off me, acting as if nothing had happened.

I left and never went back.

"I've given up searching for a cure," I told my cousins.

"There is no one else who can help you?"

"No," I said. Not after the graveyard and the lamb fat bath.

☪

Burnt

Burnt! Lit! I am on fire!
Destroyed from walls of my skin, the skin of curse
While inside of those walls damaged, it is eating me up
My blood of Arabia is now what I blame, the poison of
family
Flowing inside and out of my body
Like maggots eating away
Inside out, inside out
I scream, I shout, I have lost my red and white blood
If there was brown blood I wish that would wash away too
You took away my youth from me and who I really was
Watching me rot and rot, immune, you were my blood clots

I crack, I bleed from out and ants are crawling into my liver
I scream, I shout!
Do you hear the drumming in my heart?
Do you hear the pride that is broken so many times
I ache to the bones that hold me together, yet this tower of
human bones is crumbling
Drumming, harder and harder, it is my heart, the soldier
hiding me for dear life
I scream, I shout!
Fifteen years I suffer, no body, no flesh, only a soul that
exists yet no existence
God, why do you keep me with my soul still, its shadow of
death surroundings?
Turn it off this fire!
That burns and burns, let me rest my eyes in a sleep for
days
Please let me sleep
My muscles ready to creep and lose their tone
To life or is it hell I have settled into
The pain, oh the pain is so skin deep
Let me sleep please, tired eyes go to sleep

It hurts mama, so bad that my mouth is dry and my
stomach upset
Excruciating, mama, that the black hairs on my head have

become gray
Mama, do not cry, it burns me to my grave made by my
father and brothers
Mama please tell them to close the coffin now
And let me sleep, tired eyes go to sleep
From the pain my skin is red and purple it seems, but never
yellow, the color of love
You burnt me good, lungs escaping, separating, but they
still run
I live you say, but my soul is completely done!
Like leftover meat thrown after eaten
My heart is still a beep
While, mama, your sea of cries for me is too steep.

Chapter 35

A Letter to Oprah

With two baby boys in the house and a husband who spent little time at home, I welcomed my cousins' weekly visits. Life was not good, but it was bearable. Unfortunately, something had begun to change with Khabeeth. He grumbled more about not having money and acted as if our financial problems were my fault for quitting the perfume business.

I tried to explain that it was too difficult to run a business with two small children, and he snapped, "Then you shouldn't have gotten pregnant!"

"What was I supposed to do? Keep my legs closed." He had not talked of using birth control and certainly wouldn't have wanted to pay for pills.

I saw something change in his eyes. When my cousins came over on Friday, Khabeeth returned home only an hour after he'd left for work.

"What are you doing here?" I said. "I thought you were working."

"Does it look like I'm working?"

"No, but--"

"Get them out of here," he said, loud enough for my cousins to hear.

"No," I said. "They're my guests."

Khabeeth slammed the door on his way out.

"He's gone," I said. I was upset, but tried to pretend everything was fine. Khabeeth should have been at work anyway.

A few minutes later, the phone rang.

"Hello?"

"What do you think you are, the man of the house?" Father growled on the other end. Khabeeth had not gone back to work. He had gone to complain to Father. "Get your whore friends out and let your husband come home."

"I didn't tell him to leave," I said. "He was the one who didn't tell me he was not working today!"

"That doesn't matter. Tell the whores to leave."

"You need to leave," I told the girls.

"Let me talk to him," Ursa said. She was the boldest of the two cousins.

"No," I said. "It's my father. He won't listen to you."

She grabbed the phone. "This is Ursa," she said.

Her mouth gaped. A tear started down her cheek. I took back the phone and hung up.

"This is why I did not want you to speak to my father," I said.

My cousins went home. I was raging inside.

When Khabeeth came home later, I was washing dishes.

"Come here!" he said.

"What?"

He grabbed my arm and slapped me so hard my glasses broke. He twisted my arm until I cried out and shoved me to the wall.

I fought back. "What do you want? You want problems for nothing?"

"You are the one starting trouble." He dug into my skin with his dirty nails. I screamed from the pain. Blood flowed down my arms and dripped from my fingers. He shoved me across the kitchen and stamped out of the room.

I found him on the phone. From the conversation, I could tell he was talking to Mom.

"She has no respect for me. She knew I did not have to work today and she brought her friends here."

"He's lying," I shouted. "He cut me and I have no brothers to protect me!"

"See how she makes trouble," he said.

Mom wanted to speak to me, but there was no use trying to tell her the truth. I went to my room and cried. Eventually, I fell asleep next to my boys.

Sometime later, I heard the bedroom door open slowly.

"Get up and change so you can sit with me and chew *khat*."

I knew what that meant. Khabeeth wanted sex. By this time, he was so rough with me, it was more like rape. Tired of fighting, I did what he said. I numbed myself with *khat*. We sat like stones and he started to speak foul language. Even the *khat* could not make me relaxed enough to put up with him that night. The psoriasis was eating me from the outside while Khabeeth consumed me from the inside. Soon there would be a hollow shell and Jasmine would be gone.

"I have decided something," I said. "You need a final signature from me at the immigration office next month."

"Yeah, so what are you going to do?"

"I'm not going to sign."

He laughed, but it ruined his mood.

The next morning I mentioned it again. He turned his bald head toward the door and left. I knew he was going to my father's house, and this time it was fine with me.

Ten minutes later the phone rang.

"You think you can control a man," Father shouted.

"No, but I will not sign that paper," I said. "You cannot make me do it, Baba. It's my name they want and not yours."

I hung up on him. It felt so good to have some power of my own.

Twenty minutes later, the phone rang again.

"Okay," Father said calmly. "We agree that he starts paying you. He will pay you everything he owes me."

"I want at least seven thousand dollars," I said.

There was silence and then he said, "He can give you one-hundred dollars every week from his check."

"Agreed."

The following week, he began to pay. I wrote down the payment in a notebook. At the same time I was making plans to leave. With seven thousand dollars I could go anywhere.

☪

I don't know why I thought Khabeeth would keep his word. After I signed his immigration papers, he stopped paying. I had been taken advantage of one more time by the men in my life.

The sexual abuse continued too. Khabeeth would disturb me from my sleep by breathing heavily on the back of my neck. Without a word he would roughly turn me to my back and rape me. I couldn't count how many times he did this. The only thing that kept me hanging on was the thought that I needed to protect my children. I had to stay alive to care for them.

Even my cousins stopped visiting and my family would not talk to me. My psoriasis was so bad that my body screamed out in pain. Still, Khabeeth would not let me see a doctor.

To survive the continuous stress and pain, I asked the people downstairs if they would extend their cable wire to our TV. This would at least give me some company and my kids some cartoons. They had not even a piece of a toy, not even from the Dollar Store.

Sitting alone in the apartment, I watched the Oprah show while the boys were sleeping. I saw the terrible things that were happening out in the world, like the woman who was shot in the face by her boyfriend and lived. I cried and cried for that woman. I also saw the real hope that she offered so many people. I dreamt of sitting with her in real life, the two of us working together to make the world a better place for everyone. I started to write Oprah a letter one day. As I wrote, I repeated her name over and over in my mind, thinking to myself that if I called to her enough she would magically answer me.

I never finished the letter and my hell continued. During the day, I was alone with my boys and the pain. At night, Khabeeth came home, ate, and chewed *khat* until his sexual urges increased. Now he wasn't happy just to have sex and be done with it. He would stick his fingers and thumbs inside me, scratching me and talking dirty. I knew I had to run.

Chapter 36

Running in Place

There was no way I could run away with three children, so I had to decide who to take with me. Dignity was already staying with Mom. Solomon was only a year old and needed so much care I didn't dare take him on a trip. I decided Mohamed, who was two years of age, was the only one who could go with me.

Leaving Solomon with my family, I ran to the only place I knew would be safe, Nagat's house in Arizona. This time we took a train. I parked my car at the Amtrak station in Dearborn and said, "Fuck 'em all!"

Nagat and her husband were happy and surprised to see us. I kissed Nagat, and the first thing that came out of my mouth was, "I want to tell you I have left those cold blooded people."

"I'm so happy you came to us," Nagat said.

"I want you to tell them I am here," I said. "And this is my reason."

I opened my shirt to show them the bloody sores covering my body. Nagat gasped. "Jasmine, what have they done to you?"

"They will not let me see a doctor." I told her about my trip to Yemen and being a teacher there. "They tricked me into coming back home. Then they married me to a fourth man. I do not think I can survive from this condition."

"You're safe here," Nagat said.

"I'm pleading to you, Nagat. I cannot take this any longer. If I have a chance, I must live for my three children. I must survive to make a difference for them."

Once he knew where I was, Khabeeth called every day for two weeks. Instead of apologizing or saying he would take me to a doctor to have my psoriasis cured, he tried to guilt me into coming home.

"She has abandoned her daughter and son," he told Nagat and her husband. They had met Dignity on my last trip and knew how much I loved my daughter. They knew I wouldn't leave her behind without good reason.

When I finally spoke with Khabeeth, he chastised me about Solomon. "What sort of mother would leave a young baby behind?"

I screamed on the phone, "What kind of man will not buy his children food and clothing? What kind of man keeps his wife ill and locked in a house?"

"I can get a VISA for you to leave for Yemen in two days," Nagat said. I had never seen her so angry. Her eyes glowed with fire.

"I don't know," I said. I didn't want go there without Dignity and Solomon.

"I'll take you to my family in Sana'a," she said. "They'll take you the best doctors."

"Thank you," I said. Nagat's heart was in the right place. If only my own family would care as much.

After another week, Munsee called.

"I'm willing to pay for your ticket to Yemen," he said. "But I want you to pay me every penny back."

I agreed to his terms and we returned to Detroit on a plane. Father and Munsee were supposed to meet me, but they didn't show up. I called a taxi and asked the driver to take me to my apartment. The place was a mess, but no one was there.

Good, I thought. At least Khabeeth wasn't waiting there to beat me. A half-hour later, I heard a knock. It was Munsee.

"We need you to come to the house so we can talk," he said.

"No," I said. "You and I can talk here." The last thing I wanted was a confrontation with my parents.

"Mom cooked for you," he said. "She wants to see you. The kids are waiting too."

"Okay. Okay," I said. My brothers had learned from the Monster. They knew just what to say.

When I walked into the kitchen, Mom jumped up and down, screaming and cursing me. "You have shamed me, your own mother in the face of God. Why has my daughter done this to her mother? May God see you for the evil doer you are."

"Stop it, Mom."

"Shut up!" Munsee yelled, his face dark.

"Don't tell me what to do," I said.

"Bitch!" Munsee growled. The punches to my face came so fast I hardly saw them, but they felt like bricks impacting my cheeks. I wet my pants and staggered backward.

"You fucker!" I charged out of the house, ears ringing and jaw aching, without any of my children. When I reached the apartment,

I slammed the door shut and lay like a dead woman on the bed. I was exhausted, but my eyes could not close.

I heard the apartment door open. *It's the pervert,* I thought. Khabeeth saw me lying dead with my eyes open. Munsee followed him into the room.

"I'm not paying for your ticket," he said. "The Qur'an in Yemen cannot heal you. Nothing will. You are a cursed woman."

My heart pained with every word.

"You are a whore and a joke to our family. You are not American. You are a worthless woman that should be home with her doors locked." Munsee's tirade continued.

His words cut through my veins like knives and I bled until I could bleed no more. I wished he had beaten me physically. Words would never heal once they were programmed in my head.

"I will pay for your ticket," Khabeeth interrupted. "You just don't worry about it."

I wondered if this was some sort of game the two of them were playing. First one man would make promises and take them back, then the next. But I saw that Khabeeth was sincere. After all he had done to me I actually felt some sympathy for this man who was cold as the blizzards in the highest mountains.

I nodded my heavy head. In my mind, I was screaming, *Is there hope? Is there hope for a cure? Is there hope I will live to care for my children?*

Munsee glared at Khabeeth, eyes sharp as glass.

"I'm sending my wife to Yemen," Khabeeth said.

"I'm telling you, man, you should divorce her fuckin' ass."

With a scowl, Munsee left the room, slamming the door behind him. I looked at Khabeeth and felt a remorse or humbleness surrounding him. Something was still missing in the man, but I was not about to find it. I was just happy he had decided to help me.

Khabeeth left the room. I was spinning. The floor was spinning. *I must let go of my fear,* I thought. I would take Khabeeth at his word. I would trust him for that moment.

My boys were sent to me not long after Munsee left. When I heard Mohamed calling Mama and saw tears on his chubby cheeks, I knew he was desperately hungry for a hug. I could not do it. My soul had left my body and I was numb.

Night fell quickly and I dozed for a time.

☪

A door slam woke me and footsteps came toward my room. Khabeeth came in with a box of food. "I brought your favorite, lamb liver," he said. "Please, get up and eat something."

I felt a duty to be loyal for this rare kindness. I sat and ate a couple bites. I did not pray. I did not call for Allah even inside my head. I did nothing, but chew and swallow.

"I have put the kids to sleep," Khabeeth said. "Why don't you get up and take a shower and we will chew some khat together."

I chewed *khat*, but had nothing to say.

Khabeeth finally spoke. "What I am about to tell you is only the truth," he said. "You have shamed us in a deeper way than you will ever know. A prostitute can never bring us such shame as you have given us."

I was not surprised. I sat as if listening, but his words drifted by like so much smoke. I could not hear, smell or taste him. I was disconnected.

"I will send you with the first family to go to Yemen," he said. He pressed his face right into mine and ground his teeth. Between his grinding came the words, "But on one condition. You will go to *my* village and you will stay with *my* wife and family. Understood?"

I gazed at him through a veiled consciousness. Words came to me all at once. "I don't want to go if you do not want me to. I mean that with all my heart. If you are satisfied with this body that looks like it is burning in hell, then I am too."

He seemed to sense that I really meant what I said.

"You find a family to travel with. I will pay for a ticket only for you. You will eat what my family eats, live where my family lives, will sleep where my family sleeps."

He nodded and sat back. "Take all your clothes off and stand with your legs open. I want to see what kind of a whore I have. Did anyone fuck you in Arizona?"

I listened while I assumed the position. My legs shook from weakness. My body shivered from the cold night. I stood there for what seemed hours. I could not be helped, so I wanted abuse. I craved it like no drug in the world. He kept jabbing his penis into my mouth. He stuck his fingers in my anus one by one.

"Smell how dirty you are... huh?"

I couldn't answer. I was drowning in my own worthlessness.

☪

When morning arrived, I did my usual chores, cooked, cared for my boys, and cleaned. I lit some *bakhur* incense and a spark of hope rekindled within me. I was desperate waiting for Khabeeth to leave for work, afraid everything would unravel like a fragile rope.

I called everyone I knew, trying to find someone who was going to Yemen. I finally I located a family from Juban who were traveling. One night after Khabeeth had had his dinner and first cigarette, I told him the news.

"I found a family that is leaving for Yemen in three weeks. I even have the airline number and time, if... if you want it... I have it." Khabeeth did not look at me; we never had eye contact in our marriage.

"Fine," he said. "When I get my check we will reserve the same airline, but you better be sure this is no lie."

"Do you need anything else," I said.

He looked at me coldly. Five minutes later he answered, "No."

The next weeks were torture. My psoriasis itched so badly, I dug my fingers into my skin until I dripped blood. I could not sleep and was constantly in pain.

On the day I was to leave for Yemen, I tried to not get excited. Khabeeth could change his mind at any time.

"I am going to miss you," he said.

"I'll be back in no time," I assured him, fighting the anxiety boiling up inside me.

When Asser picked us up in his car, Khabeeth insisted we stop at my father's house.

"Why don't you come and say goodbye to your mother?" he said. I wondered if this was another trick. Had Khabeeth asked Mom to talk me out of going to Yemen? Was Father waiting with the ticket in his hand to tell me the trip was cancelled?

Munsee opened the door hard, attempting to hit my face. "Get off our property," he said. "Mother doesn't want to see you and she told me to tell you, you are not her daughter."

I swallowed my hurt and walked back to the car.

When we reached the airport, I met the family I was leaving with. As we waited for the flight, a daughter hugged her mother good bye. Why didn't I have a family that hugged instead of throwing knives at each other? Why was I born into a family of monsters?

My Husband

You are the son of my father....Grendal!
Sinful in laws of morality of marriage
Which should be prohibited to you.
You are Grendal, the child of all immoralities and
calamities
Created in your gender!
Your soul is tender
And Allah will burn you inside as he gives you the taste of
hell!
Denying your empowerment over Him
As he seizes you with your self ignorance.
You are prideful Grendal.
Created only from your father
Never from a mother or the ovaries of a Goddess!
So you dig and dig to corrupt me
And the children begotten for you
Giving only the gift of fear. The hell with you!
Shallow, you stand like a massive society against my lonely
self
A self taken away from the day I was born
In a religious culture that held my born head
You pray loudly, viciously
"May you be cursed for you are a girl"!
But you forget the speck of Allah inside you remembers
Reminding you that as hopeless as you want me to be!
You stand and remain the same!
Breaking me, have you won such cowardly victory?
I live and my mission will never be forgotten!
I will fight the forests and desert of eternal pain for my
mothers and grandmothers
I will receive the sword to my left and defeat you
On my right, my guard will protect me from anymore
scaring wounds!
My sons will be as warriors guided to destiny by truth
And victory will be with me.

Chapter 37

Final Flight

We landed at the airport in Sana'a and I donned a black veil and *balto*. Two of Khabeeth's brothers and his mother greeted me. They drove me to the city, where we stayed with one of their family members until we could continue on to the village of Hagag. We sat on faded cushions on the floor of a boxy living room with walls painted a faded yellow that made me feel tired. I wanted only to sleep, but my mother-in-law and her two sons hovered close. We talked about general things. When Mother-in-law asked about Khabeeth, I pretended everything was fine.

She asked me to lift my veil.

I hesitated.

"It is okay," she said. "My sons are like your brothers." She wore a pleased expression on her face. "You look so much more beautiful than your party pictures. You are flawless."

If you could see the rest of me, you would not be saying that, I thought.

Mother-in-law said, "Won't you show me your problem in your body?"

"No," I said. I was too exhausted. "I'll show you tomorrow."

"Oh, it cannot be that bad," she said. "Khabeeth told us it is not severe."

I smiled and kissed her on the knee. "Tomorrow, please."

She nodded, impressed I had kissed her knee. That told me that no one respected her. I had seen that look on the faces of my own mother and other Yemeni women.

The next day after breakfast, Mother-in-law found me in the living room alone.

"Can you please show me now?" she asked. "No one is here."

I removed my scarf. The scores around my hairline were not as bad as the others, but they were red below and encrusted with whitish skin above. Skin flakes fell to the floor, flushing me with embarrassment. She looked at them closely.

"They're in my hair too," I said. I was continuously combing to get the flakes out. Some days I wanted to cut my hair off and be done with it.

"It is not so bad," she said. I heard pity in her voice.

I pulled up my sleeve. Circular patches six inches across covered my arm. Some had cracked open and were bleeding. Others were covered with white skin. Mother-in-law began to understand my problem. Her wrinkled brown hands went to her mouth.

"Is this all over your body?"

"Yes," I said.

"No," she cried. I cried with her.

When her sons were informed of my condition, they took me to a special place in the city where people could be rid of the evil eye and other curses. I doubted psoriasis could be cured this way, but was ready for any healing they could offer.

We walked into the darkened hall of an old building and the cries of women echoed from all directions. I saw all kinds of craziness. All around us, women in black screamed and slammed themselves into walls. If I had not been with Khabeeth's brothers, I would have run from the place.

The sheikh was an old man with wrinkled hands and face. I knelt before him and he put his hands on me and read from the Qur'an. I kept telling myself I didn't have the evil eye, but at the same time, I wanted him to heal me. I closed my eyes behind the veil and let my body suck his words into my bones and soul.

"Your eyes are red," the sheikh said. He asked this thing to leave my body. I heard words coming from my mouth, but it was not me. Something was happening and I prayed it would work.

The healing process continued for a week before my family started to intrude. I heard that Mouzi was in town. Khabeeth's family made him come to talk to me.

"You ran away again," were his first words. He was the same old Mouzi, filled with rage.

I raised my veil and quickly showed him my arms. "This is why I did what I did, Mouzi. I am so sorry, please forgive me."

He said nothing, but at least he did not punch me in the face or the gut. When he left, I figured I would never see him again.

The exorcisms continued. One night when I sat chewing *khat* with the women, my left index finger stiffened. Then my eye would not move and I could not see.

"I'm feeling faint," I said.

I don't remember what happened next, but the women told me my eyes rolled in their sockets and my right leg shook like the tail of a rattlesnake. They called for the sheikh and he came as quickly as he could. I was diagnosed with the evil eye and a malicious ghost. The sheikh mixed herbs with honey and recited verses from the Qur'an. When I awoke, Mouzi was standing beside me with tears in his eyes. Just that morning he had bought a new Qur'an written with gold lettering. He gave it to me, but said nothing. There were too many years of hostility between us.

When the sheikh did his reading the next day, he told me my hair would fall out. I told him I had been seeing blood in my feces.

"These are good signs," he said. The sheikh shared with the men around me that I was a good woman of gifted wisdom. I felt God in his words.

Before my treatment was complete, my brother-in-law tired of the city and decided to take me to their village. I was upset. I wanted to complete my sessions because, regardless of the evil eye, the Qur'an was a cure for me.

There was nothing I could say to keep him from taking me away.

☾

After a long car ride, we arrived at the house of Khabeeth's first wife. Everyone in Juban had been hysterical when they learned I would live in the same house with my husband's first wife, but Mother-in-law had come along to protect me. In many ways, she reminded me of my grandmother, Hayla. Besides, my whole life had been a risk. I had fought with the Monster in the basement, endured abusive husbands, been raped and scarred and beaten. Living with my husband's first wife would pale by comparison.

When I received too much attention for being the "American" girl, Khabeeth's first wife held back. She tried strategies to put me on the spot, but I knew how to protect myself. I continued to treat her like a sister and even bought a bike for her son and doll for her daughter. I did not give in to her games and kept my head high. She could not get her claws into me, so she gave up.

When the rest of the family heard of my psoriasis, they were shocked that my family could leave me in such a condition in America. They took me to a psychic who made herbal concoctions to put on my skin. My sister-in-law applied them every day, telling me how stunning I was. My looks were unimportant. I only wanted to be well.

After three weeks, Khabeeth began calling me to come home.

"I need more time," I said. "I've only begun to heal."

"You have to come back and take care of the boys," he said. I missed Dignity and my boys terribly, but I didn't admit it to Khabeeth. He would only use it against me. Anyway, the boys were staying with my parents. Mom would make sure they had clothing and food.

Phone calls erupted into arguments. Khabeeth disrespected his mother and fought with his brother. Despite these disagreements, I gave in and agreed to return to America. My psoriasis remained inflamed. Maybe that had been Khabeeth's plan all along. Maybe he wanted me to be frustrated in my search for a cure. That way, I would never want to return to Yemen again.

The day I was to leave, Mouzi called. "I just want you to know that I was planning your death when I heard you were coming to Yemen. But you had a good excuse. I let you live. If you run from your husband again, I will find you and kill you in America."

I let him speak. How could I respond anyway? I knew Mouzi meant what he said. Here in Yemen and maybe even in America he could get away with killing me.

Chapter 38

Free in America

I returned to my parent's house only to find Mohamed with darkness under his eyes like an orphan and Solomon's breathing labored. I had thought my children safe, but my own mother had let them deteriorate to such a condition I barely recognized them. I gathered Solomon into my arms.

"What have you been doing to them, Mom?"

She shrugged and sat at the kitchen table with a cup of tea. "You should have been home taking care of your children, not flying off to all corners of the Earth."

"That's no excuse for neglect." Anger coursed through me once again. "How could you do this to your own grandchildren?"

She sipped tea and I saw a glimmer of satisfaction in her eyes. She had neglected them on purpose to punish me. All these years I had seen myself as Mom's protector, standing between her and the Monster and speaking for her when she was afraid to talk to him. I had thought that someday I would convince her to leave him. But as Solomon lay wheezing in my arms, I saw there was no hope for Mom. I might be caged, but she was weighted down with chains.

"You will never tell me I'm a bad mother again," I told her

She had nothing to say to that, which was just as well.

During the weeks that followed I focused on my children. I got some relief when Khabeeth decided to visit Yemen, which freed me for a time.

When he returned, our marriage escalated to a dangerous level.

"I'm out of money," I complained. "I need money for food for the boys."

"What are they to me," he said, "but sons of a whore. They should be drowned."

He would tell me to ask Father for a divorce one day and change his mind the next. It wasn't love that motivated him, but money. The fear of paying a $10,000 penalty to Father was the only thing keeping us together at that point.

My brothers told me that if I called the police about my husband's or their abuse they would kill me. The only thing I could

241

do was wait, hoping Khabeeth would ask Father for the divorce himself. I put up with meals thrown in my face and being spit at. I tolerated Khabeeth's paranoia and wasn't surprised when he told me he had bugged the phone.

When intimidation didn't work, Khabeeth tried another tactic to get us divorced without penalty. He came home from work one night and accused me of having a man in his house. At first, I thought I could ignore him, but I got a call from Tumasha.

"Jasmine, are you fucking a man, because I just received a call from a man who knows my uncle and the names of my brothers. Tell me!"

I was shocked.

"No," I said. "What man told you this?"

"I don't know," she said.

"Khabeeth put someone up to this," I said. "The prick is trying to frame me."

"Why would he do that?"

"He wants a divorce."

I doubt Tumasha believed me, but I didn't care. I did worry what my brothers might do if they thought I was seeing another man. Munsee would kill me, but I didn't think my other brothers would do more than beat me.

Khabeeth came home with a smug look on his face. He thought he had figured everything out. He would blame me for adultery and get out of the marriage free and clear.

"Sit down. I want to talk to you," he said.

"What is it?" I sat on the sofa and feigned innocence.

"I know you are fucking someone."

"What makes you think that?"

"I know every move you take. You are being watched."

"Then you know there is no other man. No one comes to this house, not even women."

"No one will believe that," he said.

"Then prove it. Who is this mystery man?"

Khabeeth hesitated.

"Father will want proof," I said. I doubted Father would really need proof, but I wanted to force Khabeeth into admitting his plot. "He'll want the name of this man."

Khabeeth ground his teeth.

"Who is he?" I asked. "A Yemeni? A Lebanese?"

Khabeeth's eyes narrowed. "You are *not* so clever," he hissed.

"I hope he has more hair than you do," I said. "I hope he's a better lover."

Khabeeth grabbed me by the throat and pushed me into the sofa cushions.

"If you want a divorce," I croaked, "you're going to have to pay for it."

Khabeeth's face went dark, his eyes cold with hate. I had seen this look before, the night Father waited for Mom with the gun.

"I have dug a hole for you and you," he said. His hand tightened on my throat. I knew his threat was real. My life was worth exactly $10,000. I stared into his eyes, ready for death.

Please, Allah, have mercy on my soul.

☪

The next morning I was still alive. *This is it*, I thought. *Either I leave for good or my children will be without a mother.* If I couldn't find the courage to run for myself, I would have to do it for them. This time I would be strong. I would free myself from the obligation I felt to Mom. I would see through Father's tricks. I would leave and not look back.

I cooked for Khabeeth and tried to act normal. He didn't say a word and left for work at the usual time. Fearing he might turn back, I watched him through the peephole until he climbed into the car with the men he rode to work with.

My stomach was filled with stinging bees and my mind became a whirlwind, trying to figure out the best way to escape. If I ran to Arizona, they would find me. Khabeeth had an old van, but if I took it, that they could call the police and have me arrested. I searched the phone book, looking for women's shelters. The ones in Detroit were too close. My family would find me there and bring me back.

I remembered Khabeeth's hands around my throat. He wouldn't stop the next time. I would be dead and my boys left with a father who wished to drown them. Fumbling, I looked through the government section of the book and discovered other state shelters, a safe house in Ann Arbor.

Shaking, I dialed the number.

"Hello," a young woman answered.

"Hello," I whispered. "I need to get out of my house. My husband is going to kill me."

"We can help," she said.

"Can I come now?"

"Yes," the woman said. "We can take you immediately."

The woman seemed friendly, but I remembered the shelter in Arizona. They had seemed friendly at first too. I would have to be careful.

While the boys slept, I packed my Qur'an and prayer rug and some clothes in a suitcase. I gathered together all the papers I thought I would need. Dignity was with my parents, so I felt she was safe for a time. I would have to fight for her later. For now, I had to save myself and the boys.

I waited until sunset, worrying all the while that Khabeeth would come home early. When the neighborhood Yemenis were in their homes and wouldn't witness my escape, I bundled the boys into the old van and drove as fast as I could to the Lebanese section of town. I stopped at an auto dealership and spoke to a gray-haired Lebanese man who owned the place.

"Please," I said. "I need your help."

"I have plenty of used cars," he said.

"I don't need a car." I told him my story as quickly as I could and asked if he could hold my van and title. "I don't want anyone to find me. Understand?"

"Do not fear," he said.

"I need to get to Ann Arbor."

"You are in no condition to drive," he said. "I will call a taxi."

When the taxi arrived, he paid the fifty dollar fare.

"I don't know how to thank you," I said. "Allah, bless you."

The next two hours we traveled highways, leaving the bright lights of the city behind. Mohamed and Solomon fell asleep and I gazed at the stars. To the west, a bright star shown above the horizon. It did not twinkle like the others. *Venus*, I thought, remembering what Gais had said. *Venus. The goddess of love. A planet of heat and poisonous gas.*

It ends now, I told myself. I would not go back this time. I would not subject myself to more abuse. I needed to heal and my sons needed to learn a better way.

At the shelter, a girl younger than me stood in the open doorway, her face and hands glowing in porch light. *An angel*, I thought. *God has sent me another angel.* She smiled. I gathered my sons into my arms and ran to her.

"Everything will be okay," she said, stroking my scarf.

Yes, I thought. The Monster and his minions had lost their hold. I felt it as I had never felt it before.

As I walked into the shelter, I imagined all the abused women of the world coming together in a single voice, a voice like a tornado or disaster siren, a voice that everyone would hear and no one ignore. No longer caged by family and culture, freed from unrealistic dreams of marrying Prince Charming, we would stand on our own, as sisters.

We would be free in America.

Afterward

My flight to the Ann Arbor shelter marked the beginning of my new life. I was transferred to a second shelter in Pennsylvania where I felt even safer. Later, I moved to a third shelter in Indiana. I plan to write a second book about my experiences dealing with women's shelters, how they helped me survive on my own, and how I think they can be improved.

While living in the Ann Arbor shelter, the Michigan courts granted me custody of my two boys, but awarded the care of my daughter to her father. Since I am now living outside of Michigan, dealing with the legal system across state lines has been impossible. To this day, I fear for my daughter's safety and wish I had the legal representation to get her back. I must put my faith in God that she will be all right.

I am now under a doctor's care and am being treated with the correct drugs to keep my psoriasis under control. Writing this book was my way of healing the psychological wounds of my past. I hope that by sharing my experiences, I will inspire other woman to seek help and escape abusive relationships. I also hope my example gives others the courage and faith to continue. In the future, I plan to develop a boot camp for abused women to teach them how to survive after living under the darkness of abuse. I want them to know that there is an end to hardship and a life of peace in the future. Praise Allah.